VISUAL
Learning AND
Teaching

An Essential Guide
for Educators K–8

Susan Daniels, Ph.D.

free spirit
PUBLISHING®

Library of Congress Cataloging-in-Publication Data
Names: Daniels, Susan, 1958– author.
Title: Visual learning and teaching : an essential guide for educators K–8 / by Susan Daniels, Ph.D.
Description: Minneapolis, MN : Free Spirit Publishing Inc., [2018] | Includes bibliographical references and index.
Identifiers: LCCN 2017039970 (print) | LCCN 2017060628 (ebook) | ISBN 9781631982866 (Web PDF) | ISBN 9781631982873 (ePub) | ISBN 9781631981401 (pbk.) | ISBN 1631981404 (pbk.)
Subjects: LCSH: Visual learning. | Visual literacy. | Visual education.
Classification: LCC LB1067.5 (ebook) | LCC LB1067.5 .D36 2018 (print) | DDC 371.33/5—dc23
LC record available at https://lccn.loc.gov/2017039970

Free Spirit Publishing does not have control over or assume responsibility for author or third-party websites and their content. At the time of this book's publication, all facts and figures cited within are the most current available. All telephone numbers, addresses, and website URLs are accurate and active; all publications, organizations, websites, and other resources exist as described in this book; and all have been verified as of June 2018. If you find an error or believe that a resource listed here is not as described, please contact Free Spirit Publishing.

Edited by Brian Farrey-Latz and Meg Bratsch
Cover and interior design by Shannon Pourciau

10 9 8 7 6 5 4 3 2 1
Printed in the United States of America

Free Spirit Publishing Inc.
6325 Sandburg Road, Suite 100
Minneapolis, MN 55427-3674
(612) 338-2068
help4kids@freespirit.com
www.freespirit.com

To April Morris for believing in me and the work of this book one
mind map and doodle at a time and every step of the way.
To Devin McGhee who has been a constant
source of insight and inspiration.

CONTENTS

List of Figures

FOREWORD by Richard M. Cash, Ed.D.

When I was a student in the 1960s and 1970s, film strips and movies on a reel-to-reel projector were all the rage in schools. In the 1980s, overhead projectors and videotapes became the visuals that enhanced teacher voices. The 1990s saw an explosion of technologies (computers and interactive whiteboards, for starters), which challenged teachers to keep pace. Now, in the 2000s, visually enhanced technologies overwhelm our daily lives. As a result, many of today's students have known nothing other than a highly visual world.

For thousands of years, we have depended on using visual elements to communicate. Today, we use visuals more than ever. From social media to outdoor advertising, from tech screens to interactive media, our students are bombarded with visuals intended to engage, encourage, and inspire. Teaching students how to use visual language to record ideas, refine thinking, and transmit ideas is an essential tool for success in this multilingual world.

Susan Daniels understands this. One of my first encounters with Dr. Daniels was at an educational conference. We were discussing new ways to engage students in learning. We both drew pictures of our ideas on napkins, placemats, and any surface that would allow for our graphics. As we did, we realized we were expressing ourselves beyond the spoken word. I knew at that moment she was the right person to write a book on developing visual learning and teaching.

So many of our students who struggle with the written word are more at ease sharing their ideas in graphic ways. In this book, Susan encourages educators to delve into visual language and communication: that which isn't spoken or written. She expertly outlines the visual triad model (VTM)—"seeing, imagining, and depicting"—as a way for students to express what they understand. Best of all, her techniques can benefit students accustomed to traditional teaching methods and students for whom visuals are the preferred way of demonstrating proficiencies.

I remember one of my teachers scolding me for doodling during class. She said I was daydreaming and not paying attention. In this book, Susan reassures us that doodling is, in fact, a mentally stimulating process through which more divergent thoughts and ideas are shaped. Allowing our students to let their pencils and minds wander can help them craft better solutions for this highly complex world.

Immerse yourself in the world of visual teaching and learning. Doodle your ideas as you read. Document your thinking visually as you progress through this text. Discover new ways to awaken your inner creative thinker and deepen your understanding of diverse ways to communicate and learn. Let yourself go as you enjoy this highly valuable text.

Richard M. Cash, Ed.D.
Educator, author, and consultant

INTRODUCTION
Why Visual Teaching and Learning? Why Now?

People have innate tendencies to express themselves visually, and visuals play a big part in how we process information. From prehistoric images to the printing press, humans have sought to communicate. Primitive cave drawings show a primal desire to use pictures in an effort to convey thought, feeling, and meaning. Even today, most toddlers seek to make meaningful marks, drawing rudimentary pictures to show what's going on inside their heads.

Despite this early inclination to express ourselves visually, our classrooms often default to verbally dominated instruction. For centuries, many educators have relied on lecturing, storytelling, and the written word to convey information. Standardized tests, in written form, emphasize verbal learning. But in a world filled with laptops, smart-phones, tablets, and virtual reality machines—all tools with graphic-centric interfaces—it becomes paramount to proactively teach students how to "read" and create visual texts and to embrace this instinct more fully or risk falling behind. As such, many teachers find themselves without the resources needed to give 21st-century students the skills they'll need to thrive in an increasingly visual world.

The Benefits of Visual Teaching and Learning
Introducing a consistent visual component to the curriculum can:

- help students better engage with materials
- develop higher-order thinking skills
- hone fundamental abilities that enable students to see and conceptualize visuals clearly
- enhance tactile hand-eye-mind connections that improve the ability to recall facts and retain learning
- serve the unique needs of learners who process information primarily through visuals, as well as increase learning for all students
- provide new opportunities to some students with learning differences and challenge students who are gifted or twice exceptional
- be an integral part of best-practice intervention methods with individuals on the autism spectrum

This book, *Visual Learning and Teaching: An Essential Guide for Educators K–8*, seeks to give educators exactly what they need to fill this void. Visual learning and teaching are exciting and creative ways to meaningfully engage students in visual literacy, visual language, and visual communication. By introducing meaningful visual elements to the curriculum, educators can help students more completely engage with the multitude of visual messages they receive daily. And becoming fluent in visual communication can help students build the skills necessary to succeed in almost all areas of their lives. The teachers I have worked with, who use visual note-taking with their students, consistently report better student scores on quizzes and tests as well as stronger essays, projects, and papers.

Defining Visual Terms

To fully understand visual learning and teaching, we need to discuss visual literacy, visual language, and visual communication.

Visual literacy has been defined many ways. As applied to classroom learning, this book defines visual literacy as the ability to do three things:

- Decode—to understand and translate communications made with visual imagery
- Imagine—to create, interpret, and manipulate mental models of visual imagery
- Encode—to express thoughts and ideas using visual imagery

I will use the visual triad model, introduced in chapter 1, and its three components: (1) see, (2) imagine, and (3) depict.

In addition, visual literacy includes the ability to be an informed critic of visual information and to ethically judge accuracy, validity, and worth. For example, when visually literate students encounter graphs and charts in their texts, they often have the ability to read and analyze the visual and verbal messages, comprehend their meanings, question irrelevant or misleading data, and create a visual or verbal response to it.

As you proceed through this book, you will come across additional visual terms that are synonymous with *mark-making*, such as: depict, doodle, draw, sketch, and illustrate. These terms, in many instances, can be used interchangeably. The definition of *depict* is "to show or represent by doodling, drawing, illustrating, or other visual means (collage, photographs, and so forth)." A *doodle* is thought of as a more basic image, and a *sketch* or an *illustration* is something more realistically rendered. *Infodoodling* is a form of doodling used to convey information. What's important to remember is that none of these words imply "artistic ability" when used in the context of visual learning and teaching. Mark-making is a tool for learners of all skill levels. (This will be discussed at length later in the book.)

Visual language is a form of communication that isn't aural, written, or gestural. By excluding the spoken word and signed words, visual language relies on marks, forms, design, color, and shapes to convey messages. Pictograms, hieroglyphs, and ideograms are simple forms of visual language. Signs and symbols for trains, planes, buses, restrooms, restaurants, and others are readily understood visual communications that don't rely on language to comprehend. This book will address both depicting and doodling as simple forms of visual language and then extend into other graphic forms, including mind maps, one pagers, presentations, picture books, and more.

Doodling is an important part of visual learning and teaching. Once thought to mean simply dallying, doing nothing, or scribbling absentmindedly, doodling has more recently been defined by Sunni Brown, author of *The Doodle Revolution*, as making marks to help yourself think. This definition, and Brown's work on doodling and graphic facilitation, form part of the foundation of this book. And infodoodling integrates words and images that are designed to record and communicate concepts and processes.[1] Depicting refers to a broader range of ways to show or to illustrate that includes detailed sketches, illustrations, designs, diagrams, photography, digital content, videos, and more. Doodling and depicting will take center stage throughout this book as important tools on the path to visual literacy.

Visual communication is something we take part in every day, both actively and inactively. We actively rely on visual communication to perform day-to-day tasks (for example, following directions on road signs). But sometimes, we are unaware of the visual conversation because it's happening constantly: images in advertising, photos in magazines, icons within emails, colors in the background of product packaging, and so on. This book will introduce skills to help you and your students become active visual communicators.

The Path to Visual Learning

Simply put, visual learning is associating information with reading, analyzing, interpreting, and creating images, symbols, icons, and other forms of visual input. It's sometimes referred to as spatial learning, or visual-spatial learning when applied to three-dimensional objects and space. On their own, verbal instructions on the whiteboard are not an example of visual language or communication. Visual learning begins when simple yet meaningful doodles or depictions are added alongside the verbal instructions. It continues when text and visual elements appear together in the form of a graph, a diagram or an illustrated text, such as a picture book or graphic novel.

It's important to note that visual literacy is not new. As infants, we take in a tremendous amount of information visually and quickly begin learning through the visual mode. For young children, visuals are an important part of how they interact with the rest of the world. Invite a child to share, "Please tell me about your picture," and a whole story will unfold. In fact, until we become proficient at written and spoken language, most of us rely on depictions to communicate our ideas and wants.

Over time, however, our visual skills—observing, looking closely, analyzing images, imagining, doodling, and otherwise depicting—can sometimes diminish as our focus turns to other forms of communication (verbal and written). But, as previously noted, the demands of the new century and the advancements of technology suggest we need to integrate opportunities to learn, teach, and interact visually within education contexts. This book will help educators reenergize and build upon these innate abilities in both themselves and their students.

A Note on Visual Learning and Technology

Graphic interfaces and iconography dominate today's students like never before. They live in a digital world as much as an analog one, and a large part of navigating the digital world is learning how to read and interpret visual imagery. However, while the formats and mediums may be novel, the skills needed to understand and create visual information are not new. While using the latest app, game, software, or device, users still need to see and conceptualize visuals clearly and make their own meaningful visual marks. The tools in this book aid these fundamental abilities, online or off, even though the tools may not reference specific technologies, which are ever-changing and shifting. Furthermore, the importance of the tactile hand-eye-mind connection when writing or drawing the old-fashioned way is difficult to overestimate when it comes to engagement with and retention of learning.

Why Visual Learning and Teaching?

When educators introduce a new teaching and learning technique, the goal is to help students better understand the material in an assigned curriculum. Visual teaching and learning methods can simultaneously address the needs of underserved learners (those who excel at processing information visually) and potentially increase learning for all students. Let's look first at how visual techniques can help students whose learning style is more visual-centric.

In her book *Upside-Down Brilliance: The Visual-Spatial Learner,* Linda Silverman identifies two types of learners—auditory-sequential learners and visual-spatial learners—and discusses the different learning preferences and characteristics of each. Silverman states that auditory-sequential learners work well with words, linear organization, and order. Visual-spatial learners work well with images, big-picture thinking, and possibilities. Most students work with both modalities but have strength in or a preference for one or the other. **Figure 1** shows a comparison of auditory-sequential and visual-spatial strengths.

FIG. 1 DIFFERENCES BETWEEN LEARNERS WITH AUDITORY-SEQUENTIAL STRENGTHS OR VISUAL-SPATIAL STRENGTHS*

Learners with Auditory-Sequential Strengths	Learners with Visual-Spatial Strengths
• Think mostly in words	• Think mostly in pictures
• Have auditory strengths	• Have visual strengths
• Are step-by-step learners	• Are whole-part learners
• Attend well to details	• See the big picture
• Follow oral directions well	• Decode visual depictions well
• Do well at arithmetic	• Prefer geometry
• Learn phonics easily	• Learn whole words easily
• Can sound out spelling words	• Can spell well by visualizing
• Learn well from instructions	• Arrive at correct solutions intuitively
• Are comfortable with one right answer	• Like problems with many possible answers
• Tend to be academically oriented	• Often, are creatively, technologically, or mechanically talented
• Can memorize math facts quickly	• Can tackle higher-level math successfully often before mastering basic facts
• Have good short-term auditory memory	• Have good long-term visual memory
• Are well organized	• Create unique methods of organization, need to "see" materials

*Adapted from Silverman, L. K. (2002) *Upside-Down Brilliance: The Visual-Spatial Learner.* Used with permission.

Because many modern classrooms rely on lecture, reading, and writing to impart information, they are set up to convey information in a manner that best suits learners with an auditory-sequential preference. But from 1999 to 2001, researchers conducted a study of 750 students in two schools and found that 33 percent of the students were strongly visual-spatial and another 30 percent were moderately visual-spatial. The results clearly showed that the majority of students have a visual-spatial learning preference. And the research suggests that many of our students with this preference are going undetected and undernourished.[2] In adopting a visual learning and teaching approach, educators can better meet the needs of these students.

Visual Learning and Students with Special Needs: Some Examples

Visual-spatial strengths and related learning needs have been found in greater incidence in some students with learning differences. Visual-spatial abilities have been identified as strengths in students who are gifted. Students with dyslexia have been found to perceive three-dimensional visual presentations with great acuity, but they often struggle with visual material presented in two dimensions and in sequence. And visual support strategies are being used extensively with individuals on the autism spectrum and are considered to be an integral part of best-practice intervention methods. Further, some students who are known as twice exceptional—particularly those who are gifted and who also have dyslexia—have been found to be creative visual thinkers.

Sources and Recommended Resources:

The Dyslexic Advantage: Unlocking the Hidden Potential of the Dyslexic Brain by Brock Eide and Fernette Eide, 2011, Plume.

Literacy for Visual Learners: Teaching Children with Learning Differences to Read, Write, Communicate, and Create by Adele Devine, 2016, Jessica Kingsley Publishers.

Twice Exceptional: Supporting and Educating Bright and Creative Students with Learning Difficulties by Scott Barry Kaufman, 2018, Oxford University Press.

Visual Support for Children with Autism Spectrum Disorders: Materials for Visual Learners by Vera Bernard-Opitz and Anne Häußler, 2011, AAPC Publishing.

But what about learners with an auditory-sequential preference? These students also can benefit from adding visual elements to the curriculum. Research by educational psychologist Richard Mayer found that using images to convey information improves a person's ability to recall facts or key steps by an average of 23 percent. When text and graphics are combined, retention increases to 42 percent.[3] So, whether students prefer auditory-sequential or visual-spatial learning, they can still benefit in terms of recall when visual elements are incorporated.

This is not to say that traditional teaching methods rooted in lecture and reading should be jettisoned wholly. Even though visual communication is becoming increasingly important, verbal and written communication are still ubiquitous and essential. Employer surveys frequently cite verbal communication skills as some of the most highly sought-after skills in potential employees. So, it's important to learn visual skills but not at the expense of other skills. This can be accomplished by introducing visual elements in tandem with existing techniques. The lessons in chapters 10 and 11 demonstrate how to do this.

About This Book

Over the years, my work in visual learning and teaching has been inspired by a number of groundbreaking pioneers whose research and ideas formed the bedrock of what is collectively understood today about how humans process information visually. The lessons learned from their work and the work of other researchers have guided many of the ideas and classroom materials I present in this book.

Dr. Jerre Levy, a neuroscientist from the University of Chicago, researched the specialized functions of each hemisphere of the brain, leading to a stronger understanding of how the two hemispheres collaborate to process visual stimuli. Her work moved us past the old concept of right-brained and left-brained learners. The traditional and dichotomous view of right-brained and left-brained learners is false. We are whole-brained learners with hemispheres and regions of the brain that both specialize and work simultaneously and synergistically depending on the task and the strengths and learning preferences of the learner.[4] Dr. Howard Gardner, of Harvard University, researched and developed the theory of multiple intelligences and showed how visual-spatial intelligence is naturally advanced in some children and adults. But—barring physical or cognitive impairment—everyone can develop the abilities associated with each intelligence to at least a proficient level.[5]

Professor of psychology Allan Paivio's dual-coding theory of cognition and literacy development is of special importance. Paivio asserts that we perceive, discriminate, analyze, synthesize, interpret, anticipate, comprehend, compose, imagine, remember, and express ourselves without text as well as with text. Further, dual-coding theory suggests that the integration of visual and verbal modes of expression in a learning context increases engagement, understanding, and retention.[6]

Finally, Robert McKim's pioneering work on visual thinking described three kinds of visual imagery: images that we see, imagine, and draw. His work closely informed my own model of visual learning, the visual triad model (VTM), which is discussed in greater detail in chapter 1.

My goal is to synthesize the knowledge of these leaders with my own thoughts and present practical, easy-to-use strategies that will help educators become more comfortable with their own visual abilities and introduce these techniques to students.

Visual Learning and Teaching is meant to be an interactive guide. As you flip through the pages and immerse yourself in the chapters, you'll find recommended activities to exercise your visual literacy skills on the spot. You will want to keep a blank notebook or journal and your favorite writing utensil handy (or a tablet or smartphone with a stylus). This will be your visual learning notebook. In it, you can make marks, doodle, sketch, and illustrate to practice your own visual skills and more closely connect with the material throughout. When you are ready to introduce these skills to your students, you can revisit the same exercises. Each student will need a notebook as well.

Most importantly, this is a resource for you to:

- acquire visual tools to fill students' visual toolboxes

- integrate visual language and visual literacy across the curriculum

- meet the needs of visual learners

- provide visual learning opportunities for all students across all grade levels and content areas

Using This Book

To help students learn visually, we need to teach visually. Many teachers express anxiety about visual teaching, believing that they aren't "artistic" enough. The truth is you do not need to be artistic, or even a visual-spatial learner yourself, to learn the skills and strategies of visual teaching.

This book will share proven strategies for building on to your innate visual capacities to enhance your instruction. You'll explore, practice, and implement these strategies throughout each chapter.

To help teachers gain confidence and to further clarify what visual literacy is all about, I've divided the book into three parts to take readers from understanding the foundations of visual literacy, to using visual teaching and learning tools with students, to incorporating visual tools and texts into different areas of the curriculum.

Depending on your comfort level and teaching goals, you might start with a careful read of part one or, alternatively, focus more on the tools and strategies in part two or the curricular applications in part three.

Part One: The Visual Teacher focuses on educators. The goal is to help teachers of all skill levels feel more comfortable with doodling and sketching, core components of visual teaching and learning.

Chapter 1 explains what it means to be a visual teacher and introduces a team of educators who adopted visual teaching techniques into their classrooms. Throughout the book, these educators will talk about their own journeys to becoming visual teachers, share their classroom experiences using visual teaching, and offer insights into how they feel their students have changed in a visual learning environment.

Chapter 2 explains the basic tools required to create meaningful marks—such as the visual alphabet and six essential design elements—and uses key strategies to connect doodling and learning in a memorable way.

Part Two: Visual Tools in the Classroom is filled with tools you can use day to day in your visual classroom. There are explicit instructional strategies with visual and verbal examples that introduce these gateway tools to students.

Chapter 3 offers insight into working with visually adept students and reluctant doodlers. This chapter includes several activities to introduce students to visual tools. The chapter also explores visual note-taking, visual vocabulary flashcards, and graphic organizers that help students put these tools to use.

Chapter 4 covers visual texts including two of the most important texts for classroom use: mind maps and one pagers. Mind maps and one pagers are both single-page formats that use visual and verbal content and are designed to represent knowledge of and information about a central concept or idea.

Chapter 5 contains a primer on informational graphics—such as icons, diagrams, and timelines. They provide readers with a visual explanation without relying on verbal decoding. Infographic posters are discussed as assignments that can be used across the curriculum. These graphics provide building blocks that allow students to communicate visually in a manner that's easy to understand and comprehensive.

Chapter 6 looks at journals and how they can become visually rich tools that can expand learning. Two types of journals are highlighted: life notebooks that document day-to-day activities and prompt personal reflection and learning, and nature journals that aid in enhancing scientific curiosity and study.

Chapter 7 delves into the world of picture books—for many students, picture books are the first visual texts they encounter—and how they can be used to convey more complex and detailed information. There is also a discussion of how comics and graphic novels have become commonplace in classrooms and how these visually rich texts can be interpreted. Resources for incorporating comics and graphic novels into the curriculum are provided.

Chapter 8 discusses the benefits of keeping visual learning portfolios of student work for assessment and reflective purposes. This chapter includes information on how to create assessment rubrics and be selective in which material to include in the portfolio. It also talks about how a well-maintained portfolio can be passed along to future teachers and provide a quick overview of student progress and abilities.

Part Three: Incorporating Visual Tools and Texts into Subject Area Lesson Plans and Curriculum includes content-based chapters that provide instructional strategies, activities, and models for integrating visual teaching and learning within K–8 curriculum across subject areas and grade levels.

Chapter 9 looks at how visual learning and teaching fits into Common Core State Standards and how to design effective, visually rich curriculum.

Chapter 10 provides sample units that integrate visual lessons into the curriculum for grades K–3 focusing on science (botany) and social studies.

Chapter 11 includes sample units that integrate visual lessons into the curriculum for grades 4–8 focusing on math and design, English language arts, and earth science.

All these lessons include the necessary tools to integrate the visual processes and products alongside their verbal counterparts. Each curriculum unit also provides assessments for visual products. Part three wraps up with a glimpse into the future of visual learning and teaching.

Supplemental materials and all the book's reproducible handouts are available in the book's digital content. See page 258 for instructions on how to download.

I hope you find the ideas and strategies within this book valuable and fun as you build your own visual thinking abilities. Further, I hope the visual content in the book inspires you to tap into and build on the visual skills of your students to help increase their retention, motivation, and engagement.

I'm eager to hear about your experiences as you implement visual teaching and learning in your classroom. Feel free to contact me in care of:

Free Spirit Publishing Inc.
6325 Sandburg Road, Suite 100
Minneapolis, MN 55427
help4kids@freespirit.com

Let's get ready to explore visual learning and teaching!

Susan Daniels

PART ONE

THE Visual Teacher

Being a Visual Teacher

All educators have the potential to be visual teachers. For many of us, this means remembering or relearning some of our earlier visual thinking abilities. Looking closely, observing, analyzing images, imagining, and doodling are abilities we typically developed as very young children. Some of these skills dwindle as we progress through school. My passion is to help teachers connect (or, in many cases, reconnect) with their ability to express themselves both visually and verbally and gain comfort and confidence in helping their students engage with their visual abilities.

My goal is to show how you may already be a visual teacher and how you can improve on these skills. This book will share proven strategies for building your innate visual capacities and enhancing your instruction with the children you teach. We'll explore, practice, and implement these strategies throughout each chapter, and I'll share insights from teachers I've been working with over the past few years.

Setting the Scene: Meet the Visual Teachers

Susan

You may have doubts about your ability to become a visual teacher. You might say, "But I don't draw" or have a dozen other reasons to feel skeptical. Don't quit before we've even begun! Let me introduce you to a team of educators who went from novices to seasoned visual teachers. All they needed was a little determination and faith.

I have been collaborating with a team of K–8 teachers to develop visually enriched and integrated curriculum ever since I provided professional development to the entire staff of a K–8 school on differentiated instruction and creativity that included an introduction to visual learning and teaching. A group of teachers expressed interest in learning more about visual instruction. They varied in their teaching experience and their background with using visuals in the classroom. What they shared was curiosity and a desire to expand their visual teaching and learning skills to better meet the needs of their students.

After the principal approved it, we made plans to meet for extended professional development to be held over one week during the summer. The first two days were a workshop during which I provided and modeled instructional strategies for visual learning and teaching. The teachers had time to practice these new strategies and discuss applications for their classrooms. The next three days were spent redesigning existing curriculum units to integrate both visual and verbal learning.

These newly developed curriculum units were implemented during the next school year. While piloting their curricula for the first time, teachers kept detailed notes of what worked and what they would do differently. We continued to meet for one afternoon on a monthly basis. The teachers piloted their resources and curricula, and we worked on revising the units throughout the year. Let me introduce the team:

These curriculum units are featured in chapters 10 and 11 to use as models or to build upon for your own use.

Kipp is a young, talented, and tech-savvy kindergarten teacher. He uses his interactive whiteboard with ease, and his students are comfortable expressing themselves in images and words. Kipp was eager to better understand the developmental needs of young children, how to incorporate more explicitly visual instruction in reading and math lessons, and how to structure his classroom as an atelier, or learning studio, for early childhood.

Carol has been teaching kindergarten and first grade for many years. Her classroom has a number of activity stations where children may go to work and create on their own. Carol is very comfortable with hands-on activities and various forms of visual expression. The curriculum that Carol has built over the years is largely project-based with small-group instruction. Her classroom provides a rich selection of materials—markers, pencils, crayons, various papers—that students may use while developing their designs and class projects. Carol came to the professional development with a lot of experience and a great deal of openness to new experiences and strategies.

Jenna is a creative and curious primary grade teacher. She has taught a second-and-third-grade combination class for several years. While she doesn't consider herself an artist, she has always been a strong visual thinker. She supports her students' learning with multiple forms of literacy in the classroom, including numerous visual activities. When first presented with the concept of visual teaching, Jenna said, "But I can't draw." Jenna was self-critical about her abilities to draw until she participated in our summer professional development on visual learning and teaching. Now, Jenna keeps a daily visual journal, and she models that "everyone can doodle" by illustrating her whiteboard work with simple doodles and diagrams.

Martin is a fourth-grade teacher who walks the walk. He is both a talented teacher and a talented artist. In his spare time, Martin sings and acts in operettas. He also designs curriculum with a strong visual emphasis. Though he is not a trained visual artist, Martin expresses himself beautifully through doodling, sketching, and drawing. These are all wonderful qualities for a visual teacher to have. Yet, Martin's talents can be intimidating to students and colleagues. Martin has addressed this by adapting his own visual illustrations in the classroom and by simplifying the methods he uses, while simultaneously scaffolding his students' abilities to express themselves visually.

Toni and Jennie are on the same sixth-and-seventh-grade team. Each teaches students in their looped and self-contained classrooms. Toni and Jennie are experienced, energetic, and passionate teachers. They regularly revise and update their curricula, and more often than not, they collaborate to do so. Toni has had the good fortune to have a classroom parent with visual design experience who has brought many ideas for potential projects, especially related to literature and social studies. Meanwhile, Jennie has been dedicated to differentiating instruction to build on students' strengths. Jennie has had particular interest in the value of illustrated science notebooks and students' life notebooks. (See page 114 for more on life notebooks.) Because they teach adolescents,

both teachers recognize that many students work best when they have a personal connection to their learning, engage in self-reflection, and can vividly see their role in the classroom and the larger community.

Becoming a Stronger Visual Teacher

I've been working for over twenty years to help teachers understand the value of visual learning and become stronger teachers. I am heartened and fueled by the feedback I get from teachers all over the country who have embraced their visual learning and teaching methods. Some of the most compelling and telling responses I've received reflect significant transformation by teachers.

For example, Jenna's first response—"I can't draw"—became:

"Thinking about visual teaching and learning has helped me see my own practice in a new way. I am a very verbal person, and words are my comfort zone. By practicing drawing and doodling, I have become more confident in expressing knowledge in a more visual way. But, more importantly, I have been able to incorporate visual learning into my classroom in ways that I wasn't before. The simple question, 'How could you doodle that?' has opened up a world of possibilities for me and my students."

And when I asked Toni about her experience:

"When I first started working with visual literacy, I shared with my class the very basics of doodling as learning. Some very simple ideas and concepts were all it took to change how my students expressed themselves. Gone were text heavy posters that simply regurgitated information. In their place were rich documents that expressed deeper understandings with color, pictures, and recomposed text that clearly had meaning for the student creators."

I have the good fortune of designing and leading professional development workshops that include rich visual resources, are highly interactive, and provide numerous opportunities for teachers to experience visual learning and teaching in a hands-on way. Part of this process involves helping teachers remember how doodling, drawing, and diagramming were natural instincts in early childhood. In early childhood and the primary grades, most of us enjoyed hands-on and eyes-on practices that incorporated strong visual components. As we grew older, into middle school and beyond, these practices were replaced with verbally loaded textbooks, classroom talks and lectures, and verbally dominated assessment practices. How sad that we lose the inclination and the confidence to pick up a pen or pencil—or tablet or smartphone with a stylus—for illustration. And how unfortunate especially when we live in a visually prolific culture.

Fortunately, many teachers recognize (or are rethinking) the value of visual teaching and learning. Some of you may have found visual modes of expression through hobbies, crafts, or the publication of books designed for business that extol the virtues of doodling. Or perhaps you have discovered online teaching tools like TeacherTube, Moodle, Edmodo, and the like. Some of you may still feel disconnected and, like the teacher at the beginning of the chapter, are stuck on "But, I can't draw." Well, this book has emerged from years of working with teachers just like you, from every grade and subject area across the country. So, let's shift our focus from the classroom to you—the classroom teacher, the classroom designer, and the curator of visual learning experiences.

The Five Ws

How do we identify a visual teacher? How do we know a visual teacher when we see one? Let's look at the basic five Ws: Who? What? When? Where? Why?

Who Is the Visual Teacher?

Teachers who are striving to increase their understandings of and apply instructional strategies that increase students' visual literacy—their capacity for decoding, imagining, and encoding visual images—are visual teachers. The teachers you have already been introduced to—Kipp, Carol, Jenna, Martin, Toni, and Jennie—did not come to visual teaching and learning with specific skill sets or prior training. What they had in common was a recognition of the value of visual teaching and learning along with a desire to learn more and reach their students. As stated at the top of this chapter, there is a visual teacher in each of us.

What Does a Visual Teacher Do?

Visual teachers optimize learning for all students by integrating visual teaching and learning across the curriculum. They understand that visual teaching and learning activates students' brains more fully than when verbal modes are used alone. They provide opportunities—work stations, visual note-taking, mind maps, one pagers—to decode, imagine, and encode visual images in all subject areas. They observe the progress that students make in visually representing their learning. They model visual learning and teaching by sharing and using their own visual representations. They doodle in front of the class. In short, they actively encourage students to combine images and text to share ideas more expressively.

When and Where Does a Visual Teacher Use the Skills of Visual Literacy?

When we become more aware of visual teaching and learning, we begin to see opportunities for incorporating visual strategies into our classrooms and curricula.

- Visual learning and teaching helps students access and share prior knowledge, develop vocabulary, learn new concepts, brainstorm ideas, and build higher-order thinking.
- Visual thinking helps students see connections, patterns, and relationships, and also helps the development and communication of ideas.

Spelling, vocabulary, language arts, math, science, technology, and social studies all lend themselves to instruction with both visual and verbal content. Once we become more aware of and deliberate in the use of visual thinking approaches, it is something we take with us everywhere. As Jenna points out on the next page, visual thinking is not reserved for the classroom alone.

"Not only am I incorporating visual teaching and learning within my classroom, I am becoming more aware of my visual surroundings: Noticing street signs and their icons, looking more closely at the visual images in magazines/TV/mail/books. Daily doodles are now a part of my life. The grocery list is an explosion of icons, and while planning for teaching, I illustrate with simple doodles too. I am becoming more confident in my own visual skills, and although it does take some extra time, I feel it is well worth it for motivating and engaging the learners in my classroom."

Why Is It Important to Be a Visual Teacher?

Visual communication is too important in the 21st century to leave its learning to chance. Unfortunately, teachers receive very little, if any, explicit instruction in how to teach with visual language and texts. To learn useful strategies for explicit visual learning and teaching, we need to fully understand visual literacy.

Teachers change and shape lives. Strong teachers seek out resources and strategies to support all learners. Visually aware teachers strive to incorporate visual thinking. Children learn in different ways, and all of our students are processing more and more information and input from visual sources each and every day. We need to bring this into our classrooms by integrating both visual and verbal literacy throughout the school day. Most of our instruction is already verbally based, so now it is up to us to meaningfully integrate visual learning. We do this by embracing visual literacy and engaging in explicit visual instruction.

Visual Literacy

Timothy Gangwer, a teacher and an author who specializes in visual teaching and learning, defines visual literacy as the ability to understand nonlinguistic communication made with visual imagery and the ability to use visual imagery to communicate. In his book *Visual Impact, Visual Teaching*, Gangwer states that individuals become visually literate by means of visual encoding—expressing thoughts and ideas in visual form—and visual decoding—translating the content and meaning of visual imagery.[7]

My own definition of visual literacy includes interpretation and imagination, nestled between decoding and encoding. So, from my perspective, visual literacy is:

- Decoding: the ability to understand and translate communications made with visual imagery
- Imagining: the ability to create, interpret, and manipulate mental models of visual imagery
- Encoding: the ability to express thoughts and ideas by using visual images to communicate

When teachers embrace visual literacy, classroom instruction is shaped by—and students are actively engaged in—the processes of decoding, imagining, and encoding visual texts.

Visual Thinking, Teaching, and Learning

When I first came to the study of visual thinking and creativity over twenty years ago, I was immediately drawn to the work of Robert McKim. McKim, a professor and designer, wrote an early strategy manual for thinking visually titled *Thinking Visually* (Yes, really!) in which he outlined three kinds of visual imagery that are essential to visual thinking.

1. Images that we see.
2. Images that we imagine.
3. Images that we draw.

Now, this may not seem revolutionary, but in 1973 and 1990, the years of the first and second versions of his book, little had been written about visual thinking. McKim's work first defined and described the processes of visual thinking and then provided activities for practice.[8]

I've built on his work and developed what I call a visual triad model (VTM) of visual thinking, teaching, and learning. My VTM is a combination of my own definition of visual literacy and the writings of McKim.

1. Images that we see. (Decode)
2. Images that we imagine. (Imagine)
3. Images that we depict. (Encode)

In my model, I changed the last word from *draw* to *depict*. It may seem like a small change, but this is an important distinction when taking into account how many people immediately believe visual thinking requires the ability to draw. There are so many other ways to visually represent our thoughts, ideas, and feelings. I felt this idea was best captured by *depict*. I encourage doodling as the most generally accessible means to depict ideas. But, we could also make collages, take photos, create digital images, and more. My experience has been that the majority of students enjoy working with simple depictions or doodles. Yet, when learners try different forms of visual expression, they benefit by having opportunities to work in the mode they are most comfortable with, or perhaps, the mode they most enjoy.

Visual Triad Model (VTM)

The VTM provides a visual schematic for how the processes of seeing, imagining, and depicting interact to support the visual decoding, imagination, and encoding of our students. In **figure 1.1**, the actions listed under see, imagine, and depict describe visually based learning and teaching strategies as applied in the classroom. These lists are an excellent resource for developing visually based learning objectives. The questions that follow provide jumping off points for discussion with students about their visual experiences and their visual products.

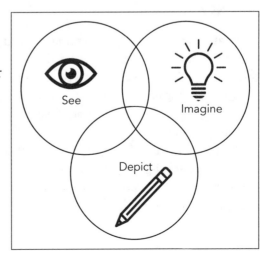

FIG. 1.1 VISUAL TRIAD MODEL BREAKDOWN

	See	Imagine	Depict
Actions	*Decode* Look View Perceive Observe Inspect Examine Identify Analyze Contemplate Investigate Evaluate	*Manipulate mental models* Picture Visualize View in mind's eye Envision Conceptualize Interpret Design Foresee Inspire Invent Dream	*Encode* Doodle/draw/diagram Represent Reproduce Chronicle Communicate Illustrate Display Model/map Compose/recompose Express Create
Questions	What did you see? What is there, and what isn't there? How are you able to think about parts and wholes about what you see? What insights have you had about your observations? What did you discover in your observation?	How have you used mental images in your thinking? What did you discover? How have you manipulated your mental images to develop a new idea? What thoughts have you used to express what you have imagined?	How have you depicted an idea, a concept, or a feeling visually? How are you able to use simple methods of depiction—especially doodling—to depict your thoughts and convey meaning? How can you elaborate on your depictions to convey a more detailed meaning? What can you do to help a viewer understand your intended meaning?

Before we go into exactly how you can use these lists to write visual learning objectives, let's think about this model for a moment, with a few examples from an educator's perspective.

1. What is significant about the images students see?

In our visual world, we are inundated by images—those we choose to see as well as those thrust in our field of vision (advertisements, pop-ups, billboard signs, commercials, and so on). Given the amount of visual information we take in on a daily—not to mention hourly—basis, we would overload if we didn't find a way to distinguish useful images from tertiary images.

Learning to identify and decode visual communications takes practice. The more practice students have with "seeing" images, the more they will start trusting their ability to see with a purpose and make viewing a more intentional act—something they actively do and not something they don't have control over.

2. What is significant about the images students imagine?

Imagination is a birthright of being human. We can conceive of possibilities not yet realized and manipulate them internally. This is an extraordinary capacity and one that is evident even in very young children. Toddlers play with pots, pans, bowls, and dishes as drums, hats, and building supplies. Socks become puppets with their own possibilities, and if you observe preschool play, you will hear "Okay, you're the mommy, and I'm the baby, and this teddy bear is really our pet dog." Imagination is important at all ages as students write original short stories, design projects in social studies, and find problems to solve in environmental science. The ability to imagine and interpret thoughts, ideas, concepts, scenes, stories, and more enables learning and undergirds all forms of creativity.

3. What is significant about the images students depict?

The images we depict allow us the satisfaction of seeing the contents of our thoughts and imaginations and the ability to share these inner experiences with others through visual communication. Again, this is fundamental to learning and creativity. Various forms of depiction or picture writing—integrating images and text (more on that later)—allow students to show what they know in varied ways with numerous forms of media. Presentations in college, career, and civic life require visual representation of ideas, designs, and data analysis. Creating and displaying knowledge, information, and findings of research are also necessary for preparing students for future career paths.

Practical Applications of the Visual Triad Model (VTM)

So, how does the VTM help us write visual learning objectives? Let's consider an example. At different times, we emphasize a variety of mental processes based on our objectives. For example, in the primary grades, picture books are often part of the English language arts curriculum. As we read through the text, we might ask students to view the pictures while they listen. Our objectives might be that:

- Students **view** illustrations in picture books while being read to.
- Students describe what they **see**, including characters, setting, and action.
- Students **analyze** illustrations in picture books and predict what might come next.

After which we might have students use their imaginations to create their own visual representations. These objectives might include:

- Students will **imagine** themselves as a character in the story.
- Students will **draw** a picture placing themselves in the setting.

You'll see the VTM in application as you study the activities and lessons throughout this book.

"Teaching the very young child can be challenging as most have not mastered basic literacy and mathematical skills. Using visual strategies—having students observe their visual world, chronicle their findings, and express their interpretation through words and images—allows students another avenue in which to express themselves. Incorporating visual strategies allows me the chance to provide appropriate learning tasks that challenge students at their level."

Kipp

You Are the Visual Teacher

It shouldn't come as a surprise that a visual teacher looks like you. You have visual skills to draw upon, and you will learn new strategies throughout this book. Take a minute or two to review the checklist on page 219 to identify your strengths as a visual teacher. Most teachers don't claim all of the characteristics and that's okay. Your response to this list will highlight approaches and skills that you already have in your toolbox and those you might still need to work on.

What I have found over the years is that most teachers are visual teachers to some degree. While reviewing the checklist, you will identify the items that apply to you now. You may also uncover and identifiy some areas of visual teaching that you would like to strengthen. Don't think of the unchecked items as areas of weakness. Weaknesses are very different than undeveloped skills. It may be that you just haven't acquired some of the skills and abilities yet, and the unchecked items may represent abilities that are not yet developed. They may represent untapped potential for you.

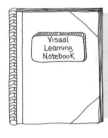

"This is a good time to break in your visual learning notebook. Based on what you marked on the checklist, take a few minutes to write and/or depict your visual strengths, and then do the same for the visual skills and abilities that you would like to acquire or strengthen."

Susan

Your Growth and Development as a Visual Teacher

To become more fluent in visual communication and to nurture these abilities in your students, it's important to develop a broad sense of the visual. The best way to do this is to build a visual vocabulary. Some educators may not be comfortable with speaking this visual language due to not having practiced it in a while. However, just like learning and mastering any second language, the more you immerse yourself in visual language and surround yourself with visual vocabulary, the more natural it will feel. An articulate visual teacher is one who attends to visuals throughout the day and who works to build their own visual vocabulary and visual communication skills.

Moving On

Incorporating meaningful mark-making into your classroom is a readily attainable skill. In the next chapter, you'll learn about using the visual alphabet to create simple doodles and begin building a visual vocabulary, the first step toward supporting students' visual learning and your own visual teaching.

The Visual Toolbox—
Doodle, Design, and Depict

This chapter is a hands-on and purposeful introduction to the fundamental tools and strategies of meaningful mark-making. The information and activities can be used in your own learning and teaching and can be imparted to your students. The act of mark-making isn't just for fun. Plenty of research supports the importance of doodling, design, and depiction in the classroom to increase engagement and retention.[9]

Making a Case for Doodling:
Meaningful Marks Make a Difference

Doodling has gotten a bad rap in the past. It has notoriously frustrated teachers who feel their students are wasting time and cannot possibly be paying attention. Several teachers I have worked with questioned whether students could doodle and listen to lessons at the same time. When I speak at conferences I ask, "How many of you think doodling may help learning?" and "How many of you think that doodling is a definite distraction?" It's not uncommon to have a split in the audience's response to these questions, even among those who are coming for my presentation on visual learning and teaching. More recently, doodling has received extensive positive attention in the world of business. Books like Dan Roam's *The Back of the Napkin* and *Show and Tell*, Mike Rohde's *The Sketchnote Handbook*, and Sunni Brown's *The Doodle Revolution* have received national and international attention for their portrayal of doodling as a positive element of learning and problem-solving. These authors conduct workshops and give TED talks on how to represent the most intricate ideas and solve complex problems with the most simple of visual representations: doodles.

In *The Doodle Revolution*, Sunni Brown notes that Albert Einstein, John F. Kennedy, Marie Curie, and Henry Ford all used doodling while engaged in deep thinking and problem-solving. Her book includes a photo of JFK's doodles at a cabinet meeting during the Cuban Missile Crisis. "There is no such thing as a mindless doodle," Brown asserts. Further, she notes that there is considerable evidence showing doodlers are most often concentrating intently, connecting neurological pathways with previously disconnected pathways, and engaging in deep and necessary information processing. Doodling, according to Brown, is making spontaneous marks to help you think—be they abstract doodles, such as margin designs or random sketches, or representational doodles, which are made to help illuminate the information being processed. At the highest level, Brown defines what she calls *infodoodling*, which uses simple representational doodles integrated with words, numbers, or symbols to optimize meaning.[10] The idea of infodoodling underpins much of what is to come in this chapter.

Doodling and Recall

Integrating words and doodles to enhance attention, retention, and learning has deep roots in cognitive psychology and neuroscience. Research on the picture-superiority effect, published by Whitehouse, Maybery, and Durkin in the *British Journal of Developmental Psychology*, shows that when ideas and concepts can be expressed with an image, as well as words, the brain remembers the information to a much greater extent than with a verbal only text. **When students doodle to represent concepts and ideas, they synthesize information and encode it in memory for easy recall and retrieval.**[11] Further, Jackie Andrade, who researches the effects of visuals on learning, documented the effects of doodling on retention and recall in the research piece titled, "What Does Doodling Do?" Andrade determined that even abstract doodling while listening to material that was not of interest to the listener increases retention by 29 percent over listening alone without doodling.[12]

I have always felt that the students in my classes who doodled, even abstractly, had greater recall. I once observed a top-performing student in a residential high school for advanced math and science students doodle abstract designs while listening to high-level physics lectures. When I interviewed her and asked how she could both doodle and remember what was said, she showed me that she took brief standard notes, as required by the teacher, on a separate sheet at the same time. And she could recount what was being said throughout the lecture by looking at various parts of her abstract design. She said, "Doodling actually helps me stay focused. It doesn't distract me; it keeps my mind from wandering." Some students are not inclined to doodle and may even find it distracting. However, findings from action research studies conducted by my graduate students, who are concurrently classroom teachers, have consistently produced overwhelmingly positive feedback from students who are allowed, even encouraged, to doodle while listening to lessons.

Why Doodle?

Doodling is an essential visual teaching, learning, and literacy skill. From a visual perspective, it is as essential to be able to decode and produce meaningful doodles as it is to be able to read and write texts. Doodling builds cognitive skills—pattern recognition, image recall, analysis, comparison, synthesis, evaluation, and more—as well as conceptual understanding. Doodling is important because it is a visual skill that is accessible and achievable by students and teachers alike.

In Practice

As we go through the exercises in this book, take a leap of faith and create your own doodles and sketches. Keep in mind, while some might question their ability to draw, *everyone can doodle.* You don't need artistic talent, just a willingness to make marks on a regular basis. You will become more comfortable with a variety of visual teaching and learning strategies as you learn—or relearn—how to doodle. And you will be more comfortable teaching your students how to integrate visual and verbal modes to optimize their learning as you do so yourself.

Inevitably, the first few weeks of doodling in their visual learning notebook feels uncomfortable for the teachers I work with in professional development programs and workshops. Given lots of opportunities for practice, however, their comfort increases over time and their responses to reflection questions are overwhelmingly positive. Doodling does not require great skill in drawing since doodles most often consist of basic shapes.

Hands-On: A Teacher's Visual Toolbox

I once gave a workshop for K–8 teachers. After we had worked with some basic aspects of doodling, designing, and depicting, we developed the following materials to guide teachers as they honed their skills in the practices of visual communication. Note: While both abstract and representational doodling are beneficial for engagement and retention, the remainder of this chapter will focus on representational doodling, because it is the more deliberate and specific of the two types.

"Everyone can doodle" needs to become our slogan. So, pick up your pencil and let's dive into the hands-on activities that will enhance your visual skills and fill your visual teaching toolbox.

Visual Alphabet: The Foundation of Representational Doodling

The visual alphabet, introduced by Dave Gray, the founder of XPLANE, a visual consultancy firm, is comprised of twelve shapes called letters. These visual letters serve a function similar to alphabetic letters. The straightforward marks and shapes can be combined and recombined to create a wide variety of symbols, icons, and images that communicate both simple and complex ideas. The possibilities for creating representational doodles from the letters of the visual alphabet are almost limitless. We use the visual alphabet with elements of design in our depiction of academic content and personal meaning throughout the book.

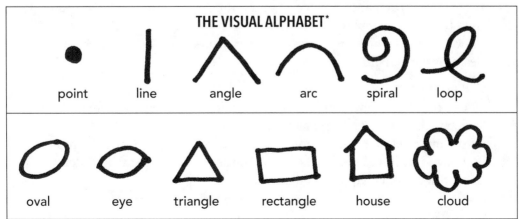

THE VISUAL ALPHABET*

point line angle arc spiral loop

oval eye triangle rectangle house cloud

*The Visual Alphabet was created by Dave Gray and is used with permission.

ACTIVITY VISUAL ALPHABET

1. Set aside part of your visual learning notebook (say, the first ten pages) to create a doodle dictionary. A doodle dictionary is a visual repository of representational doodles you can use again and again. I'll go more into the doodle dictionary later in this chapter. For now, designate part of your notebook as the dictionary and do this exercise on those pages.

2. Re-create the visual alphabet on the inside cover of your notebook to make it easier to access whenever you need it.

3. On your doodle dictionary pages, using only the letters of the visual alphabet, create a doodle of each of the following:

   - an animal
   - a place
   - a thing
   - an action

For example, in the step-by-step illustration below, I started with a rectangle and then used triangles for the neck and head. Next, I used lines for legs, a beard, and an ear. Then, a spiral for a horn, a dot for an eye, and "Voilà!" it's a goat. A good resource for these visual step-by-step directions is Ed Emberley's *Drawing Book: Make a World*.

For further practice, try doodling these in your notebook:

- bike
- camera
- cat
- clock
- dog
- Earth
- fish
- house
- lightbulb
- pen
- pencil
- school

The visual alphabet is our go-to source for elements that illustrate complex thinking in simple doodles or designs. We will revisit it again and again as we practice forming its shapes and letters like we did when we were first learning our verbal alphabet.

Extension Activity

Create one or two new representational doodles in your visual learning notebook each day. It's great practice and becomes a fun daily activity. A two-minute doodle break reinforces and validates doodling while also providing a visual interlude. Teachers have consistently reported that students look forward to their quick doodle breaks.

Six Essential Design Elements: Where Visual and Verbal Meet

As you continue to use the visual alphabet, you may begin to notice that your own personal style will influence your strokes and make them distinctly "your marks." This instinct to design can be nurtured and cultivated through practice to move you from basic mark-making in the form of random, abstract doodles to meaningful doodling that is intended to communicate things and ideas to other people.

In this section, we will integrate the visual and the verbal within doodles to create meaningful images and expand our capacity for enhanced communication. As discussed in the introduction, dual-coding theory recognizes that the integration of visual and verbal modes of expression in a learning context increases engagement, understanding, and retention. Let's explore the six essential design elements that will further help shape your visual and verbal communication.

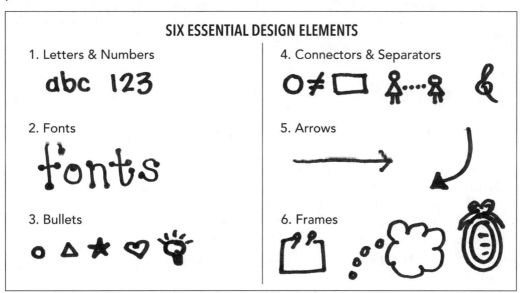

DESIGN ELEMENT 1: LETTERS & NUMBERS

AbcdEFI234567890 **BOLD** *ITALIC*

We use letters and numbers every day to make words, to communicate, to label, to identify, to count, to quantify, but letters and numbers can be rich and effective design elements in their own rights. On any given day, you probably see letters and numbers being used as a form of visual design. A neon sign in the window with the words "hot pizza" alight in glowing red gas conveys a different effect than if the same words were text on a page. Letters and numbers take up space. They are shapes, and their shapes can be elaborated on or further designed, as we'll discuss in the next section on fonts. For our purposes here, we will want to consider some basic aspects of working with letters and numbers. Even without other visual elements, the shape and detail of letter and number forms provide a host of options for communicating.

ACTIVITY LETTERS & NUMBERS

1. Write out the verbal (Roman) alphabet and the numbers 0 through 9. Don't give this any forethought, just let your pencil flow across the space and make the marks.

2. Write the alphabet and the numbers as though you are writing them as the most beautiful letters and numbers you have ever written, slowly and carefully. Think of each character as a miniature design of its own.

3. Write the letters all in capital letters and the numbers as boldly and deliberately as you can.

Writing in this way moves us from our regular everyday handwriting into forming letters as elements of design. Hand-lettering that incorporates elements of font design makes letters and numbers more distinctive and takes the written word to a new form of visual and verbal expression.

DESIGN ELEMENT 2: FONTS

thin **THICK** ≡FAST short Round hot Fancy

You might consider using any of the numerous digital fonts found on your computer when creating materials for your classroom. But for our purposes here, we are focusing on handwritten fonts—or hand-lettering—that you can create and reproduce upon a page, a whiteboard, a poster, or in a notebook. With handwritten fonts, text can take on the attribute closely associated with the word's meaning and gain the ability to carry emotion, meaning, and action. This allows the viewer to see both the verbal and visual representation simultaneously. For example, in the image above, the word *short* is written in short letters, *hot* has flames on it, and *fast* has motion lines behind it, suggesting that it is moving across the page.

Creating font styles with hand-lettering gives us a visual, verbal, and tactile experience that reinforces learning and creativity. Hand-lettering provides an outlet for personal, and even artistic, expression. Carrie and Alton Barron, coauthors of *The Creativity Cure: How to Build Happiness with Your Own Two Hands*, emphasize the importance of working with your hands to enhance overall health and well-being. The book asserts that until recently, people were commonly engaged in handwork (writing by hand, needlework, crafting, building, sewing), a practice that has cognitive, physical, and emotional benefits.[13] In the past, a child's introduction to handwork often began with learning to draw shapes and print both letters and words. Today, teachers I've worked with often report that their students will spend time on hand-lettering in journals and on posters but they might balk at pages of cursive handwriting practice.

ACTIVITY FONTS

1. Create your own fonts to both show and tell the content of the following messages:
   - Through thick and thin
   - What goes up must come down

- Honey, it's cold outside
- Slow down, curves ahead

2. Now look back at each of your messages and ask yourself the following questions:
    - Can you see thick and thin visually and verbally?
    - Do up and down actually visually guide you in either direction?
    - How cold is your cold?
    - Does slow convey motion, and how much curve do your curves have?

The concept of visual resonance applies here. When the design of letters and words represent their meanings, the word both shows and tells its meaning. We respond to the word on a verbal and visual level.

DESIGN ELEMENT 3: BULLETS

When I say, "Let's make a list," what is the first thing that comes to mind? Shopping list? To-do list? Pros and cons list? Packing list? Regardless of the type of list that springs to mind, I'll bet all of our lists have something in common. We all most likely separated the items on our list by starting a new item on a new line, with or without a bullet for emphasis.

Visual bullets serve as a simple form of a graphic organizer (see more about graphic organizers on page 50). Bullets are used to anchor text on the page and to delineate and organize information that is important or that goes together in some way. Bullets separate lines of text and tell our visual cortex to distinguish a list from what otherwise might be an incredibly long run-on sentence. Bullets can be formed by using almost any shape or image. They may be made to resemble an object that relates to a theme or a purpose of the point: a pencil might indicate an assignment; a lightbulb might be a brainstormed list of good ideas; an eye could be a list of things to look for, or a check mark might represent assignments that have been completed.

ACTIVITY BULLETS

1. You're going to create a grocery shopping list divided into categories such as dairy, meat, produce, canned goods, and so on.

2. Start by creating a key for easy reference. Designate each category with a different type of bullet. You might choose a milk bottle for dairy products or an apple for produce. You might also choose simpler bullets, like dots, diamonds, or check marks. Use a different symbol for each category. The key will remind you what each bullet stands for.

3. Brainstorm a list of items you need, putting the appropriate bullet next to the item name on the list. Each item on your list may not have a unique bullet but each category should. Even if your list starts to feel overwhelmed with clutter, the bullets should help you see the items and categories on your list more clearly.

DESIGN ELEMENT 4: CONNECTORS & SEPARATORS

Connectors and separators may not seem as glamorous and eye-catching as the other design elements; however, they are essential for visual communication. Connectors help us pull things together while separators distinguish differences. Without connectors and separators, it would be hard to distinguish where something begins or ends. As a design element, connectors can be tenuous, represented by a dotted or dashed line, or they can be definitive and seemingly unbreakable, represented by a thick black line.

A common separator that we all use is a period (.); it's a visual reminder to stop. That simple speck of ink is a very powerful separator within written communication.

Some graphic forms, such as a Venn diagram, are both functional connectors and separators. These simple, yet powerful, elements help us process relationships among visual and verbal information. They are used in diagrams, flow charts, mathematical equations, mind maps, family trees, geographical maps, street signs, sentences, paragraphs, and visual directions.

ACTIVITY CONNECTORS & SEPARATORS

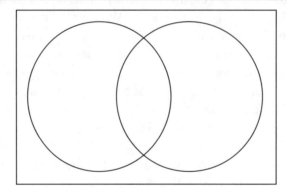

1. Draw a Venn diagram like in this illustration.
2. Label the left circle "Straight Lines Only," label the right circle "Curves Only," and label the almond-shaped section where the circles overlap "Lines and Curves."
3. Write each letter of the verbal (Roman) alphabet in the diagram, placing it in the appropriate category.
4. As you form your letters—uppercase and lowercase, if you are feeling adventurous—practice your own personal mark-making style with the printed alphabet.

DESIGN ELEMENT 5: ARROWS

For our next design element, we need to ask ourselves a few questions:
- Which way should we go from here?
- Where should we look?
- What comes next?

Arrows are useful tools and design elements. We learn about arrows at an early age. Most often, our first lesson is that arrows direct our attention, show us where to go. But their meaning can vary based on context.

Arrows can be used to:
- represent directional movement (as seen in street signs)
- show action
- convey the next step in a cycle
- draw attention to an important idea or aspect

As a design element, arrows can be useful tools when you want to create emphasis.

ACTIVITY ARROWS

Using lines (straight or curved) and triangular shapes, depict arrows that represent each of the following:
- merging
- divergence
- growth
- decline
- up/down or right/left
- above or below

DESIGN ELEMENT 6: FRAMES

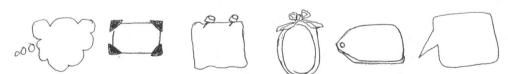

The sixth and final design element is the frame. Frames are useful for infodoodling, mind mapping, visual note-taking, and other forms of graphic recording and organizers.

Frames serve to both set apart and highlight the content they contain. In their simplest form, frames are just shapes. Squares, rectangles, circles, ovals, starbursts, clouds, and thought and speech bubbles to name a few. These shapes, when used as frames, contain specific messages and ideas so that they can be synthesized and taken in as a complete picture. Frames probably come to mind as the structure behind flowcharts, blueprints, and engineering diagrams. To enhance visual learning and teaching, we want to incorporate frames into our visual and verbal modes of expression daily.

ACTIVITY FRAMES

1. Depict a thought or speech bubble of something someone might think or say while standing in line at the grocery store.
2. Use a frame to contain the images and text someone might use for a lost pet flyer.
3. Use a frame to depict an item that is for sale.
4. Use a frame to contain a memory.

Depict: Make It Your Own

Now that you have explored the visual alphabet and the six essential design elements and practiced using them in your visual learning notebooks, your visual toolbox is growing. These elements form the basics of visual expression and the possibilities for using them in your work are almost endless.

Armed with these basics, it's time to take it to the next level. In the next section, we'll be creating faces and figures to enrich our doodles and designs, building a personal visual library of doodle images (a doodle dictionary), and putting all the visual pieces to work in visual warm-up activities that you can also use in the classroom.

FACES & FIGURES

Faces and figures are prominent in meaningful doodles, since our classroom subjects, especially in ELA and social studies, often involve people. Incorporating human depictions into our visual learning helps create a sense of self and community. It also provides opportunities to express emotions within and toward the content, which can deepen connection and retention of learning. Visual tools such as storyboards, picture books, mind maps, and journals all benefit greatly from doodles and depictions of faces and figures.

And yet, however useful figure drawing may be, this is probably where I have heard teachers say, "I can't draw" the most. Ask any preschooler or early elementary student to draw a person, and they happily go about it, not really concerned with any realistic features. They proceed to make faces and figures, even if they just sketch out a quick smiley face on a stick figure. But, there is something about being asked to draw a person that sends adults into a tizzy.

This is where we can learn from our younger selves and just start with the very basic of doodles: the smiley face. Don't worry about body figures for the moment. It's really quite amazing that an oval and four marks—eyes, nose, and mouth—can convey a wide range of emotions.

Take a look at the images. Most of the faces are made up of five simple shapes: an oval for the head, two round shapes for eyes, a dot or a squiggle for a nose, and a line or a circle for the mouth. Look at all the different expressions these simple marks can make. Adding just two more marks (as eyebrows) extends the range of emotions even further.

Look at the faces from left to right. The first is happy with upturned features. The second from the left is sad with downturned features. The third is tired with eyes closed. The next is angry with a furrowed brow and a scowl. And the last face looks neutral with a minimal expression, or perhaps a bit perplexed. You may find that, after practicing these basic faces, you will be ready to introduce a few more marks—ears, hair, clothing—to create faces with even more character and variety.

ACTIVITY FACES

1. Be sure to use a pencil for this exercise. You may want to erase certain features as needed.

2. Depict the following four basic faces. Don't add more details at this time and don't overthink this. Just make the given marks and enjoy the process.
   - Make an oval and add four marks to depict a happy person.
   - Make an oval and add four marks to depict a sleepy person.
   - Make an oval and add six marks to depict an angry or a worried person.
   - Make an oval and add four to six marks to depict an emotion or expression of your choice.

3. Depict three fuller faces as follows:
   - Make an oval or a circle and add four to six marks that are a little more styled for a surprised facial expression. Then add ears to round out the face.
   - Make an oval or a circle and add four to six marks that are a little more styled for a goofy-grin facial expression. Then add ears to round out the face; try placing ears in varying positions to see how it affects the outcome.
   - Make an oval or a circle and add your own marks to depict an emotion or expression of your choice.

4. Re-create two of your previously depicted faces and add some hair, additional facial features, and/or accessories to polish them up. Add embellishments like earrings, hair, eyelashes, dimples, or clefts to the chin.

This is where your personal mark-making style will begin to reveal itself. This stage may feel awkward, but the more you practice, the more comfortable you will become.

Having the ability to depict faces showing a wide range of emotions and expressions is a skill that will be put to use throughout the rest of this book and throughout your visual teaching. However, a time may come when you will want to convey movement with your characters and when you will want more than a floating, bodiless face. This is where figures come in. Whether or not they have a face, figures can be made to express emotions and movement with just a few strokes of the pen.

Most of the figures that we'll be exploring will be faceless, but not featureless, and they will tell a story on their own. Take a look at the images on the next page. All of these figures are made up of the same parts—head, body, and limbs. Yet, they are each quite distinct. For example, do you see one that is just standing around? Can you spot one that seems to be marching? Stick figures, in the first row, are the most basic and probably the most well-known of all the figures. The card figures that occupy the second row, seem to carry a little more weight. The last row of assorted figures shows ways you can vary basic figures, thus allowing you to develop a personal style.

The simplest way is to start with a stick figure. Begin with a circle for the head, one line for the torso, four lines for the limbs, and a small shape for hands and feet. From there you may embellish your stick figures with hair and clothing, and you can choose to make them taller or shorter to illustrate adults and children.

ACTIVITY FIGURES

1. Depict several basic stick figures using only a circle for a head and lines for limbs:
   - an adult standing with a child
   - a person jumping for joy
   - a person sitting in a chair
   - a person marching
   - any other figure in action

2. Try your hand at depicting card figures. Using only a rectangle for the body, an oval for the head, lines for the limbs, loops for feet, and random marks for hands, depict the following figures:
   - a confident speaker
   - two friends
   - a card person in any action

3. Experiment with giving the figures different types of bodies. Maybe a figure with a star or a spring for a torso. Use your imagination to create fun, unusual body styles and poses.

Inevitably, as humans, we will include representations of people in our visual work. Ed Emberley's *Make a World* has step-by-step visual directions for making a wide array of human characters, animals, buildings, vehicles, and more. This is a worthwhile resource to check out as you collect your doodles and develop your own doodle dictionary.

BUILDING A DOODLE DICTIONARY

Now that we have the visual alphabet, the six essential design elements, and faces and figures to use in our visual toolbox, let's create a personal doodle dictionary. Just as writers turn to a dictionary, thesaurus, or writer's guide to find the perfect word to use, visual teachers also need a resource to consult. A doodle dictionary is a resource that will grow with you over time. In it, you can log samples of meaningful doodles that you can show students, either to demonstrate a point or inspire them to create a doodle dictionary of their own. Some doodled images, designs, and figures you and your students will likely want to use again and again, so having examples of these favorites means you won't have to continually re-create them.

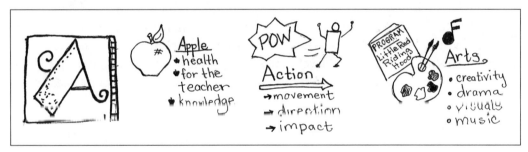

From this example, you can see that the doodle dictionary is organized alphabetically for ease of use and consistency, with each letter of the alphabet having its own page or pages. When you add entries, you can depict an image and then make a bullet list of all the possible ideas, words, and meanings that the image can convey.

As you begin to add images and symbols to your doodle dictionary, don't get hung up on attempting to make them look realistic or perfect. Remember, you want to doodle an image that is meaningful to you and represents an idea, a thought, an item, or an action. You may find that a three-ring binder is the best way to organize your doodle dictionary, so you can insert pages over time.

ACTIVITY DOODLE DICTIONARY

1. Create your own personally styled letter *A*, then create doodled symbols and images for the following *A* words, making sure to leave lots of space around each doodle:
   - award
   - above
   - alarm clock
   - arts
   - apple

2. For each image, add a bullet list of words that the image could represent— these are akin to definitions. If you created a blue ribbon to depict

award, your bullet list might include winning, 1st place, recognition, and trophy as possible associations for the image of *award*.

3. Create your own personally styled letter *B*, and then create symbols and images for the following *B* words, making sure to leave lots of space around each doodle:
   - ball
   - balance
   - book
   - butterfly
   - below

4. For each image, add a bullet list of words that the image could represent. If you created an open or closed book to depict *book*, your bullet list may include reading, story, novel, learning, studying, diary, notebook, and journal as possible definitions for the image of *book*.

Something important to keep in mind: the work we're doing now in the doodle dictionary is an exercise. We're brainstorming and listing as many ideas as possible. As you hone your visual teaching skills, you'll want to narrow the definitions in your dictionary. It's important that, as a class, you develop an agreed-upon vocabulary. For example, if you were to write on the whiteboard "Take out your" and then draw a picture of a book, this might mean different things to different people. Does it mean take out the textbook? A library book? The life notebook? The journal?

The solution is fairly simple: add enhancements that clarify what the doodle means. Perhaps, as a class, you decide that a book symbol with a picture of a sun on it means "life notebook," or a book symbol with a fraction on it means "math textbook." In a class, it is likely that there will be common symbols that everyone agrees upon and symbols that have personal meaning for individual students. This is something you can develop over time. But, for now, let your imagination run wild as you come up with significant symbols and their potential meanings.

The more you practice doodling—whether as an exercise in this book or just as a whim during your free time—the more you will discover new entries for your doodle dictionary. You may find yourself doodling absentmindedly or while thinking about something else. Then, upon closer examination, you will notice that you have doodled the perfect depiction of whirlwind, turmoil, tornado, chaos, funnel, force, confusion, spiral, and twisted—all with a single swirling stroke. These mark-making moments can be transferred to your doodle dictionary and then incorporated into your visual learning and teaching.

VISUAL WARM-UPS

We have all heard—and probably repeated—many sayings that revolve around the need to practice. Quite simply, practicing any skill will make you better. However, doing the exact same thing over and over again isn't always interesting or engaging and can stifle creativity. So how do we practice visual learning so we can teach visual learning skills and nurture creativity instead of stifling it?

One option is to flip back to the beginning of this chapter and run through all the activities again, honing your own personal mark-making style. Another option is to add five new entries to your doodle dictionary every week, extending your comfort with depicting new ideas, items, or actions. Or, you can choose any of the activities compiled in the following visual warm-ups to provide you with hours of engaging and ever-changing practice opportunities.

The added benefit from practicing these visual warm-ups is that you will be well-versed in the activities and comfortable and confident introducing them to your students when they begin visual learning. These warm-ups provide a foundation for many of the more complex visual tools presented in later chapters, such as visual note-taking, graphic organizers, mind maps, one pagers, and infographics.

These simple activities will help you develop your mark-making abilities. Remember to use the letters of the visual alphabet, some or all of the six essential design elements, faces and figures, and your doodle dictionary.

1. Doodle Colors Without Colors: Practice your mark-making and doodling as you depict and label things that are:

- red
- orange
- yellow

- green
- blue
- purple

2. Doodles Are Shaping Up: Practice your mark-making and doodling as you depict and label things that are:

- round
- square
- oval

- rectangular
- spiral
- looped

3. Doodle the World Around You: Practice your mark-making and doodling as you depict and label things that are:

- Nouns
  - People: doctor, police officer, clown, woman, man, child
  - Places: school, airport, skyscraper, barn, garden, playground
  - Things: art, bananas, caterpillar, dog, doll, elephant, food

- Verbs
  - Actions: leaping, walking, spinning, jumping
  - Activities: teaching, playing, building a snowman, driving

4. Squiggle-Doodle Sheet: Practice your mark-making and doodling as you stretch your creativity to complete an image. Have someone make a squiggle (random mark or marks on a page) and use this as your starting point.

Take the starting squiggle and add your own marks and doodles to complete the image, making it into anything you can imagine.

5. Squiggle-Doodle Stories: Once you've completed a squiggle-doodle, create a scene around the doodle design, and write a short story about it. You can use the blank squiggle-doodle template in the appendix on page 221, or you or your students can create your own.

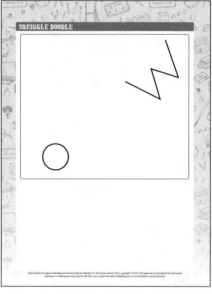

6. Doodle Note-Taking: Incorporate doodling into your note-taking. Watch an instructional or informational video and take visual notes on the video's key points. This is just like regular note-taking but you'll combine text with doodling. In doing so, you are accessing what's called the picture-superiority effect—a phenomenon that can increase retention and recall—while practicing your personal mark-making style. Recall that Sunni Brown calls doodle note-taking *infodoodling*. It's doodling that integrates images, shapes, words, symbols, numbers, and colors to create an informative visual display. We create personal infodoodles for learning while taking in or recomposing information and material from one format to another format. Some ways to do this are:

- Watch a five-minute TedEd video and take notes with an emphasis on doodling.

- Read a chapter in your favorite book and summarize what happens with a doodle.

- Watch a how-to video (DIY or cooking) and depict the parts of the process with doodling and visual note-taking.

"I never realized that doodling would help me—and my students— remember so much more, and I couldn't imagine that I would get comfortable doodling in my notes, my planner, and my class handouts—much less enjoy it!"

Recomposing

When we ask students to imagine different possibilities and to depict their knowledge in a visual format, we are often asking students to recompose from text or graphics. Steve Moline, author of *I See What You Mean: Visual Literacy K–8,* talks at length about recomposing as an essential visual thinking skill. **Recomposing involves reading information in one format and summarizing or expressing it in another format.** For example, we might read a text on the battles of the Civil War and summarize them in an illustrated timeline. Or, we could read a cycle diagram showing the phases of how planting a seed can lead to a full-size oak, then describe this in an expository paragraph. This involves reading information originally in a diagram and recomposing it as a paragraph. Moline says recomposing is both an effective research strategy and a powerful aid to comprehension.[14]

Recomposing requires students to find a different way to express the same information. This activity brings higher-order thinking—analysis, synthesis, and evaluation—to the fore. It also requires students to connect visual and verbal modes of expression. Students must take the following steps:

1. Analyze the information presented (for instance, weekly vocabulary, textbook paragraph, list of events, parts of a cell).

2. Evaluate what alternative format would be best to present the information, choosing a format that integrates words and images: timeline, infographic, one pager, poster, visual vocab cards, graphic organizers, presentation, and more.

3. Choose and design the format to recompose the information.

Moving On

After working through the activities in this chapter, you are equipped with more skills and tools to help you integrate visual teaching and learning in your classroom and across your curriculum. As you continue reading, you'll acquire more strategies to teach these skills to your students, be better equipped to incorporate visual learning opportunities into your lessons, and have several curriculum examples that thoroughly integrate visual teaching and learning into your own curriculum.

PART TWO

Visual Tools IN THE Classroom

CHAPTER 3

In the Hands of Our Students—Putting Visual Tools to Work in Our Classrooms

The majority of learning that takes place in classrooms revolves around communication. We teach students to read and write so they can receive and send ideas, thoughts, and messages. Writing is how we express our verbal thinking; depicting is how we express our visual thinking. As we use the verbal and visual together, learning and the ability to communicate are increased.

It is important to keep in mind that even though visual communication is increasingly important, verbal and written communication are still ubiquitous and highly valued. Employer surveys frequently cite verbal communication skills as some of the most highly sought-after in potential employees. So, it's important to learn visual skills but not at the expense of other skills.

In the first part of this chapter, we will look at a curriculum map that will guide you through the process of teaching your students about the visual alphabet, the six essential design elements, doodling and drawing people and things, and developing a doodle dictionary. These four tools become the springboard for all other visual learning tools presented in this book. The sample lessons that follow will teach your students to use visual tools and essential visual skills along with verbal text to optimize their learning.

In the second part of this chapter, we will dig a little deeper into our toolbox for more tools to use daily as you reinforce visual learning alongside verbal learning in your classroom.

Carol

"Susan once said, 'Make a circle, give it two eyes and a line for a mouth. Now name it.' Many of us laughed. It broke the ice. It helped the reluctant doodlers in the room feel more comfortable. We need to do that same thing for our students. Doodles are not art. Doodles are a way to show our thinking. So, it is important that we don't critique our students' doodles as artwork but that we discuss the ideas they represent."

Curriculum to Get Visual Tools into the Hands of Your Students

The following unit, titled "Learning with the Visual Alphabet and More," poses the essential question: "How can doodling and drawing help with learning?" The unit questions explore doodling with the visual alphabet and the six essential design elements.

The curriculum map for the unit includes both essential questions and unit questions. Essential questions are big picture questions that help define the breadth and depth of the curriculum. Unit questions are more specific to the current topic of study. We will discuss essential and unit questions more in-depth when we go over the creation of curriculum maps in chapter 9. This chapter's map also includes content standards, content topics, academic skills, visual skills, and both unit project and unit product options. The map also focuses on the essential aspects of learning to use the visual alphabet, the six essential design elements, and individual mark-making in all learning activities. Four lesson plans are included. Notes, doodles, and drawings are completed in the students' visual learning notebooks and on handouts provided by the teacher. The unit clearly follows the guidelines of the visual triad model (discussed in chapter 1) and provides a solid foundation for developing the skills of visual literacy. Students are guided through the processes of decoding, imagining, and depicting visual representations through simple doodles and drawings.

Strategies for Encouraging Reluctant Doodlers

- Let students use personal whiteboards, chalkboards, or electronic tablets so students can play and take risks with their doodling. Mistakes can easily be erased and students can start anew with a fresh surface. This is helpful for people who lack confidence in their doodling abilities and don't want to commit to paper.

- Good erasers make mistakes bearable for those with perfectionistic tendencies.

- Triangle pencil grips may be helpful for writing on paper.

- Have a classroom library of books on how to draw. This can inspire even the most tentative drawing/doodling/depicting students.

- Model your own visual mark-making. Use every opportunity to doodle and sketch in front of the class.

- Have a "class doodler" who comes to the whiteboard to doodle next to your written notes.

- Believe it or not, playing a simple game of hangman reinforces doodling without being obvious.

- Pictionary, Memory, and other visual-perceptual games can be highly motivating.

Learning with the Visual Alphabet and More: Cross-Curricular K–8

You may already use curriculum maps in your school. The maps we'll use, incorporating visual tools and visual learning strategies, will be slightly different. In chapter 9, you will be guided through the process of using these maps to design curriculum. You'll also find examples of curriculum maps with units containing visual strategies across grade levels and subject areas.

Unit Narrative

Buying into the research supporting the need for visual learning in the classroom is easy. The data clearly shows that using visual drawings and doodles can help reinforce learning and increase retention. But integrating doodling and drawing into the academic curriculum can feel daunting. The following lessons are a road map for how you might introduce doodling and drawing to your students for everyday academic tasks.

Curriculum Map

Subject: Visual learning

Unit/Theme: Learning with the Visual Alphabet and More

Essential Questions
1. How do doodling and drawing help with learning?
2. How do visual and verbal communication work together?

Common Core State Standards and/ or State or Provincial Content Standards	Content Topics
CCSS.ELA-Literacy.CCRA.R.4 Interpret words and phrases as they are used in a text, including determining technical, connotative, and figurative meanings, and analyze how specific word choices shape meaning or tone.	Doodling Drawing Visual Alphabet Design
CCSS.ELA-Literacy.CCRA.R.7 Integrate and evaluate content presented in diverse media and formats, including visually and quantitatively, as well as in words.	
CCSS.ELA-Literacy.CCRA.SL.5 Make strategic use of digital media and visual displays of data to express information and enhance understanding of presentations.	
CCSS.ELA-Literacy.RH.6–8.7 Integrate visual information (e.g., in charts, graphs, photographs, videos, or maps) with other information in print and digital texts.	

Unit Questions
1. What is the visual alphabet?
2. What are the six essential design elements?
3. How can you use the visual alphabet to draw people and things?
4. How can you use the six essential design elements to add meaning to doodles, drawings, and more?

Skills	Visual Skills	Projects/Products
Conveying ideas Storytelling Compare and contrast	Making pictures: conveying ideas Making pictures: telling stories	Visual alphabet stories Doodling with the visual alphabet Basic people drawings Doodle dictionary

LESSON 1 THE VISUAL ALPHABET

Subject: This lesson can stand alone or be used while teaching other subjects.

Duration: This lesson will take approximately forty-five minutes but can vary depending on the length of discussion time or if you allow students to create additional images.

Materials Required
visual learning notebooks or plain paper, copy of the visual alphabet symbols available to students (see page 220)

Key Vocabulary
visual alphabet, visual language

Learning Objectives
- Students will begin to understand the concept of visual language by using visual symbols to tell a simple story.

Visual Objectives
- Students will copy the twelve letters of the visual alphabet into their visual learning notebooks.
- Students will learn the visual alphabet and use it to express thinking through visual representations.
- Students will transfer learning and apply skills of doodling and depiction in content area lessons, homework, and projects.

Lesson Introduction
Explore the word *visual* with students. What does it make them think of? Build on this by asking what a visual alphabet might be and how it is the same as or different from the regular alphabet. Follow up with a discussion on how kids learned the regular alphabet. Explain that students will learn the visual alphabet in a similar way, by writing it and using it to share information.

Procedure
Project or disseminate a copy of the visual alphabet. Ask students to copy the alphabet in their visual learning notebook. Once this is complete, choose five students—one at a time—to each pick a different symbol. Draw these symbols in a single framed box for students in such a way that you create a simple image. For example, you might create a house with a tree next

to it and the sun and clouds overhead. Repeat the process again, but let the students dictate the placement of symbols to create the image. Finally, challenge students to draw a frame in their visual learning notebook to tell their own story, using just five letters of the visual alphabet. Emphasize that the visual symbols are the storytelling method to be used. Students can exchange drawings with each other to see if their stories are clear or if they need more detail. Debrief this activity with students to begin a list of how you might use this alphabet in the classroom.

Assessment/Evaluation

Formative Assessment: Teachers will observe students as they complete their doodles, looking for effort and evidence of story development.

Summative Assessment: If a summative assessment is necessary, stories can be collected and evaluated to determine if the storyline created from the shapes is clear to the viewer.

LESSON 2 DOODLING WITH THE VISUAL ALPHABET

Subject: This lesson can stand alone or be combined with other subjects.

Duration: This lesson will take approximately an hour but can vary depending on the length of discussion time.

Materials Required
visual learning notebooks or plain paper, copies of the "Visual Alphabet Doodle Exercise" handout on page 222 for each student

Key Vocabulary
visual, doodle, doodle dictionary

Learning Objectives
- Students will define and describe the unique features of the visual alphabet.

- Students will combine the letters of the visual alphabet to create doodles of various people, places, and things.
- Students will begin depicting visual entries in their doodle dictionary.

Visual Objectives

- Using the letters of the visual alphabet, students will create simple doodles to represent a variety of people, places, and things.

Lesson Introduction

Distribute copies of the "Visual Alphabet Doodle Exercise" sheet to each student and read the following directions aloud: "Use the handout to explore your doodle skills and the use of the visual alphabet. Create a doodle for the word in each of the boxes."

Procedure

Have students complete the doodle exercise sheet. Then have students discuss with a partner or table buddy which of their own doodles they like best and in which ways their doodles are similar to or different from their partner's.

Building a Doodle Dictionary

Students can develop their doodle dictionary by recording doodles of people, places, and things for each letter of the verbal alphabet. A doodle dictionary can be part of students' visual learning notebooks or you might have them create it as a stand-alone reference guide.

1. Have students select a blank page in their visual learning notebooks (or in a stand-alone notebook). This will be the first page of their doodle dictionary.

2. Have students write the letter *A* at the top of the page.

3. Have students copy their depiction of *airplane* from their "Visual Alphabet Doodle Exercise" onto the *A* page. Remind students that just as there are many words to a page in the dictionary, there will be many depictions per page in their doodle dictionary. They will need to leave room on the page for future depictions.

4. Have students neatly write *airplane* (or a different, age-appropriate word) alongside their depiction and ask them if there are any other words or meanings that the image could convey. Have them add more words in a bulleted list under the initial word.

5. Have students designate one page per letter of the verbal alphabet for collecting, creating, and recording doodles over time.

To see an example of what a completed doodle dictionary page might look like, you can show students the sample from chapter 2 on page 31.

Assessment/Evaluation

Formative Assessment: Teachers will observe students as they complete their doodles, looking for effort and quantity of responses.

Summative Assessment: Students' doodles will be evaluated for accurate content and clarity in their depictions.

LESSON 3 THE SIX ESSENTIAL DESIGN ELEMENTS

Subject: This lesson can stand alone or be combined with other subjects.

Duration: This lesson will take approximately an hour but can vary depending on the length of discussion time.

Materials Required
visual learning notebooks or plain paper, copy of the six essential design elements available to students (see page 220)

Key Vocabulary
visual, element

Learning Objectives
- Students will view, analyze, and reproduce the six essential design elements.
- Students will begin to combine the six essential design elements with the visual alphabet in the creation of doodled images.
- Students will incorporate the visual alphabet in doodles and drawings to convey information.

Visual Objectives
- Students will use the six essential design elements to convey ideas.

Lesson Introduction
Review the visual alphabet and share the image of the six essential design elements. Ask students: How are the elements the same and how are they different? Where else have students seen the six elements? What makes something an element?

Procedure
Have students illustrate a series of vocabulary words using the visual alphabet and the six essential design elements.

Assessment/Evaluation
Formative Assessment: Formative assessment of the use of the visual alphabet and the six essential design elements is based on observation and providing comments for students. The teacher will walk through the class observing students at work, noting effective use of the depiction and making suggestions when needed.

Summative Assessment: Vocabulary word illustrations will be assessed for effort, quality of design, use of space, and integration of words and images.

LESSON 4 DOODLING FIGURES

Subject: This lesson can stand alone or be combined with other subjects.

Duration: This lesson will take approximately an hour but can vary depending on the length of discussion time.

Materials Required
visual learning notebooks or plain paper, copies of the "Doodle Figures Activity" handout for each student (see page 223)

Key Vocabulary
visual, element, expression, embellish

Description
Students will learn how to use the visual alphabet to add human elements to their drawings.

Learning Objectives
- Students will learn two different methods for expressing human elements in drawings to incorporate the idea of self in student work (for example, in visual note-taking, mind mapping, comics, visual journals, and so on).

Visual Objectives
- Students will learn the star method and card method for drawing people to effectively add human elements to their drawings.

Lesson Introduction
Begin the lesson by displaying an image of a stick figure and asking students to identify which of the visual alphabet letters are present. This is a good way to review previous work.

Procedure
Show students the image of the completed "Doodle Figures Activity." Starting with the star style, ask students to think about how they can use lines to give their figures "expressions." Discuss the importance of the various expressions and how they can change the meaning conveyed in the drawing.

Then discuss the card style for drawing people. Be sure to point out how simply tilting the rectangle body can convey motion or mood. Discuss the concept of embellishment and how simple shape details can enhance meaning.

Give students copies of the blank "Doodle Figures Activity." When students are done, have them compare drawings with a partner to see how different approaches and combinations can be used to convey the same ideas.

Assessment/Evaluation

Formative Assessment: Formative assessment of doodling figures can be ongoing with the teacher observing use of the card and star method of figure development and making suggestions for how to vary the figures: making adults, children, different actions or occupations, and so forth.

Summative Assessment: Doodles will be assessed for content and clarity of depictions.

Doodle Every Day with a Doodle of the Day

Like any skill, doodling needs to be practiced regularly to be of use. The next section is about how to get everyone doodling regularly (even reluctant doodlers).

"I'll never forget the first time I modeled doodling to my students. We needed to bring in an assortment of recyclable objects—cardboard tubes, plastic cups, etc.—for a recyclable art project, and I needed to be sure the students would remember. So, I used doodles and words for their 'Recyclable Art Supply List.' The results were remarkable. Everyone—literally all of my students—brought their materials. Honestly, that NEVER happens."

Susan

When I am leading visual teaching and learning workshops for teachers and students, we start with the visual alphabet and create doodles with personal content familiar to the learner. Then, we move on to doodles with academic content. After practicing making designs and basic symbols and icons using the strokes and shapes of the visual alphabet and the six essential design elements, I ask participants to do a doodle of the day: a doodle that shows either part of or the whole of their day.

See the examples. Hannah, a fourth-grade student, doodled the sequence of activities that got her day off to a good start with a smile.

HANNAH'S DAY

Elizabeth, a sixth-grade teacher, doodled the complete contents of her day as she experienced it in a "doodle montage." A doodle montage is like a collage, except that the components displayed together are created by hand rather than using magazine clippings or the like.

This doodle of the day activity can be intimidating to some who still hold fast to the belief that they cannot draw. For those who may feel this way, try a mini-square daily doodle. The mini-square daily doodle offers a much smaller canvas that is less intimidating and truly requires little more than the mark-making abilities that come with learning the visual alphabet. These are roughly the size of a large postage stamp (1.5" square), and they integrate simple doodles with words for optimal meaning in a compact space. After committing to a doodle of the day every day, my graduate students' responses included:

"Take a few minutes and create your own doodle of the day in your visual learning notebook."

Susan

- "It's a habit now and one I intend to keep."

- "I never realized how much information you can include in a one-inch square."

- "I can't wait to introduce this to my students!"

MINI-SQUARE DAILY DOODLE

Looking for even more ways for your students to practice their visual alphabet and doodling skills? The assortment of visual warm-ups introduced in chapter 2 can be used to practice visual expression and doodling skills with your students as well.

Once the visual alphabet, six essential design elements, faces and figures, and visual warm-ups have been introduced and incorporated into a classroom, they enable students to use many other visual tools. The remainder of this chapter will be dedicated to examining and using these tools.

Visual Note-Taking and Graphic Organizers

Using the visual alphabet, six essential design elements, and faces and figures, we can create more complex doodles, including stories. Visual note-taking and graphic organizers, along with mind maps (see chapter 4), provide ways of organizing visual language and are designed to process and keep a record of students' learning. Think of these as more elaborate and structured visual tools to organize and document learning. They might be developed as a study tool for students or as a finished assignment to be evaluated.

Graphic organizers are visual ways of constructing knowledge and organizing information. The result conveys complex information in an easy-to-understand manner.

Graphic Organizers: Practical Classroom Applications

Graphic organizers help students construct meaning. The graphic organizers included here help students visualize how ideas fit together. You can also use them to identify the strengths and weaknesses of your students' thought processes.

The following visual learning tools may be used with any book or lesson and may be applied across all grade levels. Use them as an informal way to assess your students' understanding of what they are reading, or the content of a lesson, or in response to viewing a video. The visual and verbal recordings in these graphic organizers enable you to observe your students' thinking processes on what they read as a class, as a group, or independently.

VISUAL VOCABULARY FLASHCARDS

Let's begin with a very basic yet effective tool that students can use as they start using visuals alongside their verbal counterparts. Visual vocabulary flashcards provide students a way to depict their vocabulary terms with a simple doodle representation on one side with the word definition on the back.

Visual Vocabulary Flashcard Instructions
Visual vocabulary flashcards are typically created on blank 3" x 5" cards. Larger may be used, if desired.

- On one side, write the vocabulary word with a sketch or doodle of its meaning.

- On the other side, write the definition.

NOTE:
- Students should have fun with this and be creative.

- Students should include details that have meaning and aid memory.

- Students are not to be graded on artistic abilities.

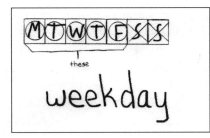
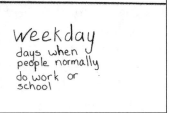

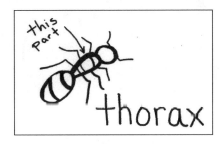

VISUAL VOCABULARY CHARTS

Once students have created visual vocabulary flashcards, they are ready to create visual vocabulary charts. Visual vocabulary charts create meaning by listing the vocabulary word, providing a definition, and illustrating the word's meaning with a doodle picture. Then students can turn over the chart and use the word in a sentence on the back of the page. A visual vocabulary chart may include vocabulary studied across content areas or one chart may be created for the specific vocabulary in a piece of literature or an individual unit of study (see page 224 for a blank chart).

Once the vocabulary lesson is over, students will be able to keep their visual vocabulary charts for use in later lessons as reference material or as an evolving "image/picture" dictionary. Keeping these in a three-ring binder or a designated folder can be a great reminder to students that they can create and doodle and draw.

> Visual vocabulary flashcards and charts are not just for vocabulary words. Visual vocabulary charts are great to fold in half and use as bookmarks. When students come across a word they don't know, they can write it on the chart along with the sentence it was found in. Then, they can look up the word and create a meaningful depiction to help them remember the meaning.

VISUAL NOTE-TAKING FORM

The "Visual Note-Taking Form" (see page 225) provides a solid format for keeping notes and recording ideas that may be developed further through individual or small-group projects. Visual note-taking works well for young children who are just learning to write, as well as for high school and college students who can use them with more advanced concepts and content.

In this form of note-taking, two columns are used to record information. Key events or concepts are listed on the left, and simple doodle illustrations are created on the right.

See a sample student form from a unit on the Trojan War. This student took visual notes during the lesson, listing significant figures and actions on the left in words and providing simple illustrations on the right.

Visual note-taking forms can similarly be used while reading or listening to a piece of literature, documenting a process in science, diagramming math problems, and explaining with simple text and doodles. Visual note-taking is a simple and effective way to keep learners engaged with recording their learning during any type of class lesson. Plus, the form provides a way to engage both modalities while studying.

Visual Note-Taking Guessing Game

A fun way to incorporate visual note-taking in any unit study is to pair off students using a list of the unit's key terms or vocabulary. Have each student choose three to four words from the list and visually depict those words to the best of their abilities on their visual note-taking forms. After both students have depicted their words, they swap forms and begin guessing or decoding the images. The goal is to have their partner decipher what the terms are based solely on the depictions.

SEE-HEAR GRAPHIC ORGANIZER

The "See-Hear Graphic Organizer" (see page 226) outlines key information about a topic at the top of the page with a small cluster-shaped graphic organizer. Underneath that, the students can further document their understandings in two columns: the "See" column and the "Hear" column. Both visual and verbal language are integrated for better engagement and retention. See the sample of a student's work on the Boston Tea Party.

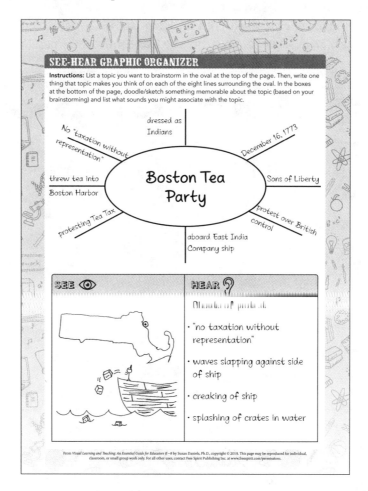

A fun way to incorporate this graphic organizer is as an extension activity that can be completed before and during any class activity, event, outing, or field trip.

Give students the graphic organizer prior to the event. Ask students to fill in the center of the starburst with the event, activity, or field trip location. Then have them predict what they may see or hear while at that location or event and fill in the spokes of the starburst with those words, phrases, and small depictions. This can even be used with young students (grades K–3), if together the class brainstorms ideas and develops a word bank. This is a good warm-up that develops a word list for student reference.

When students arrive at the event or trip location, give them a few minutes to take in their surroundings and tune their senses to the environment. Have them focus on what they are taking in visually, and give them time to doodle or depict these images in the "See" column. Then have them focus on the sounds and doodle or depict what they hear in the "Hear" column.

When students return to class, give them some time to reflect on what they had predicted they would see and hear compared to what they actually saw and heard.

Storyboard: A Go-To Graphic Organizer

Storyboards depict a linear sequence of events using a series of frames or boxes. They have been used to communicate even the most complex ideas through images in various cultures and across time. Storyboards with pictographs, hieroglyphs, and most recently comics and graphic novels have been used to communicate everything from the events of a hunt, to various fairy tales, to complex technical or scientific processes. The Chinese language was built using pictographs and the Egyptians used hieroglyphics to illustrate events in frames that, in sequence—like storyboards—showed the passing of time.

For classroom applications, storyboards use simple picture writing and sequencing and are a clear choice for analyzing stories. As you can see in the example, a simple three-square storyboard is useful for identifying and illustrating the beginning, middle, and end of a story. Storyboards can have any number of panels, and multiple-square storyboards may be used as an assignment or as a means to draft the story for another project. Storyboards can be used to draft, or to sketch out, a story that may later be translated into a picture book, a comic, or another form of graphic text.

The logical sequence of a storyboard accompanied by a student's original picture writing integrates both critical and creative thinking in the learning process. Developing the story is a creative activity; sequencing the story is a critical thinking activity.

Storyboards lend themselves to application across subject areas. They are low-tech examples of picture writing that can illustrate complex ideas in very simple ways. Using stick figures and simple doodle representations, hand-drawn storyboards can be generated in very little time. The practice of depicting with marks and shapes with small amounts of text helps students visually clarify their ideas. The advantages of doodling and simple drawing over using clip art or other media is that students can create as they go and revise easily. Plus, the act of creating these simple images is informative in itself.

For example, a storyboard used within a science lesson can show the chronological stages that a seed goes through to become a plant. As we follow the story of our main character, the seed, we can see the traditional beginning, middle, and end, but we can also see stages in between.

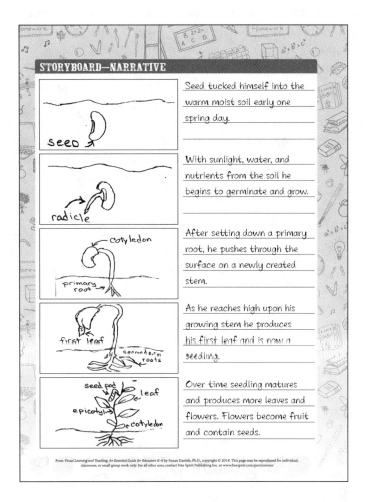

You'll find more storyboard templates on pages 228–230 to use with your students. The comics template can be used to create a page of comics or a graphic novel. The narrative template gives students more room to write brief descriptions of the stages of their story; the five panels with connected text can be cut apart and students can rearrange their stories as they go. The nine-panel template also offers room to write and gives students nine frames to work with. Storyboard graphic organizers can be used in almost every situation where students want to express themselves or their understandings visually.

Visual Four-Square Graphic Organizer

The visual four-square graphic organizer (see page 231) is particularly useful for literature, history, and social studies. Its unique four-square outline guides students logically through their retelling of a writing, lesson, or viewing. Very similar to the storyboard in its ability to record events in a chronological order, the four-square design also captures all the pertinent information both verbally and visually. Students begin by identifying the major events and then sketch and label these with as much detail as they can squeeze into the square. (Hint: One way to get students to fill in squares with representations of their learning is to give them several small squares instead of one blank sheet.) Then they proceed to draw, sketch, or doodle representations of the people or characters in their reading selection, labeling as they go, and they conclude the activity by naming and listing big ideas and key terms.

There are no multiple-choice options here. The students identify what the big ideas are from the lesson, and they also choose which key vocabulary to record. This not only helps them think critically about the lesson as they search for the big ideas, but it gives teachers insight as to what the students view as key vocabulary. Visual four-square graphic organizers can also reveal which students are struggling and at which level of vocabulary, so you can offer scaffolding or differentiation to further student learning.

The visual four-square graphic organizer example is based on a sixth-grade student's response to reading *Surviving the Applewhites* by Stephanie Tolan.

This graphic organizer sets itself apart from the storyboard because the box at the bottom can be adapted to capture final thoughts, summaries, and take-away ideas for each lesson. It can also be used for students to ask follow-up or connecting questions. It can be used as an informal assessment while increasing student creativity and critical thinking.

Moving On

The emphasis in this chapter was to integrate visual language and verbal language to enhance the learning process. We began with a visual curriculum using simple doodles to record and express personal experiences. Then we used doodles explicitly to increase student engagement, and then added a variety of graphic organizers to illustrate student learning. The following chapters will build upon these fundamental tools of visual language and learning and extend opportunities for creating visual texts, mixed-media projects, and culminating products.

CHAPTER 4

Visual Pages—Mind Maps and One Pagers

Your and your students' toolboxes are now filled with some basic visual tools and it's time to practice putting the tools to work to create visual presentations and products. What follows is an introduction to a wide variety of visual texts with examples that show how to see, imagine, and depict using each of these texts.

We begin with two single-page formats that integrate verbal and visual forms of expression and record, review, and express learning. Mind maps and one pagers both are simple to design using just a few basic guidelines, yet they can communicate complex concepts, content, and scenarios.

Mind Maps

A mind map is a visual display of a concept or process. It combines graphic elements (lines, doodles, colors, icons, and sketches) with verbal components (words, phrases, and numbers) in a diagrammatic representation of an idea.

In a mind map, each word or phrase connects to another and links back to the central topic or theme. Icons and images are used in interplay with words and numbers to convey the greatest meaning in an economy of space. Imagine a tree with many branches. The trunk illustrates the central topic, and the branches illustrate subtopics and themes.

Originally attributed to ancient Greek philosopher Porphyry of Tyros, mind mapping was used to graphically visualize the work of Aristotle in the third century BCE. Leonardo da Vinci is also credited with using the technique, employing mind maps to develop his creations in art, science, engineering, and literature.

While there are recorded instances of individuals using mind mapping after da Vinci, including such notable thinkers as Albert Einstein, Charles Darwin, Winston Churchill, and Pablo Picasso, the use of graphic mapping in support of visual thinking and learning was not popularized until the 1960s, when British author and educational consultant Tony Buzan used the technique "as a universal key to unlocking the potential of the brain."

Since our memory is associative rather than linear, mind maps mimic our thought processes and enhance creative thinking. More than illustrated notes or an outline, mind maps enable the student to link new ideas to previously understood concepts; mind maps emphasize connections between ideas and stimulate the creation of new thought.

In his book *How to Think Like Leonardo da Vinci: Seven Steps to Genius Every Day*, Michael J. Gelb explains how some of the world's most creative minds have employed this organic approach to note taking. He states that mind mapping "frees you from the tyranny of premature organization, which stifles your generation of ideas. Mind mapping liberates your conceptual powers by balancing generation and organization while encouraging the full range of mental expression."[15]

While mind maps often have the structure of the main idea in the center (trunk) with subtopics as branches, the maps may be varied with different shapes and graphic structures. This way, students can create a design that helps them make connections to the material they are learning in a manner that's meaningful to them. Sometimes mind maps are born organically as teachers and students begin documenting their brainstorming or discussion session on a whiteboard.

Mind maps thoroughly integrate visual and verbal learning. This example represents ideas and things that are important to middle schooler Jessica. Her mind map is divided into sections for each related subtopic.

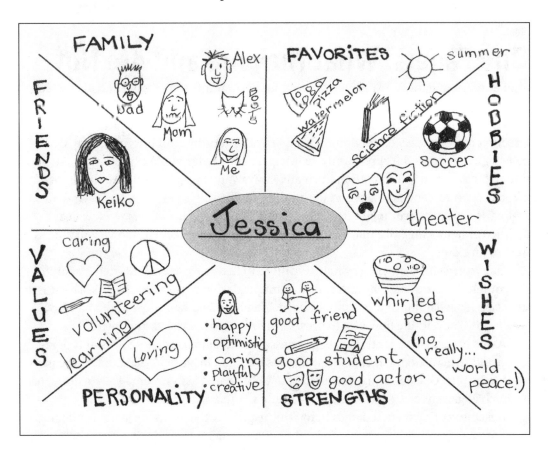

Benefits of Mind Mapping

As mind maps require planning and design, students achieve a deeper understanding of a topic when creating one. As such, mind maps are a way to develop the higher-order thinking skills of analysis, synthesis, and evaluation while organizing information in a clear structure.

Beyond simple note taking, mind maps nurture creativity and support visual teaching and learning. Through the incorporation of words, numbers, pictures, and colors, many students find the learning process more engaging and their retention of information is enhanced.

Likewise, the nonlinear nature of a mind map encourages divergent thinking and students develop ideas quickly, with one concept stimulating connections between previously understood ideas. Studying often becomes easier and more enjoyable as mind maps present a topic along with connections drawn and ideas illustrated.

You can offer multiple opportunities for your students to use mind maps to show their learning. They can be used in place of, or in addition to:

- a book report
- a report on a historical event
- a report on a historical figure
- a biography of a famous scientist
- an overview of a notable artist's life and work
- a summary of a class field trip

One Pagers: What They Are and Are Not

Similar to mind maps, one pagers are assignments that integrate verbal and visual representations of knowledge. Using one side of a single page, students use images—hand drawn or photographic—and text to illustrate their understanding of a piece of a class lesson. It represents each individual's unique understanding and interpretation. One pagers give students the opportunity to integrate knowledge while expressing their understanding and interpretation in creative ways. A one pager could take the place of a book report for language arts and the student could sketch a favorite scene. Or for a history lesson, a student might depict Roman architecture. One pagers work well as a finished assignment, a summative assessment of student work, or as a review before a quiz or an exam.

One pagers are, by their very nature, differentiated assignments. Students analyze the content they are studying and craft the unique design of their one pagers. The students decide what information should be included on their one pager and what should be left out. They decide how best to present their content in words and visuals.

A one pager is *not* a random collage or assortment of images and words. It is organized and structured. It has specific objectives outlined in a teacher-created rubric that need to be met. One pagers are not an easy or abbreviated assignment. They require just as much engagement, time, and effort as a fully written response.

Designing one pagers activates both critical and creative thinking skills. Students most often enjoy creating one pagers and find the depicting and designing aspects to be fun. With one pagers, students are actively engaged in constructing meaning and are also using higher-order thinking skills. Designing and illustrating involves application, analysis, and synthesis. Students must ask themselves: "How can I best illustrate these quotes? How do I want to create an illustration of these quotes?"

Research continues to document the learning advantages of the picture-superiority effect—the idea that we learn and retain more with images—and, of special importance for our purposes, the drawing effect—the idea that understanding, memory, and recall are increased through the integration of semantic, visual, and motor experiences. As

Wammes, Meade, and Fernandes noted in *The Journal of Experimental Psychology*, when we engage in writing and drawing, we are building on dual-coding theory and encoding meaning through three systems: verbal, visual, and motor.[16]

Viewing and Interpreting One Pagers

Following is an examination of a variety of one pagers. Let's start with a teacher's one pager designed during a workshop on visual teaching and learning.

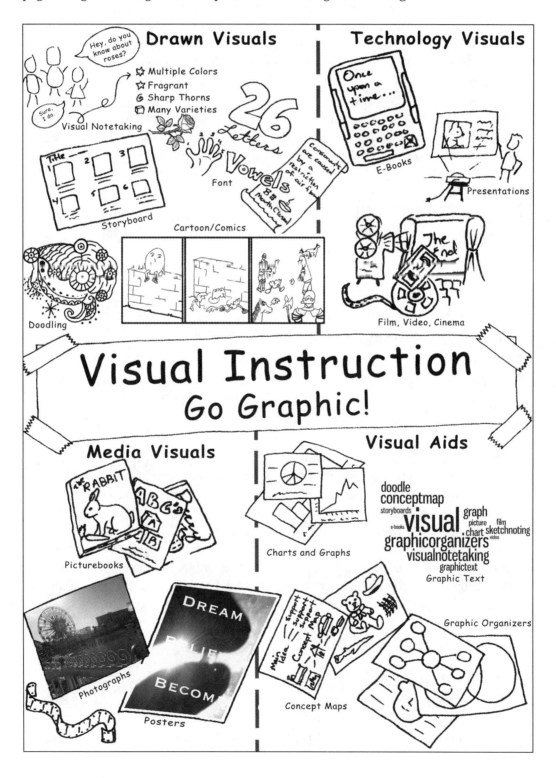

Elizabeth created the "Visual Instruction: Go Graphic!" one pager to summarize and illustrate her understanding of the applications of visual learning and teaching for herself and her fourth-grade classroom. Her one pager is divided into four sections: drawn visuals, technology visuals, media visuals, and visual aids. It's a bit different from most of the other examples, because she incorporated doodles, hand-drawn sketches, and computer-generated images and text. This was meaningful to Elizabeth, because her school just received a technology grant. Elizabeth made plans to integrate visual instruction and technology into her teaching during the upcoming school year.

Before I assign one pagers in a class, whether it be a class of young students or a university class, I always provide examples of one pagers from prior classes as models for the students. I save a variety of one pagers, so students can see samples of different styles from different subjects. Students learn that one pagers can be designed in a variety of ways.

I encourage the class to take time to view the samples. Taking in information with our eyes yields a lot of data without having to analyze it. Awareness happens as you glance over an image, and observations take form as you really begin to study it. From observation, it is logical for questions to start forming, and this is where the practice begins. Building visual skills requires practice, structure, and opportunities for viewing examples. Following are some discussion guidelines to get you started.

ONE PAGER "SHOW AND TELL": DISCUSSION GUIDELINES

When viewing one pagers, consider using these questions to lead discussion and analysis.

- What do you notice first when viewing this one pager?
- What is the topic or focus of this one pager?
- How do the visual images and text work together to communicate understanding?
- In what ways is this one pager most
    - interesting?
    - informative?
    - creative?
    - effective?

When we start exploring these questions, we start noticing more details and getting a sense of how students interpret academic content in their own unique ways. One pagers may be used individually by students to share their responses to reading a novel—with each child reading a different book. Or, the entire class may read the same text, and the one pagers will still be unique, since each student's understanding and experience of the text will vary from the next. Students may be illustrating and writing about the same content, but the way they interpret and recompose the content will create individual interpretation and creative expression. One pagers can be used across the curriculum to document understanding of most units of study in language arts, social studies, math, science, and electives.

Creating One Pagers

Creating a one pager is something that most students can do (across all grade levels), and it can be a valuable assessment tool—informal, formative, or summative—to show their comprehension. However, creating a one pager isn't done without planning and design.

Students can use a "One Pager Worksheet" (see page 232) to guide them through the following four prompts to develop their one pager design.

1. Brainstorm a list of key words, phrases, and ideas related to your one pager.
2. List key visuals that will be used in your one pager.
3. Select quotes (if required for the assigned one pager).
4. In the space provided, create a thumbnail sketch of the design planned for your one pager. Be sure to include:
   - the title in a prominent place with strong lettering
   - doodles or sketches of the key ideas you've identified placed in such a way to fill the page while leaving room for quotes
   - the quotes you've chosen to represent the key ideas from this assignment (if applicable)

CREATING A ONE PAGER FOR ASSIGNMENTS

One pagers can be used to help students visualize what they have read, explore a text on a variety of levels, and identify the most important points and central theme of the text. For example, when used in an English language arts curriculum, one pagers can be used for a variety of assignments: doing a book report, mocking up a book jacket, offering literary critique, and summarizing the story of a book.

Directions for Creating a One Pager for English Language Arts

Here's one way to use a one pager for creating a book report. This assignment required students to pull two quotes from a book of their choosing that they felt were important. Feel free to change the details to fit your curriculum.

- Complete the "One Pager Worksheet." This worksheet includes important ideas, the quotes you chose, and a thumbnail sketch for the design of your one pager. This is your plan for your one pager.
- For this English language arts one pager, get a blank sheet of white paper and write the title of the book in decorative letters that are easy to read. Pay attention to the placement of your title to leave space for all the other elements.
- Include the name of the author and put your name in smaller writing.
- Create a textbox somewhere on the page. It should be big enough to fit five to seven sentences.
- Copy the two quotes you chose onto your one pager exactly as they appear in the text. Be sure to use quotation marks and include page numbers of the quotes.
- Create visual illustrations based on the thumbnail sketch on your worksheet that match the quotes you chose. The illustrations may depict the whole quote or a part of it.
- Begin with pencil, then go over the text and illustrations with a black pen.
- Make your one pager clear and colorful but also consider leaving some white space too. You have the option to fill the whole page, but sometimes leaving space is effective for highlighting parts of the one pager.
- When you have finished the items above, write a short paragraph (five to seven sentences) in the textbox you created that explains why you chose these two quotes from the story. Describe the meaning behind them and why they are so important to the story.

A one pager for *The Three Little Pigs* was created by a sixth grader whose class was doing a unit on picture books. The students read a variety of picture books and created one pagers for the books they read before creating their own picture books. (The picture book project is discussed in detail in chapter 8.) This one pager met all of the requirements of the assignment, including illustrations, quotes, and an expository paragraph.

GRADING ONE PAGERS

Teachers often ask about how to grade one pagers and other visual assignments without grading students' artwork. Here is the rubric that was used to assess the previous English language arts one pager assignment. The rubric incorporates the following four criteria: (1) the use of quotations, (2) the illustrations, (3) the written response, and (4) the appearance and organization.

ONE PAGER RUBRIC

	4 pts	3 pts	2 pts	1 pt	0 pt
Quotations	The one pager contains two quotations from the text. The quotes are copied exactly, including quotation marks and page numbers.	The one pager contains two quotations from the text, but they are incomplete, there are spelling errors, and/or they are missing quotation marks or page numbers.	The one pager contains one or more quotations, but they have spelling errors, are incomplete, and/or they are missing quotation marks or page numbers.	The one pager contains just one quotation. It may also be incomplete or have spelling errors, and/or be missing quotation marks or the page number.	There are no quotations on this one pager.

CONTINUED ▷

ONE PAGER RUBRIC, CONTINUED

	4 pts	3 pts	2 pts	1 pt	0 pt
Illustrations	The illustrations were created with care and effort. They are clearly visible and clearly represent the two quotations.	The illustrations were created with some effort, and they represent the quotations.	The illustrations were created with little effort and do not necessarily represent the quotations.	The illustrations do not indicate effort. They are sloppy and/or do not clearly represent the quotations.	There are no illustrations on this one pager.
Written Response	The written response indicates a thorough understanding of the text.	The written response indicates a clear understanding of the text	The written response indicates a limited understanding of the text. The information may be too simple or too general.	The written response indicates a very limited understanding of the text. The writing may include some flaws.	The written response contains significant errors. It may be inaccurate or irrelevant.
Appearance and Organization	The one pager is neat, clear, and shows evidence of thought and effort, and the content is well organized.	The one pager is not as neat, but shows evidence of thought and the content is organized.	The one pager is sloppy. It appears that little effort was made, and the content is not well organized.	The one pager is sloppy and poorly organized. It appears to have been rushed or done at the very last minute.	The one pager is very sloppy and disorganized or sections are missing.

"On our team, we grade for the academic content and visual effort not for the quality of the art. As we have come to understand, simple doodles and drawings can be a very effective way to illustrate complex ideas. The visual representation is not dependent on artistic ability."

Jenna

One pagers have great versatility. They can be used for almost any subject that has a strong illustration and textual explanation. For example, shapes in the primary grades or geometric forms in the upper elementary and middle school grades can be presented with descriptions and discussion of where the shapes or forms are found. A one pager could be used to depict a visual model of a cell in science. One pagers can be used to provide an overview of the life of a historical figure or the main character of a picture book or novel. Once you start using one pagers, you will start to see many opportunities to work them into your curriculum.

CREATING A ONE PAGER AS A FORM OF ASSESSMENT OR FOR REVIEW

Using one pagers in tandem with a particular assignment or unit is a micro example of how they can be used. But one pagers can also help students process a macro view of what they've learned over the course of time. Students can express their comprehension of, reactions to, and connections with a specific content area or topic of study through creating a one pager.

Directions for Creating One Pagers for Review and Assessment

In this example, sixth-grade students were told to make a one pager that used text and images to depict everything they'd learned across four subjects: identity (a middle school health unit), science, reading, and social studies.

- Complete the "One Pager Worksheet." Using your texts and notebooks for each subject area, fill in the worksheet with important ideas and concepts you have learned, meaningful quotes from the subject areas, and a thumbnail sketch for the design of your one pager. This is your plan for creating your one pager.

- For this review and assessment one pager, get a blank sheet of white paper and sketch in pencil the overall layout of your subject areas. Make sure to use decorative or bold letters for the subject headers. Pay attention to the placement of your headers. Leave space for all the other elements.

- Include your first and last name clearly displayed in smaller writing on the page.

- Give your one pager a title that represents the assessment period or the subject being reviewed. Make sure it stands out. For example, put the title in a frame and use decorative letters. Or center it on the page using boldface capital letters.

- Include visual images and phrases from your worksheet for each subject area. These should vividly illustrate what you learned in the unit or units of study. Design the page so there is sufficient room for both your chosen text and images.

- Explain the importance of what you've learned in each area of study with the statement, "The most important things I learned in _____ was/were: _____."

- Begin with pencil, then go over the text and illustrations with a black pen.

- Make your one pager clear and colorful but also consider leaving some white space too. You have the option to fill the whole page, but sometimes leaving space is effective for highlighting parts of the one pager. This is your one pager, and you have the freedom to represent your learning in a personal and unique way using text and images!

Kokoro, a sixth grader, created a one pager to showcase everything she had learned during her first semester. Her one pager is divided into four sections, one for each of her four topics of study, and she integrated visuals with text and phrase. You can see retention, understanding, and both complex analysis and complex design depicted in Kokoro's one pager on the next page.

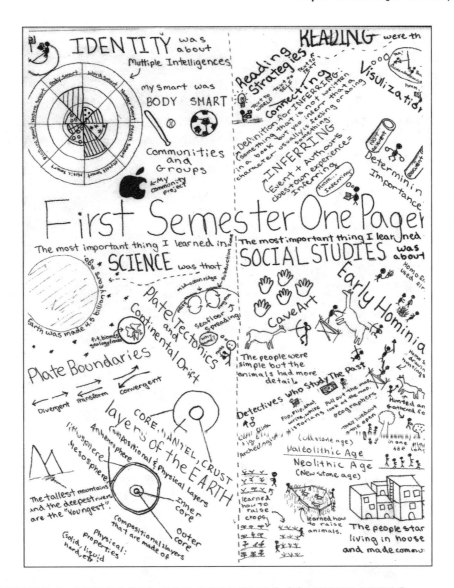

CREATING A ONE PAGER FOR ACADEMIC CONTENT AREAS

One pagers can also be used with unit studies. For example, at one school, part of a social studies unit on ancient civilizations included a focus on Egypt. Students were asked to depict a minimum of six aspects of the Egyptian culture. They were given the "One Pager Worksheet" and then set out to create their products.

Directions for One Pagers in the Content Areas

- Complete the "One Pager Worksheet." Using the text or unit study materials, fill in the worksheet with important ideas and concepts you have learned, meaningful quotes from the text or unit study, and a thumbnail sketch for the design of your one pager. This is your plan for creating your one pager.

- Include your first and last name clearly displayed in smaller writing on the page.

- Create vivid visual illustrations for the unit of study, making sure to include the visual images from your worksheet that best depict the text or unit of study subject area.

- Insert important phrases or quotes from the text or unit of study as applicable, making sure to include the quotes from your worksheet.

- Provide support of and explanation for your illustrations and the learning they represent with a personal statement. Begin your statement with "I most enjoyed learning_____ because_____."

- Begin with pencil, then go over the text and illustrations with a black pen.

- Make your one pager clear and colorful but also consider leaving some white space too. You have the option to fill the whole page, but sometimes leaving space is effective for highlighting parts of the one pager.

Below is an example of one student's "One Pager Worksheet," and his final one pager is on the next page.

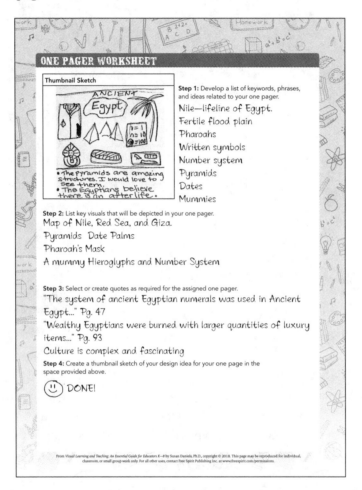

Simple shapes and mark-making combined with text create a personalized record and remembrance. A one pager can also be placed in a student's visual learning portfolio to be used as a summary of learning and as a study aid for the end of the unit test. (Visual learning portfolios and assessment are discussed in chapter 8.) One pagers are good work samples to share with parents at semester conferences too.

As you incorporate one pagers into your teaching, whether through an assignment, an assessment, or a review, you will be providing students the opportunity to clearly display their knowledge while also expressing their understanding and interpretation in creative ways. Not only that, you will also be helping your students sharpen their visual literacy skills as they practice seeing, imagining, and depicting daily.

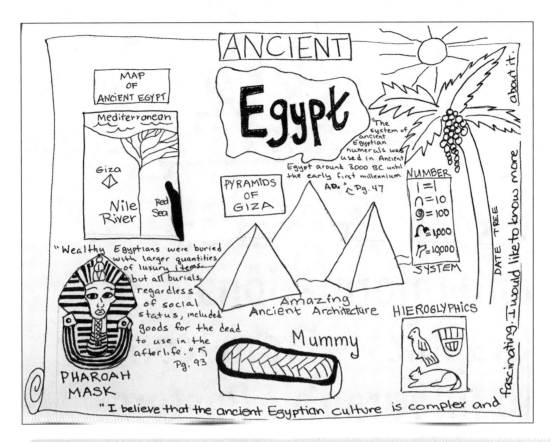

While there are many good reasons to have students create one pagers by hand, Glogster.com and PiktoChart.com are websites that facilitate digital one pagers. Creating a digital one pager isn't any less demanding than a hand-rendered version, and it can be a great tool to help asynchronous students express high-level thoughts without being limited by difficulties or struggles with handwriting.

Moving On

Visual pages that use both simple text and basic doodles are excellent tools to get students thinking about the link between what they're learning and how it can be expressed visually. Mind maps and one pagers have provided our entry point to other visual texts. From here, we will explore what develops when many images are curated and compiled with meaning and intention.

Visual Information and Informational Graphics—From Icons to Infographic Posters

Sometimes the need to get a message across effectively and succinctly can be accomplished with simple or complex images that complement or replace words. In this chapter, we'll look at several different types of visual texts, which all fall under the category of informational graphics. Informational graphics are texts that depict information visually. They are meant to provide the viewer with a visual explanation without the need to rely heavily on verbal decoding. Some, but not all, of these graphics involve the doodle and depict skills we've been using so far.

Informational graphic texts:

- are richly visual

- integrate basic words and pictures in a fluid, dynamic way

- are flexible in that multiple forms of data can be incorporated in one text to provide different perspectives or to include related information

- most often have dominant visuals where the text supports the visual

Figure 5.1 provides a list of different types of informational graphics. Once you "see" visual representations and informational graphics for what they are—a form of visual communication that makes faster, more consistent understanding possible—you'll begin to see them everywhere.

FIG. 5.1 INFORMATIONAL GRAPHICS GUIDE

Informational Graphic	Description	Example
Icon	A simple symbol, image, or picture that represents its object or action. Icons are a type of graphic shorthand. They may stand alone or appear as part of other graphic representations.	
Diagram	1. A drawing or plan that outlines and explains the parts and workings of something (for example, the wing of an airplane). 2. A Venn diagram that uses circles to represent sets, or categories, and their relationship.	
Graph	A visual that represents data or a system of related information.	
Map	A representation of an area with details showing respective forms, sizes, and relationships of places.	
Illustrated Timeline	A visual representation that illustrates events on a linear display as they happened, linking an image with a date.	
Infographic Poster	A specific type of informational graphic. Infographic posters are visually rich texts that integrate words and language to support the image. They are unique in that they can incorporate other types of informational graphics, such as graphs.	

Icon: The Oldest Informational Graphic

Icons hold a special place in human history. They were essential to the development of the first forms of visually based communication. Icons first appeared as petroglyphs in prehistoric times and evolved into hieroglyphs in ancient cultures, particularly in Egypt and Mesopotamia. The ancient Egyptians are famous for their iconic art in paintings and carvings. Painted frescoes, found in the tombs of Egyptian priests, consisted of icons that represented significant stories and mythological subjects. Icons have been used to convey essential meanings via simple images throughout time. The roots of iconography—the study of images and illustrations—run deep.

Icons represent communication within and across cultures through commonly recognized symbols and culturally specific symbols. They are most often a sign or a symbol that stands for a person, place, object, or action. Many icons are easily identifiable and understood, and others require a deeper understanding of the context in which the icon was created. It might be a representative image, such as an outline of a dog on a leash for a dog-friendly, dogs-on-leash park area. Or it might be three arrows making a continuous path in the shape of a triangle, a visual analogy for recycling. Whereas, the meaning of the dog and leash are immediately clear, the three arrows require explanation and experience to decode their meaning.

Icons can also represent corporate brands and commercial identities. Sometimes, companies choose an icon that is more literal, such as Apple's bitten apple icon. Other companies might take a more abstract route, choosing something simple and memorable even if the link between the image and company isn't immediately apparent: for example, Nike and their "swoosh." Whatever path is chosen, it takes repeated exposure to a certain icon before people associate it with a given brand. This demonstrates the power of icons: to evoke an idea through mere association.

We're exposed to icons at a very young age, even before we learn to read. Elevators, stairways, hospitals, restrooms, hotels, parks, gas stations, and recycle centers are all identifiable with graphical symbols. As young children we come to understand, even without direct instruction, what the icons represent. For example, we learn that the colored circles on traffic lights give instructions to drivers even though no words are printed on or around the lights. A simple circle of color relays a very direct message: green is go, yellow is slow, and red is stop. These colors, used in this manner, are commonly recognized and convey the same message in many, if not most, roadways across the globe.

As we made our way into the world as pedestrians (walking to and from school, the library, or the park), we also began to notice some very familiar informational graphics. The red hand icon relayed the message to "wait" or "stop where you are," whereas the brightly illuminated human walking icon visually announced permission to "proceed" or "continue" along your way. And, when in need of a restroom, we knew which door goes to a restroom—as opposed to a tool shed—based on the images on the sign. Icons are compelling in their graphic simplicity and in their ability to convey meaning in multiple contexts, thus solidifying their place as essential forms of communication in the world in which we live.

Viewing and Interpreting Icons

When we address icons within the framework of the classroom, we are not starting from scratch. Most of our 21st-century students have known about the language of icons for much of their lives. When you explain the concept of icons and ask students where they have seen icons, most students will likely mention how they see icons on their computers, their digital devices, their phones, or even their TV screens.

Some students may even contribute icons in the form of logos that are pervasive in the media aimed at their demographic. However, we want to make the distinction between these commercial icons that are all about brand recognition and the icons that are used to convey information about people, places, and activities.

Commercial icons or logos represent product brands and convey meaning about the identity, intended audience, attractiveness, and desirability of a product.

Informational icons are found on web pages and in printed texts, manufacturers' instructions, and public spaces with buildings, parks, and streets signs, and they provide information about people, places, and activities.

Your students most likely have a basic level of proficiency in viewing and interpreting icons given how prevalent icons are in the digital age. But we want students to develop a deeper understanding of how icons can be used to convey important information.

We want students to go from being *proficient* in identifying icons to being *fluent* in identifying and using icons. Fluency may sound like a lofty goal, but it engages a process that underpins the viewing, interpreting, and creating of other forms of visual communication.

ACTIVITY JUDO ICON WALK-THROUGH

When introducing icons to students, we want to help reinforce visual language and strengthen visual literacy skills. We can do both by leading students through some prompts that engage their visual thinking.

Use the icon that represents judo at the Olympic games (at right). Show it to your students but don't tell them what it is. If possible, isolate it on a plain background without context so they can focus on it.

Ask the following questions:

- What's going on in this icon?
- What features of the icon make you say that?
- What else, or what more can we see?

These questions engage your students as they come up with various meanings and opinions on how they view the icon.

Next go a little deeper and have students re-create the icon in their visual learning notebooks and answer the following questions beneath their depiction.

- What do I see?
  - What details can I make out?
  - What else could it be?

- What does it make me think of?
  - Where have I seen this before?
  - Is it similar to something else?

- What is its purpose?
  - What message or statement is it trying to convey?
  - What would happen if we didn't have this icon?

Once they've answered these questions, explain what the icon is meant to represent. Ask students why they think Olympic officials chose this icon for judo. Also ask what, if anything, students would have chosen differently.

These prompts help students look past the literal translation of the icon and reach into their own experience and ideas about the meaning and the effectiveness of the icon.

Extension Activity

Show the judo icon, alongside other Olympic event icons. When viewed in this context, many students will spend less time coming up with answers to "what else could it be" and may move on to discussing its purpose and significance. Ask them to decode what sporting event each icon represents. Have them each choose a sport (one not already represented by an example icon) and discuss what actions involved in that sport would make an instantly recognizable icon. For example, what familiar actions in American football might make a recognizable icon? A player passing the ball? A player crouching at the line of scrimmage? Students can better understand how all aspects of a sport can be distilled into a single icon when they discuss what they know about the sport.

For a variation on this activity, introduce the "escalator up" icon, and ask students to decode its meaning. Then show the icon along with other travel-related icons and discuss their meanings.

After students analyze an icon on its own and then within the context of other icons, you may want to have students look for a variety of icons in the world around them or online. They can present their findings to the class and discuss how effective they feel the icons are.

ACTIVITY ICON SCAVENGER HUNT

Learning Objectives
- Students will identify icons in their school, neighborhoods, and communities. Further exploration can be done online.

Visual Objectives
- Students will create a visual vocabulary chart to record the design of each icon they locate.
- Students will write descriptions of each icon's meaning on the chart.

Materials
- blank "Visual Vocabulary Chart" handout (see page 224) for each student, textbooks, reference books, and internet, if available

Procedure
Provide students with a blank "Visual Vocabulary Chart" and instruct them to identify icons in their environment. Once they find an icon—be it a gas station symbol, a public library icon, a picnic area sign, or a warning around a construction zone—they sketch, depict, or doodle their representation of the icon along with a written description of what they interpret the icon to mean.

This activity incorporates both the act of viewing (looking for icons instead of overlooking them) and interpreting (decoding the meaning of an icon based on its properties and the context of the environment where it was found) as students complete their chart.

The icon scavenger hunt is a flexible activity that lends itself to any grade and can be a short-term assignment (How many icons can you find while riding the bus to the field trip?) or it can be expanded to cover an entire term (How many unique icons can you find this term?). Either way, students will expand their icon awareness, and they will rapidly become fluent icon finders and interpreters.

Once the activity has been wrapped up, students can use their icon charts to discuss what they discovered. Ask the class about the features of effective icons, including:

- Is the design legible?
- Is the icon both simple and understandable?
- Does it clearly show the key idea?
- Are the visual features—color, shape, and size—appropriate?

Students could also graph the most and least seen icons (more about graphs on page 86).

Creating Icons

The key to creating an effective icon—that is, a simple symbol capable of encapsulating a single idea—is to think with a minimalist view. Sports icons are great examples that distill the essence of the activity they represent. Archery icons typically depict an archer with a bow. Bicycling icons often show a cyclist on a bike, leaning forward as a racer might. Icons that focus on a singular, highly identifiable quality of the idea being depicted are decoded with a higher degree of accuracy.

As previously mentioned, cultural differences can make it difficult to create "universally recognized" icons. The icons for the Olympic games come closest. Every four years, thousands of Olympic athletes, coaches, trainers, and spectators arrive at a different host country for the games. What will all these people from all over the world have in common? They don't all speak the same language. How will all these people know where to go to participate in or watch an event? How will they get around the Olympic Village or the city streets of the foreign country? Icons make traveling—local, foreign, and event—easier.

ACTIVITY TRAVEL ICONS AT THE OLYMPICS

In this activity, students create their own icons. Keeping with the Olympics theme, students design icons that represent their favorite sport, event, athlete, and so on. Or, they might choose to make a travel icon to help foreign visitors quickly recognize important landmarks (restaurants, restrooms, museums, and so forth).

Learning Objectives
- Students will analyze existing Olympic and travel icons.
- Students will evaluate the messages of the icons.

Visual Objectives
- Students will design an original Olympic icon that represents a sport, an event, or a nationality. Or, they might choose to make a travel-related icon to help visitors get around.

Materials
- white paper, pencils, black markers

Procedure
Display icons used for Olympic events and travel—road signs, airport and train signs—so students can see them.

After a brief review, have students create their own icons, framing them with any shape they feel fits the message they want to convey. Emphasize that they shouldn't use text in their icons.

This is an example of an icon that a student created to depict a location for food. The student combined a well-established icon (the fork and knife) with a more contemporary icon (the map point or "you are here" icon) to create an icon that has personal meaning.

Icons can relay a lot of information, meaningful messages, and important facts without the need for language. As we explore even more visual texts, you may find many opportunities to incorporate icons into your classroom activities and lessons.

VIEWING AND INTERPRETING ICONS

Ask students purposeful questions that not only help them relate an icon to its concept, but that also draw connections between the icon and its concept.
- What does this icon mean?
- Does it tell you to do something?
- Does it **stand for** something else?
- Does it **show** something else?
- Do you think it is a good way to **represent** it?
- What about it tells you more about what it represents?

ACTIVITY CREATING ICONS

Ask students to create an icon that represents something about themselves. Do they have a favorite activity or hobby that could be easily conveyed by an icon? Would they like to represent their family or their pets? Is bike riding, swimming, or soccer a favorite sport? Have students explain their choices verbally or in writing. Even young children can understand that an icon can represent something that is important to them if the icon illustrates the object or activity.

Discussion and Extension

Thinking/Skills	Questions
Knowledge and Understanding	• What defines an icon? • How are icons used in everyday life? • Describe different types of icons. • Where do you find icons? Print? Signs? Technology? Other applications?
Application	• What examples have you found of commercial icons and informational icons?
Analysis	• How are commercial icons and public information icons similar? How are they different?
Evaluation	• Does the icon you are studying demonstrate legibility, simplicity, clarity of key ideas, and appropriate visual features like color, shape, and design?
Creative Thinking	• What aspects of the sport did you choose to represent when you created your Olympic icon?

ICON CREATIVE EXTENSION

Ask students to design an icon that depicts an aspect of their personalities, who they are, what they like, or what they do. Remind them that icons should be designed to be as simple as possible while conveying the most information. This can be a challenge and may take several attempts to refine a first idea.

ICONS IN EARLY ELEMENTARY

"Reading" and comprehending visual texts involves skills that develop gradually. In early elementary, children learn that certain graphic representations correspond to specific concepts or meanings. For example, a yellow house-shaped sign with an adult and a child crossing a crosswalk is a school crossing sign. Elementary students also see examples of icons on the badges they can earn in Scouts and other clubs.

However, students need scaffolding to effectively interpret complex icons and build their iconic vocabulary. Scaffolding can also help the cognitive process of abstracting a concept and representing it with an icon. To start the process, it may help to define phrases like *stands for* or *represents*. Breaking down the idea of how an image can replace a concept can be beneficial to early education learners. For example, a merit badge with a needle and thread represents completion of a sewing project. A badge with a bandage stands for completing first aid tasks successfully.

"Grab your visual learning notebook and depict an icon that represents a message or a location that is meaningful to you. For example, you might consider creating icons that represent notable locations within your school (library, gymnasium, principal's office, and so on)."

Susan

Diagrams: Explaining What You Know

Whereas icons *represent* information, diagrams *explain* information. Diagrams range from simple line drawings to more complex sketches. Maps, bar charts, engineering blueprints, and architect sketches are all examples of diagrams. They often, but not always, include text and symbols.

In their many forms, diagrams need to be read to be understood. Ask a football, soccer, or basketball player about the last thing they read and they might cite a textbook or a novel assigned for class. They might not think back to the last time they sat in the locker room where the coach created a diagram of Xs and Os to discuss various plays. Many students associate the word *read* with verbal reading or the written word. They may not recognize that, when they study a diagram to gain information, they are also reading. And just as we can read a textbook and recall and restate the data within, we can do the same with diagrams.

Obviously, athletics aren't the only place our students experience diagrams. They might be familiar with the diagram-centric instructional booklets that come with LEGO sets. Or maybe they've helped their families assemble furniture pieces using IKEA's wordless diagram instructions. Both IKEA and LEGO have become known for their visual instructional diagrams. From a dual-coding perspective, integrating images and text might be beneficial.

DIAGRAM GUIDES

There are three categories of diagrams: analytic, process, and structure. Analytic diagrams analyze intricate designs, process diagrams delineate specific steps (often, but not always, linear), and structure diagrams draw logical correlations among pieces of data. Students most likely encounter examples of several types of these diagrams in K–8 science and social studies texts and resources. Each category includes several different types of diagrams as shown on pages 79–81.

FIG. 5.2 ANALYTIC DIAGRAMS

Diagram Type	Definition	Example
Enlargement/ Exploded view	Enlargement diagrams depict at a larger scale what is too small to see clearly. Exploded-view diagrams depict the order of assembly of the various components or parts of an object.	isotonic blood cell enlargement Exploded Diagram
Floor plan/Blueprint	Floor plans are drawings of a physical structure or space that shows the view from above. These are typically drawn to scale and show the relationship between the various areas and spaces of a structure. Blueprints are a design plan (technical drawing) of a structure and are typically used in the building or creation of an object or structure.	DESK
Cutaway/Cross-section	Cutaways are three dimensional representations that have selected exteriors removed so that the inner workings of an object can be seen. Cross-sections are diagrams showing what would be exposed by making a straight cut through something. A cross-section of Earth would reveal all the layers of the planet.	Peach cross-section Human brain cross-section

FIG. 5.3 PROCESS DIAGRAMS

Diagram Type	Definition	Example
Basic flowchart	A flow chart shows the step-by-step actions that are taken in any specific procedure or process by means of using basic geometric shapes and connecting lines.	
Storyboard	A storyboard uses images or illustrations in sequence to visualize the stages of a procedure, process, or story.	
Cycle	A cycle diagram depicts how items are related to one another in a repeating cycle with no beginning and no end.	
Play diagram	A play diagram is used mainly in sports. Players are represented on a playing court or field with a series of symbols (X and O). Arrows and lines depict motion or movement so players can visualize their relation to other players and their relation to a specific location on the field.	

FIG. 5.4 STRUCTURAL DIAGRAMS

Diagram Type	Definition	Example
Venn	A Venn diagram uses circles to designate and represent data sets and their relationship to each other. Venn diagrams are used to compare and contrast data.	
Pyramid	Pyramid diagrams are mostly used to depict and relate data that is hierarchical. A common elementary pyramid diagram is the food web energy pyramid.	
Web	Web diagrams visually represent relationships between concepts, actions, or things through the interplay of words, shapes, connectors, and other visual elements.	
Tree	A tree diagram has branching connecting lines that represent different relationships and processes.	
Tables	Table diagrams organize and display facts or figures in columns and rows.	

Diagrams convey facts, plans, or processes. Using diagrams in our instruction, we can help students see how pieces of history, parts of a machine, members of a food chain, layers of the soil, or parts of a story fit into a bigger picture.

Viewing and Interpreting Diagrams

As with many concepts in this book, the best way to help students view and interpret diagrams is to find examples from everyday life. Discuss common examples, such as the aforementioned LEGO or IKEA instructions, food pyramids, food chains, or the water cycle. This can get students engaged in analyzing the images for directions, processes, and how aspects of the diagram relate to each other. Ask students to share examples of diagrams they've seen.

Use the following activity to give students a clearer understanding of what diagrams are and what they look like within different areas of their lives (school, home, sports).

ACTIVITY DIAGRAM SHOW-AND-TELL

Learning Objectives
- Students will identify five or more types of diagrams.

Visual Objectives
- Students will depict the basic format of each diagram in a simple sketch.
- Students will record the source of each diagram.

Materials
- blank "Visual Vocabulary Chart" handout (see page 224) for each student, pencils/pens, science texts, magazines, newspapers, and other textbooks as references

Procedure
Diagram Show-and-Tell is a fun way to get everyone looking for a variety of diagrams. By searching for, identifying, and interpreting diagrams, this activity reinforces students' abilities to recognize diagrams in all forms and their understanding of the visual vocabulary surrounding diagrams. You might facilitate this activity by making sure several diagrams or resources with diagrams in them are placed about the room.

Start by showing students the "Diagram Guides" (see pages 233–235) on a regular or an interactive whiteboard. As you briefly discuss each diagram type, ask students to name any examples they've seen. The diagram guides should remain visible during the activity so students can reference them while they proceed with the show-and-tell activity.

Assign students to pairs or working groups. Have students scour the classroom looking for five or more different types of diagrams listed on the diagram guide.

Some examples are:
- emergency exit floor plan/map
- cycle of life posters
- magazines

- newspapers
- various instruction guides or booklets
- texts

As students move around the classroom, they can use a blank "Visual Vocabulary Chart" to document the diagrams they find.
Have students document their finds by:

- Writing down the type of diagram.
- Sketching a reasonable depiction of the diagram.
- Citing the source: location, page number, or other identifying data.
- Either writing out or orally stating what the diagram's purpose is and describing their understanding of it.

When all pairs or groups are finished, or when allotted time is up, hold a brief show-and-tell. Have each pair or group choose one of their diagrams to share with the class, restating the information they collected on their visual vocabulary charts.

Creating Diagrams

While most diagrams are very straightforward and easy to read (as they're meant to be), more complex information may require more complex diagrams. When first seen, these intricate diagrams can be overwhelming for some students and they may require additional decoding.

For example, students may encounter 3-D cutaway diagrams or 2-D cross-section diagrams in STEM texts and materials. Without a proper explanation, these diagrams can be daunting. They illustrate what is beneath the surface—or inside of—plants, animals, areas of the earth, and structures. They can also be used to show the mechanics of how machines work. Often, they are so detailed that some students shy away from creating their own due to their perceived inability to "draw well."

We can easily provide an opportunity for students to gain confidence in their abilities to depict and construct their own cross-section diagrams in the classroom. A simple, yet also challenging and enriching lesson is to create a cross-section of a piece of fruit.

Bring a piece of fruit (or vegetable) for each student to study before creating a cross-section diagram. Providing actual items will help students see the features and details as they create their own cross-section diagrams.

ACTIVITY CREATING A FRUIT/VEGETABLE CROSS-SECTION

Learning Objectives
- Students will define the components of a cross-section diagram.

Visual Objectives
- Students will analyze the internal structure of an object by viewing a cross-section.

- Students will sketch the internal structure of an object by representing its cross-section.
- Students will label the parts of the cross-section they have chosen.

Materials
- fruits or vegetables (soft enough to easily cut), plastic knife, paper plates, white paper or visual learning notebooks, pencils, pens

Procedure
To help students understand the purpose and function of cross-section drawings, bring in a variety of fruits and vegetables for them to examine and draw. Peaches (used here as an example), lemons, green peppers, strawberries, squash, celery, and even bananas exhibit a great variety of details and are fun to draw. Even very young students can produce accurate and detailed drawings when encouraged to take their time and look closely.

First, cut open the fruit or vegetable and place the samples on paper plates. Allow students to examine the samples and ask questions. When they're done examining, ask them to draw what they see. This sketch should be basic: an outline and notable features. Next, allow them to examine the sample with a magnifying glass. Help them notice smaller details. After viewing the enlarged image, have students add new details to their original drawing.

This might lead to questions about what students are seeing inside the specimen. Have students list their questions on a piece of paper and use textbooks or the internet to find answers and learn the vocabulary for naming/labeling the parts of the fruit or vegetable. Finally, with the cross-section diagram drawn, labeled, and colored (if appropriate), have students write a caption and a title for their diagrams.

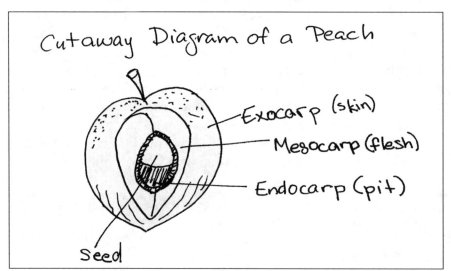

This activity can be repeated several times throughout the year with different types of fruits and vegetables. As students get more practice, they may discover more details and more insights into the inner workings of whatever they choose to examine.

FACILITATING DIAGRAMS IN EARLY ELEMENTARY

As students begin their journey in early literacy, they often choose to express their thoughts and ideas with illustrations before they've acquired alphabetic knowledge to do so. Here are some activity suggestions to set our youngest students on the path to illustrating diagrams purposefully.

- Emphasize how the visual alphabet can be used to represent common objects. Embed mini-square daily doodles into routines, like morning meetings or morning messages.

- If students are responsible for designing thinking projects in a maker space, have them diagram their projects before building them. Set guidelines and routines for students and remind them of their visual alphabet tools before they start.

- Have students build a creation out of LEGOs and ask them to diagram their creation.

- Have students collaborate and draw their classroom or community with the goal of representing as much as they can remember without worrying about full accuracy. The goal is to have students create abstractions of their environment on a two-dimensional medium.

Discussion and Extension

Thinking/Skills	Questions
Knowledge and Understanding	• What features define a diagram? • Why are diagrams used today? • Describe different types of diagrams.
Application	• How could we use a diagram in our study of _____?
Analysis	• Compare and contrast different types of diagrams. Can diagrams be used interchangeably?
Evaluation	• How would you evaluate which diagram format would be best for a given application?
Creative Thinking	• How might you depict a process using two, or combining two, different diagrams?

DIAGRAM CREATIVE EXTENSION

Start with everyone making a family tree in the traditional tree diagram style. Then have students choose another diagram type and attempt to express the same information in the new type. After everyone tries, lead a discussion about which diagram types worked best and which were more challenging.

"Grab your visual learning notebook and create a diagram that is relevant to something you are passionate about. Love to cook? Create a cross-section of an ingredient. Love to read fiction? Create a Venn diagram listing the traits of two characters."

Susan

Graphs: Data Can Tell a Story

Graphs, like diagrams, are designed to illustrate information. However, graphs emphasize ranking and ordering relational data more so than labeling parts or depicting a process. Visually depicting quantity without the use of graphs would quickly become unmanageable and unfeasible.

Some of the most common types of graphs found in K–8 instructional settings are listed in **figure 5.5**.

FIG. 5.5 GRAPH GUIDE

Graph Name	Definition	Visual Image of Graph
Pie chart	Pie charts represent categories of data. They are circles with divided segments that represent the portion each category contains in relationship to the other segments and to the pie as a whole. Percentages and segments can be compared to one another or to the whole. The entire pie chart always equals 100 percent. Creating the divided slices in the proper size needed to represent the data can be a bit challenging for younger students. It is important to start with simple pie charts in the lower grades—a pie chart divided into halves, thirds or fourths—and then introduce more complex pie charts as you move into the intermediate and upper grades.	 FAVORITE PIES
Bar graph	Bar graphs represent and compare data. Two types of bar graphs are the most common: horizontal and vertical. Bar graphs are easy to understand and easy to make, because the bars vary in height or length in relationship to the quantity they represent.	 FAVORITE DESSERTS
Line graph	Line graphs organize and show relationships between and among points of data. Line graphs are distinct in that they have the potential to project the results of data not yet gathered.	 October Bake Sale
Pictograph	A pictograph is a representation of data on a chart or graph using images, icons, or pictures.	 October Bake Sale Purchases

CONTINUED ▷

FIG. 5.5 GRAPH GUIDE, CONTINUED

Graph Name	Definition	Visual Image of Graph
Stacked bar graph	Stacked bar graphs use bars to depict differences between groups of data and have the ability to isolate and compare the many parts of a whole. Each bar stands for a whole, with each individual segment in the bar representing various parts of the whole.	

Viewing and Interpreting Graphs

For the purposes of visual literacy, it's not necessary to teach students about every type of graph. What's most important is to help them see that graphs exist to convey facts. We need to teach students how to read a graph for the intended meaning. Bar graphs are most often the first to be taught since even young students can usually create simple bar graphs and understand the one-to-one correspondence of students' responses to a question and their representation by a number on a bar graph.

ACTIVITY RAISE YOUR HAND

In this activity, you will create a simple bar graph from student responses to help them understand how graphs are designed and how they are to be read and interpreted.

Learning Objectives
- Students will identify personal characteristics as a source of data.
- Students will recognize multiple types of graphs and describe their purposes.

Visual Objectives
- Students will depict data in a bar graph of their own design.

Materials
- whiteboard or chart paper to keep a tally count and to display a bar graph during the lesson

Procedure
Graphing and visualizing personal data can be an engaging way to help students understand the purpose of graphs. In this activity, students keep a tally of the class's responses to a variety of questions. The teacher will track the totals of each response on a simple bar graph presented on chart paper or a whiteboard.

Tell the class they will be gathering information about the characteristics of each student, and their responses will be data for creating a graph. To begin, write the numbers one through eight on the board and tell the class that the numbers correspond with questions you will ask them. Leave room for tally marks next to each number.

Ask the following questions and have students raise their hands if they agree with your question or statement.

1. How many of you are involved in a sport?

2. How many of you love to read?

3. Who likes to participate in the arts?

4. Who likes to play video games?

5. Who enjoys writing in their free time?

6. How many of you like to build or make things?

7. Who enjoys listening to or playing music?

8. Who enjoys cooking or preparing food and meals?

Keep a count for each question and then create a simple bar graph like the example to depict the students' responses. First, draw a vertical line (the Y axis) with six equally spaced marks labeled in increments of five (0, 5, 10) until you've exceeded the number of students in class by five. Then, draw a horizontal line (the X axis) that intersects with the right edge of the vertical line. Make eight equally spaced marks along the horizontal line, labeling each with one of the activities mentioned in the questions. As you work at filling in the graph, call upon students to provide you with the numbers from the tally for each question.

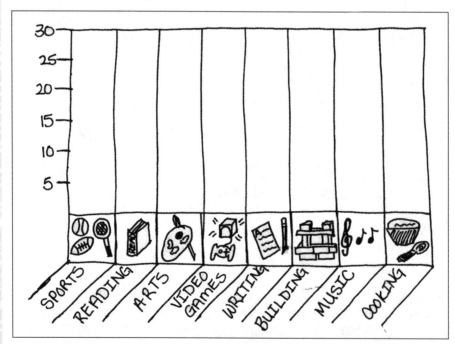

As the numbers get filled in, and the vertical bars of the graph begin to grow, ask the following questions about what the graph is telling you, and give students an opportunity to "read" the results on the chart.

- Can you tell what the favorite activity is? How do you know?
- Are there two activities that have the same number of responses? How does the graph show that?
- How do we create a bar when the number of students doesn't match the numbers on the Y axis? For example, if seven students love to read, where do we place that value when the numbers are in increments of five?

This activity captures a lot of information and data and models for students how to depict data they've gathered in a simple graph.

Next, introduce students to other types of graphs. Display images of graphs on a whiteboard alongside their names and definitions. Give students a new "Visual Vocabulary Chart" so they can copy each image and create their own graph reference sheet to add to their visual learning notebooks. Present samples of each type of graph while discussing the strengths and purposes of each as outlined in figure 5.5. Ask students why they think each type of graph might be better for a specific type of data.

This class graphing activity will reinforce students' understanding of the visual power of graphs and will give them experience in creating their own.

Creating Graphs

We are always asking students quantity questions: How many? How much? How big? How much more or less than? Introducing graphing, even to very young students, provides a place for all this information. When the questions pertain to the students or class—How many books have you read? What is your favorite color?—tallying and graphing the data becomes personally relevant.

ACTIVITY GRAPH YOUR CLASS

Opportunities for gathering and graphing student/class data are as readily available as questions you have to pose. In this graphing activity, personal responses provide the data that will be graphed.

Learning Objectives
- Students will recognize personal experiences as data points.

Visual Objectives
- Students will learn to express experiences as visualized data.
- Students will graph raw data on a bar graph based on responses to questions about personal preferences.

Materials
- graph paper, pencils/pens, colored pencils/pens, access to peers to survey

Procedure
In this activity, each student will create a question similar to the ones in the Raise Your Hand activity.

Suggest the following prompt questions to any students having difficulty coming up with a question. Students will use these questions to create their own categories. Tell students that "other" or "not listed" are possible categories. Examples include:

- How many states have you visited? (create categories, such as less than five, five to ten, more than 10)
- What month is your birthday? (list the months)
- What is your favorite color? (primary colors or colors of the rainbow with "other")
- What hobbies do you have? (reading, sewing, video games, drawing, collecting, "other")
- What sports do you play? (soccer, swimming, softball, gymnastics, football, "other")
- How many siblings do you have? (0, 1, 2, 3, 4 or more)

After students have chosen their questions, they need to gather data. Have students create a tally sheet by writing their question and related categories on a piece of paper. Post the tally sheets around the room, and have students move from one to another entering their individual tally marks on each sheet.

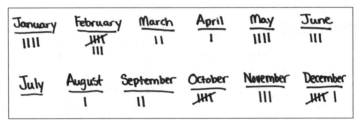

After gathering their data, students can proceed to share their results by creating a bar graph on graph paper. First, begin by reviewing the bar graph created in the Raise Your Hand activity so students can again see how the numbers translate onto the graph. Students then practice graphing skills by labeling their graphs and graphing their data. Have students compare their data to the graph to make sure the data is correctly represented on their graph. Students can share their graph with others in a small group.

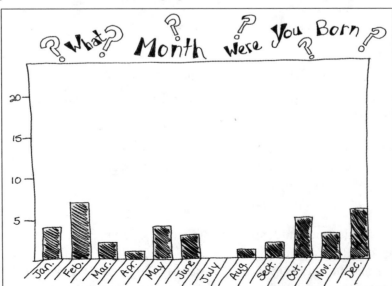

Discussion and Extension

Thinking/Skills	Questions
Knowledge and Understanding	• What defines a graph? • What are different ways that graphs are used? • Describe different types of graphs. • Where did you find graphs in the environment? Print? Signs? Technology? Other applications?
Application	• How would you use data found in a graph?
Analysis	• How are different graphs used to depict different data sets?
Evaluation	• What qualities make the design of a graph effective and why?
Creative Thinking	• What would be a visually creative way to design a meaningful graph?

GRAPH CREATIVE EXTENSION

Pie charts can really excite students. (Maybe it's that they involve the word *pie*.) Offer students the opportunity to flex their math muscle a bit by polling their classmates about their favorite flavor of pie. This activity works well with students who are currently learning or have already learned how to calculate percentages. Once the data is collected and the pie segments are calculated and drawn, students can get creative by filling in the segments with doodles, images, colors, icons, or other depictions that represent the choices.

"Grab your visual learning notebook and create a bar graph that depicts how you spend your time in an average day. Try to make the bars visually compelling. The goal is to create a graph that can be interpreted by a wide range of people of varying verbal abilities. This is a great time for you to practice your graphing skills."

Maps: Show Me Where to Go

Maps have been around for thousands of years. Some of the very first rudimentary maps were inscribed into clay tablets by Babylonians, painted on silk by the Chinese, or recorded by Egyptians to document property boundaries.

Maps are often more than just records of land and space. They can also be vehicles of communication. Maps enable those who have never ventured out of an area to "see" what other places look like, what resources they contain, and what avenues of travel—roads, trains, ferries, bridges, airports—they offer. All of this is made visible through learning to read a map.

Maps provide a visual representation, usually on a flat surface, of an area and its features. This might include a country, a state, a neighborhood, a house, or even a room. Maps can show geographical content, including continents and landmasses, bodies of water, natural resources, roads, railways, other transportation routes, population centers, and so much more.

Closer to home, maps can show the layout of a room or a home. When a home is being designed or built, these maps are called *plans*. (Students often enjoy mapping their own home or room.) Maps can also show areas of public spaces—both inside and outside. For example, a museum brochure often shows exhibit locations on various floors. For an outdoor setting, a map of a public garden can show where different types of plants can be viewed, perhaps arranged by region. This map could also show various walkways through the gardens and any bridges connecting them.

Viewing and Interpreting Maps

One of the most commonly used maps is a roadmap. Of course, to use a map effectively when traveling, it helps to know where on the map you are currently. Your destination might be the city park, which you can see outlined, shaded in green, and labeled with *City Park*. But to get there, you first need to figure out where you are in relation to the park. This is where the skills of reading and interpreting a map come in handy.

A well-rounded geography curriculum might include basic map reading and interpreting skills: how to recognize and use cardinal directions, a compass rose, legends, scale, inset maps, coordinates, latitude and longitude, and so on.

Most people assume they'll only find maps in a geography lesson. But maps can be useful in many other subjects. In English language arts, you might use a map to get a clearer idea of what the fantasy world in the novel looks like. In social studies, a map can tell you about resources in different regions. Displaying maps of local areas with civic, cultural, and industrial importance helps students relate the features of their own communities to a representation on a map.

Each type of map in **figure 5.6** illustrates and emphasizes different types of information.

FIG. 5.6 MAP GUIDE

Map Name	Definition	Example
Climate	Climate maps represent the climate and the precipitation (rain and snow) of an area. Different colors are used to indicate different climate zones.	Tropical Monsoon / Tropical Savanna / Tropical Steppe / Sub-tropical Steppe / Subtropical Desert / Mountain
Physical	Physical maps represent the water features and landforms of an area, including mountains, rivers, and lakes. Different colors are used to illustrate water and the type of different landforms.	

CONTINUED ▷

FIG. 5.6 MAP GUIDE, CONTINUED

Map Name	Definition	Example
Natural Resource	Natural resource maps represent the natural resources and most prominent economic activities in a given area. Icons are used to illustrate the locations of natural and economic resources on the map. For example, apple icons on a map of Washington show that apples are grown there.	
Political	Political maps show state and national boundaries. They also depict major cities and capital cities.	
Road	Road maps show highways and roads, airports, railroad tracks, cities, and other points of interest in an area. Road maps are most often used to plan trips. In the past, they were also consulted for driving directions, although GPS is used much more often now.	
Topographic	Topographic maps use contour lines to represent the shape and elevation of an area. Lines placed close together represent steep terrain, while lines placed far apart represent flatter terrain.	

ACTIVITY MAPS ARE ALL AROUND US

Learning Objectives
- Students will define and describe different types of maps.
- Students will analyze different features of maps.
- Students will analyze maps of familiar places.
- Students will evaluate which type of map is best for a given purpose.

Visual Objectives
- Students will view and compare different types of maps.

Materials
- either physical or online copies of several types of maps: subway maps, bus/transit maps, intercontinental railway maps, interstate maps, natural resource maps, literary maps of fictional lands, images of globes, topographical maps, street maps, national maps, and treasure maps

Procedure

Show students a variety of maps and map terms on the whiteboard, and/or provide hands-on examples of the maps in the materials list. Have students look for commonalities and differences among the maps. For example, compare and contrast the information in a political map to a topographical map. Or compare a roadmap to a subway map from the same city.

Encourage students to use the "Visual Note-Taking Form" (see page 225) to depict and sketch different types of maps and map terms as they are introduced and discussed. Guide the discussion with these questions:

- What are the uses for each map?
- Which map tells you the most about the natural landscape?
- Which map would be useful to navigate your city?
- Who uses maps today? Which ones? Why?
- What are the features (or parts) of the map?
- Can maps tell a story on their own?

As students become more familiar with different types of maps, they can begin creating and incorporating maps into their work.

Toni

"One of the biggest advantages of incorporating visual learning and teaching in my classroom is that I feel that I am helping students develop a lifelong tool for increasing learning and memory that will last well beyond my classroom walls. Reading graphs, maps, timelines, itineraries, and data presented in tables are essential skills of visual literacy."

Creating Maps

An easy way to introduce students to mapping is to have them map an area they know well. This might be their house, neighborhood, or school. Often, through the process of mapping a familiar place and making decisions about what to include and what to exclude, students begin to see what they thought they already knew from a different perspective. Mapping the familiar helps strengthen the powers of observation.

Another way to introduce mapping is to give students a bit more freedom and let their imaginations run wild. Mapping a fictional place lends itself to using different types of maps. (Mapping a castle? Try using a blueprint. Mapping a fantasyland? Try a topographical map.) This type of variety is a great way to exercise creativity.

ACTIVITY ANOTHER TYPE OF STORY MAP

I have found that using the following map activity based on fictional lands makes map making a bit more inventive and creative. Students explore the content of imagined lands before creating direct representations of existing locations.

Learning Objectives
- Students will analyze the features of maps in works of literature.
- Students will compare and contrast examples of these maps with actual travel maps.

Visual Objectives
- Students will imagine the design of a map to represent a work of fiction of their choosing.
- Students will construct a map to depict the locations in the work of fiction they have chosen.

Materials
- copies of any of the books listed, paper, pencils, pens, visual learning notebooks

Procedure

Gather as many of the following books as you can, making sure they are appropriate for and relevant to your students and their interests:

ELEMENTARY

Peter Pan, J. M. Barrie
Winnie-the-Pooh, A. A. Milne
The Tale of Peter Rabbit, Beatrix Potter
Where the Wild Things Are, Maurice Sendak
Charlotte's Web, E. B. White

MIDDLE SCHOOL AND HIGH SCHOOL

Murder on the Orient Express, Agatha Christie
Robinson Crusoe, Daniel Defoe
Lord of the Flies, William Golding
The Curious Incident of the Dog in the Night-Time, Mark Haddon
The Old Man and the Sea, Ernest Hemingway
Brave New World, Aldous Huxley
The Dark Tower series, Stephen King
The Lion, the Witch and the Wardrobe, C. S. Lewis
Moby Dick, Herman Melville
Eragon, Christopher Paolini
The Golden Compass, Philip Pullman
Treasure Island, Robert Louis Stevenson
Gulliver's Travels, Jonathan Swift
The Hobbit/The Lord of the Rings, J. R. R. Tolkien
Around the World in Eighty Days, Jules Verne
Twenty Thousand Leagues Under the Sea, Jules Verne
The Island of Doctor Moreau, H. G. Wells

- Give students ten minutes to examine these books and the maps inside them to see how these maps are similar to or different from street maps or topographic maps. Have students create a Venn diagram in their visual learning notebooks to document the similarities and differences.

- Have students choose a book they have already read, or one that they would like to read, and analyze the features of the map it contains.

- Ask students why the maps in the books are important and what they add to the story experience. From the samples provided, have students identify what characteristics best help them understand the map (such as the compass rose, legend). Make a list of their responses and post it in a visible location.

- Ask students to each choose a favorite piece of literature: a story, a picture book, or even a movie. It doesn't have to be from the preceding list of books. But it's important they pick a story they know well from memory.

- Have each student sketch a map related to their chosen work. This should be an original map, not a replica of one that already exists in the chosen work. Remind students to include any of the map characteristics from the list they created in the third bullet, if they are relevant (or any other characteristics that the students feel are important).

Visualizing the setting or location of a story, through words and images, requires students to really connect with the written word. Depicting what they see in their minds requires students to use their perception, comprehension, and memory in addition to imagination and personal creativity. Making story maps may seem simple, but the visual learning can significantly increase learner retention.

ACTIVITY MAPS: MAP MAKING FOR EARLY ELEMENTARY

The following instructional activity has been written for use in the early elementary grades to introduce mapping with a hands-on, real-world activity. I have successfully used the activity with students in fourth through eighth grade as well.

Learning Objectives
- Students connect places in their community with two-dimensional representations on a map.
- Students apply knowledge of visual elements in recognizing places on a map.

Visual Objectives
- Students create a map of their community using the visual alphabet and the six essential design elements and justify their choices.
- Students create maps with varying degrees of detail (scale, directional relationships, and so forth), depending on the learning goals of the larger unit of study.

Materials

- book(s) on beginning cartography, including *Me on the Map* by Joan Sweeney, *Mapping Penny's World* by Loreen Leedy, and if possible: computer, projector, screen, Google Maps, chart paper/whiteboard, blank paper or cardstock, butcher paper, writing utensils, "Visual Alphabet and Six Essential Design Elements" handout (see page 220).

Procedure

- Read students a book on beginning cartography. Point out what has been mapped in the book and ask students what they have seen in their environment that they think could appear on the map.

- Show students a map of their school from Google Maps. Start with the street map mode, and then move to satellite imagery if available. Ask them what shapes and elements they see on the map and what the shapes could represent.

- Model creating a map of the school grounds, school buildings, and outdoor spaces on the whiteboard. Create the shape of the grounds first, and then discuss placement of the other features with the class as you add them one at a time on your whiteboard drawing. Talk through the process with the class as you draw. For example, you might say, "Okay, where does the school building go? How about the playground equipment?" and so on.

  Next, start exploring the surrounding neighborhood. Point out noteworthy landmarks, or, if possible, community resources like the library, grocery store, and so forth. Students will usually want to see their own neighborhoods. Explore students' neighborhoods as a class; ask students what community resources they've seen as they travel through their neighborhoods in the car, on their bicycles, or walking, and how they see these places placed on the map. As students respond to the questions, write their responses on the whiteboard or chart paper for use later.

- After brainstorming what is in their community and making a list of what they saw on Google Maps, ask students to depict places/resources in their community on blank paper. Oftentimes, students will represent their homes, favorite restaurants, sports fields, and so on. At this stage, don't worry about accuracy. That will come as their map skills develop. As the class finishes their depictions, begin taping students' smaller maps into a larger class map. Inevitably, there will be gaps and whole sections of the community that are not depicted. This is when you have an opportunity to have students exercise their memory and ask them to tell you what is missing.

- To wrap up this activity, have students review each other's work and discuss different ideas on how maps were created, what students noticed that their peers included in their maps (and how), and what they would change about their own maps.

Discussion and Extension

Thinking/Skills	Questions
Knowledge and Understanding	• What are different types of maps used for? • Which maps tell more about the natural landscape and natural resources?
Application	• What types of maps might be most useful in daily life? • What types of maps might you use only rarely?
Analysis	• Compare and contrast different types of maps. Can maps be used interchangeably? • Are there any maps that are more or less helpful when needing to navigate city streets? • Which of these maps would you find helpful if you were a tourist in a new city, state, or country? • What else can a map convey besides directions? Classify different types of maps. • Which maps give a bigger picture from a geological point of view?
Evaluation	• Which maps help tell or help support a story? How so?
Creative Thinking	• After creating your own map for a story that you've read, what ideas do you have for how else you might use maps that you have created in the future?

MAPS CREATIVE EXTENSION

Ask students to create a map for a land of their own imagination. Have them develop a key for the different features they choose to include in their map. Tell them to name the land and to write an accompanying story, if they choose.

This example is a story map drawn by Hannah, a fourth-grade student, to illustrate the fantasy land from a story she wrote. She wanted the reader to see how Calidor was in the center of Morynil and how it was inevitable that it become the main city of power in that position. Note how she used the letters of the visual alphabet to depict the forest, the rivers, the plains, and the mountainous regions.

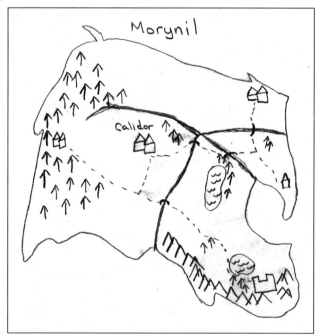

"Grab your visual learning notebook and create a map to a buried treasure. Get creative while limiting your use of words. Use your mark-making skills, the visual alphabet, and everything that you have learned so far to depict as much detail as possible."

Susan

Timelines: From Here to Then

Common in the study of history and biography, a timeline lists events and the order in which they occurred. Timelines are effective for bringing history into focus, especially when they illustrate the different life events of significant people alongside key cultural and historical events. Even in their simplest form—a straight line, hash marks, and text denoting significant moments—timelines are a form of visual learning.

To kick it up a notch, we need to talk about illustrated timelines. Whereas a more traditional timeline may be solely text based, illustrated timelines use graphic representations in addition to text to depict the chronology of events over time. For example, an illustrated timeline showing the history of man-made transportation might have images of a wheeled cart, a boat, a bicycle, a car, an airplane, and a rocket, all plotted along a line next to a date that reflects the first use of each.

But illustrated timelines can be used for more than teaching historical and cultural events. Because they primarily help lend context to time through visualization, illustrated timelines can be used to catalog day to day tasks. You can delineate important milestones in a project or create step-by-step details for a trip itinerary. Most prominently, you'll see them used in bus and train schedules. As timelines creep more and more into our everyday vocabulary (you'll see what I mean later), it's become more important for students to be able to accurately interpret and read timelines.

While illustrated timelines help students gain a better understanding of how time passes, they become even more meaningful when used to depict the personal experiences and significant events in your students' lives. For example, a timeline that depicts important events in a student's life (losing first tooth, seeing a movie at a theater for the first time) could show how these milestones fall in relation to noted world events that occurred during the same time period. Suddenly, students can see where their lives fit in the "big picture."

Viewing and Interpreting Illustrated Timelines

There are several important factors to take into account when viewing and interpreting a timeline. For example, is there significance to how time is distributed along the line? Are there evenly spaced hash marks that indicate equal amounts of time (a year, five years, ten years, for example)? Or are events listed at whatever time they occurred, with no significant times serving as anchors (is there an event in 1984, one in 1997, and another in 2001)? Or does the chronology take a back seat and the milestones are more about the events than when they occurred?

To better interpret and read a timeline, it's best to understand the several different types that exist. **Figure 5.**7 on page 100 shows the varieties.

FIG. 5.7 TIMELINE GUIDE

Timeline Name	Definition	Example
Horizontal	Horizontal timelines are perhaps the most common. They are read from left to right.	
Vertical	Vertical timelines are created and can be read either from bottom to top or from top to bottom. The most well-known vertical timeline is Facebook (see how timelines are creeping into our lives?)	
Meandering	Meandering timelines signify a process or a journey that did not follow a linear path. For example, a meandering timeline may depict Peter Rabbit's journey through the garden patch as he sampled the various delicacies.	
Mapped	Mapped timelines show the progression of distance, place, and time on a journey by placing the timeline directly on the map. For example, a mapped timeline might represent westward expansion in the United States or other migrations of people or animal life.	

CONTINUED ▷

FIG. 5.7 TIMELINE GUIDE, CONTINUED

Timeline Name	Definition	Example
Parallel	Parallel timelines show events that occur concurrently among different people or places. Parallel timelines lend themselves to being stacked. For example, in the classroom you might put a student's life events on the top and local or world events on the bottom.	
Illustrated	Illustrated timelines are a distinct form of timeline. They include images that represent significant content and convey significant information, yet they can be quite simple in their design. We can turn any of the other types of timelines into an illustrated timeline by adding depiction of the events in addition to written labels or descriptions.	

The following exercise will help students explore various types of timelines and offer criteria to determine which is the best type to use for a given assignment.

ACTIVITY A CLOSER LOOK AT TIMELINES

We begin by engaging students in a discussion of different types of timelines. Although several types will be reviewed, our main focus will be on illustrated timelines.

Learning Objectives
- Students will describe and define multiple forms of timelines.
- Students will compare and contrast multiple forms of timelines.
- Students will analyze timelines to determine their best applications.

Visual Objectives
- Students will use a "Visual Note-Taking Form" (see page 225) to depict and sketch different forms of timelines.

Materials
- examples of horizontal, vertical, illustrated, meandering, mapped, and parallel timelines, and "Visual Note-Taking Form" handout for each student

Procedure
Begin by showing students examples of different types of timelines (use figure 5.7 to help you track down as many kinds as you can find). Introduce

and give definitions of horizontal, vertical, meandering, mapped, parallel, and illustrated timelines.

As you show the examples, lead the class through the following discussion questions:

- What is this timeline trying to tell us?
- What span of time is it covering?
- What is the beginning or initial event?
- What is the ending event?

Encourage students to use the "Visual Note-Taking Form" to depict and sketch different types of timelines as they are introduced and discussed.

Creating Illustrated Timelines

Illustrated timelines do not have to be elaborate or intricate to be impactful. The goal is to depict events (either those that have happened in the past, or those that will take place in the future) in a way that clearly conveys pertinent information.

Planning for a field trip is a great opportunity to sharpen your students' visual thinking skills. Why not incorporate an illustrated timeline activity into your next classroom excursion?

Students can express their creativity and show that they understand the plans for the day in the following activity.

ACTIVITY FIELD TRIP

Learning Objectives
- Students will identify a chronological sequencing of events and show their knowledge and understanding in the form of an itinerary.

Visual Objectives
- Students will depict an itinerary in the form of a visual timeline.

Materials
- "Illustrated Timeline" template (page 236), visual alphabet, pencils or pens, colored pencils/colored pens

Procedure

Hand out a blank "Illustrated Timeline" template to each student and ask students to fill it out. Remind them to use their visual skills to doodle or depict the plans for the day.

Two days before the field trip, discuss the itinerary with the class. Begin by stating what time the trip will begin and where students will need to meet. This will most likely be along the lines of: "We will meet in the classroom at 8 a.m. like usual." Allow students a few moments to depict this in the first cell of their timeline, making sure to note the time in addition to the images.

Continue stating each step of the day verbally while students continue to fill out their forms. You may wish to model visual images to help students struggling with how to depict something.

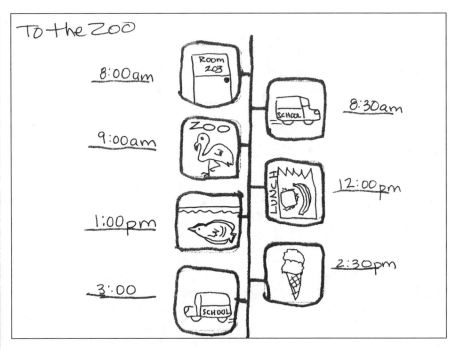

When finished, students should each have an illustrated timeline depicting the itinerary for field trip day. Have students share their depictions with a partner or group.

Also, discuss with students what to do if activities run later than expected. What needs to be done to adjust the timeline of an itinerary accordingly? For example, if the bus leaves fifteen minutes later than planned, how will that affect the schedule for the rest of the day? What adjustments need to be made?

Another way to use timelines in the classroom is to develop a class timeline as the year progresses. The timeline might be at shoulder height and wrap around the perimeter of the room for maximum viewing opportunities and individual students, or small groups of students, may supply the images or illustrations. For example, a class photo may mark the start of the school year. Photos from a field trip or open house may come next.

Schedules can be very important to some special needs students. Last-minute changes can upset students who adhere to a rigid time structure. Unexpected changes happen all the time (the bus arrives late to school, traffic makes the journey slower, and so on). It may be helpful to write the timeline in pencil. This way, start times of events can be easily adjusted to account for changes. This may help lessen anxiety in certain students.

This same activity also works to create back-to-school night agendas and other school-wide events. Having students create illustrated timelines for an event can also help them become better communicators. Encourage them to take the timeline home and share pertinent information with their families. Illustrated timelines really help convey the message and the meaning of events in the past and those on our itinerary in the future.

"Using the visual timeline activity engaged all of my kids. It gets them to focus on a moment, to grasp their understanding with an image and to be provided with visuals that increase their memory. Images help them understand events over time—personally and historically."

Martin

Discussion and Extension

Thinking/Skills	Questions
Knowledge and Understanding	• What features define an illustrated timeline? • Where are illustrated timelines used today?
Application	• How might you use an illustrated timeline?
Analysis	• Compare and contrast different types of timelines. • Can different types of timelines be used interchangeably?
Evaluation	• How would you evaluate which timeline format is best for a given application?
Creative Thinking	• How would you design the illustrations for your illustrated timeline?

ILLUSTRATED TIMELINES CREATIVE EXTENSION

This extension is particularly effective for social studies. Parallel timelines are complex texts with multiple timelines placed under another with their dates lined up.

For additional instructional activities that incorporate visual timelines, see chapters 10 and 11.

This format shows what events have happened simultaneously in history. It also helps compare and contrast unrelated events that happened at the same time. Students can create parallel timelines by making an illustrated timeline of their major life events and then making a timeline of major regional, national, or world events parallel to their own timeline. This activity can lead to a rich discussion of comparing and contrasting events of the students' lives with cultural and historical events of the time.

"Grab your visual learning notebook and make time for timelines! Copy the 'Illustrated Timeline' template onto a blank page and illustrate your day. Use color in each of the cells to emphasize your mood at that particular time of the day. Then, add details to depict what you were doing. Don't forget to write down the time. Illustrated timelines are a great way to doodle your day in a compact and linear fashion."

Susan

Infographic Posters: Data Made Beautiful

Infographics may seem on the surface like a 21st-century visual literacy skill, but the origins of information graphics began in 1801. William Playfair invented line charts and pie charts as a way to help people understand complex issues. He wrote how important it is to make data interesting, saying that appealing "to the eye when proportion and magnitude are concerned, is the best and readiest method of conveying a distinct idea." (He also addressed engaging children with the visualization of data. He said that imprinting visual data at sensitive periods of development would lay the foundation for building an accurate and valuable knowledge base.[17]

Contemporary infographic posters are graphically and verbally rich, and they are rapidly becoming a preferred way to present and receive information. The visual representation of data presents the data in a more impactful way. Infographic posters often integrate many forms of data representation and visualization, including those we've already discussed in this chapter: graphs, maps, icons, diagrams, timelines, and more.

Contemporary infographics use graphic design elements rather than pages of text to illustrate essential facts and information. They can eliminate the need for trifold brochures that read like a mini newspaper, with every possible inch covered in factoids and important information. Infographics deliver information quickly, effectively, and aesthetically.

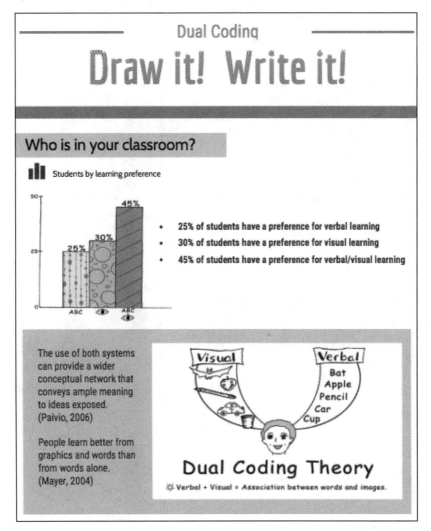

The infographic poster titled "Dual-Coding: Draw it! Write it!" on the previous page combines a graph of data showing students' learning preferences in percentages, quotes about dual-coding theory, and a visual depiction of dual-coding theory into a single page.

Before we teach students how to view and interpret infographics, we need to look at the pertinent vocabulary. As mentioned earlier, infographic posters incorporate a variety of illustrations and data representation within a single page. For example, an infographic might incorporate some combination of the components in **figure 5.8**.

FIG. 5.8 INFOGRAPHIC POSTER COMPONENTS GUIDE

Parts of an Infographic Poster	Definition	Example
Headings	Title and subtitles that name the subject of the data being presented.	
Sidebars	A short vertical area located to the side of the page that highlights related data.	
Illustrations	Images, depictions, doodles, clip art, and other pictures that connect the data on a visual level.	
Graphs	A diagram showing the measurable relation between variables.	
Timelines	A graphic representation of the passage of time as it relates to the data.	

CONTINUED ▷

FIG. 5.8 INFOGRAPHIC POSTER COMPONENTS GUIDE, CONTINUED

Parts of an Infographic Poster	Definition	Example
Icons	A simple picture, image, or depiction that represents a noun, a verb, or a concept/idea.	
Forms	Visual shapes that create structure within an infographic.	
Facts	Data, evidence, or pieces of information that have been researched and cited.	

Viewing and Interpreting Infographic Posters

Most curricula in the sciences and social studies require students to engage in analysis and interpretation to derive meaning. Common Core State Standards define college and career readiness, in part, as the ability to "integrate and evaluate content in diverse media and formats, including visually and quantitatively, as well as in words" (CCRA.R.7). Infographic posters are an excellent tool for developing these capabilities in our students, both when they interpret infographics and when they create them.

The viewing and interpreting activity that follows requires you to present a variety of infographic posters to discuss as a class. To enhance opportunities for analysis, evaluation, and critique, show both well-crafted infographics and poorly constructed or incomplete ones for students to review and discuss. Engage students in analysis and evaluation. Give them time to consider how they might design or redesign an infographic.

Need examples of well-crafted or poorly constructed infographic posters? Check out the Learning Network site at the *New York Times* (tinyurl.com/26kxu93). They provide an extensive repository of infographics appropriate for the classroom, especially in social studies, science, politics, and current events.

The website Media Matters (www.mediamatters.org) presents information on errors in the media—including poorly crafted or misleading infographics.

ACTIVITY INTRODUCING AN INFOGRAPHIC POSTER

Learning Objectives
- Students will select an infographic poster that is interesting to them.
- Students will analyze the components of the infographic poster.
- Students will evaluate the infographic poster for clarity, accuracy, and creativity.

Visual Objectives
- Students will decode the visual components of their chosen infographic poster.

Materials
- infographic poster samples; students will choose one to work with (online or printed), "Infographic Poster Components Guide" handout for each student (see pages 237–238)

Procedure
- Display the sample infographic posters on your whiteboard, and ask students to describe what they see using infographic vocabulary. This is an opportunity for students to view and interpret the posters as a class before breaking into smaller groups.
- Have students work for twenty to thirty minutes with a partner or in small groups to find sample infographic posters on the internet that interest them. They will analyze and evaluate the components and effectiveness of the infographic posters in conveying messages and information.
- Have the groups discuss and write responses to the following questions:
  - What is the main topic or message of this infographic poster?
  - How can you make use of the information?
  - Do the visuals and text work together or do they clash?
  - Can the presentation be improved? How?
  - If you were to redesign this infographic poster, what would you do?
- When students have finished their analysis and have written their responses, they can share the infographic poster they chose along with their responses to the questions with the class.

The infographic poster on the left at the top of page 109 is a good example of how students can show what they know in a format that is both visual and verbal. This student presented facts about assorted birds in a visually appealing and clear format. The student also added eye-catching text boxes that contain a unit vocabulary term with its definition and a relevant lifespan fact.

A fifth-grade student created the pineapple infographic poster on the right to share his research project with the class. He chose several key facts from his research and found creative ways to depict this data with both words and images. There is a lot of data being presented in this infographic, yet the poster as a whole does not feel overwhelming.

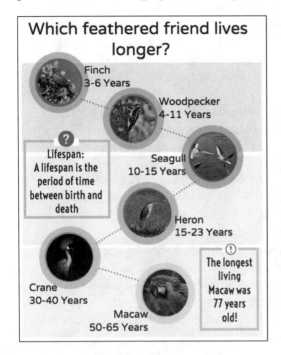

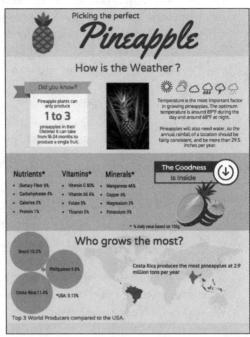

Data in the Information Age

There's no magic formula for creating an effective infographic. Should you use a pie chart or a bar graph? Or both? How many icons should you use? Most of the decisions will depend on the data being depicted. It may take several attempts to find a design that's pleasing to the eye—not too cluttered and not too sparse—and informative. Typically, students rely on their own personal aesthetics to find the balance between graphics and text. But it may also help to show students examples of professionally created infographics and discuss the factors that make them visually appealing and clear in their messaging.

Beyond the layout, it's also important to take into account the source of the data. Just as you can't believe everything you read on the internet, it's important to remember that not all data is created equal. When creating an infographic poster, consider the following qualities.

SEVEN QUALITIES OF EFFECTIVE INFOGRAPHIC POSTERS

1. It's focused on an important topic.
2. It represents interesting and meaningful data.
3. It presents information simply and clearly.
4. It creatively visualizes data and information with the use of graphics and design.
5. It isn't too long or too short.
6. It provides clear takeaways.
7. It includes sources for the data provided.

Critical Thinking: Assessing Credibility, Data Manipulation, and Misleading Information

We teach students early on that academic integrity is important and twisting the truth to send a different message is not acceptable. We don't allow students to plagiarize a research paper. We also need to remind students, as they begin creating infographics, that it is unethical and unacceptable to purposefully misrepresent or manipulate data.

Entire books are written about the misrepresentation and manipulation of data. For our purposes, we will address these issues in the most useful way for raising awareness in our students as they review resources and data representation.

There are many ways to misrepresent or manipulate data—whether deliberately or by accident. Not all misrepresentation is intentional. As students search for data, they will come across many different sources. Learning to carefully examine these sources is a very important first step.

In the age of citizen journalism, instant information, and Wikipedia, students—as part of a holistic literacy program—now also need to be able to evaluate online resources for credibility, reliability, and scholastic value. Scholastic.com, the Harvard College Writing Program, and the Purdue Online Writing Lab offer extensive resources on what to consider when leading discussions on reliable sources. Some points to consider:

- Who is the **author**, and what are his or her credentials? Is there more than one author? Are there too many authors for this source to be reliable? With which organization(s) is the author **affiliated**? Who has funded the publication?

- **When** was the source published? When was it last updated? If this information doesn't seem to be available, does the information presented seem reasonable?

- What is the **domain** of the website? Is the site hosted by a reputable top-level domain, such as .edu, .org, or .gov? Carefully consider the organization behind the website.

- How does this particular source **compare** with other sources on the same topic?

ACTIVITY CREATING INFOGRAPHIC POSTERS

Learning Objectives
- Students will identify an infographic poster as a distinct form of data visualization.
- Students will identify a topic that can be represented through an infographic poster.
- Students will select relevant data to represent their topic.
- Students will select and create forms of graphic representation to include in their infographic poster (icons, diagrams, graphs, and so on).

Visual Objectives
- Students will create an original infographic poster combining visual and verbal content based on a topic of their choosing.

Materials

- reference texts, paper, design materials, pencils, pens, rulers, online infographic design sites

Procedure

- Have students work in pairs to think of a topic and find related data that they would want to share with others.
- Tell students to select research on the topic. Students should use and cite a variety of reputable sources. If they have trouble finding enough data, have them choose another topic.
- Instruct students to plan a draft of an infographic poster for their topic. Have them create a sketch that uses at least three types of informational graphics from this chapter.
  - icons
  - diagrams
  - graphs
  - maps
  - illustrated timelines
- Students should depict their data and facts using both verbal and visual text.
- If possible, have students include color as a design feature of their infographic poster.
- Remind students to choose graphics that are crisp, clear, and easy to discern.
- Remember that white space is an asset. Encourage students to illustrate meaningfully without visual clutter.
- Keeping it simple is the key. Help students identify areas that may be confusing and make suggestions on how to revise for clarity.
- When students are finished, have them present their infographic posters to the class.

The following teacher-friendly websites are great resources for jump-starting infographic poster design ideas.

- **Easel.ly** is a free web-based tool that has many predesigned themes to help your students get started. Once students choose a template, they can begin the design process. Its drag-and-drop interface is user friendly.
- **Piktochart** provides users with images and graphic tools to design infographics online. The site includes access to over 4,000 images, unlimited creations, full editor functions, and the ability to download and share full-size files.
- **Venngage** is a free web-based tool that has limited predesigned templates so students can create professional looking infographics quickly.

Discussion and Extension

Thinking/Skill	Discussion Questions
Knowledge and Understanding	• What is the main topic of this infographic poster? • What is its message?
Application	• How can you make use of the information presented? Explain.
Analysis	• How was the information arranged and presented? • How do the visuals and text work together? • What did the author do to be sure the message was understood? • Does the infographic include sections, titles, graphs, multiple perspectives? Be specific. • Does the infographic present a particular viewpoint or perspective? If so, define and describe it.
Evaluation	• Can the presentation be improved? How? • Was this infographic created to make you feel a certain way or to persuade you? • If yes, how does it make you feel or what is it trying to persuade you to do? • Is some part of the presentation inaccurate or incomplete? • How were the colors or images used to create a desired effect? • What conclusions can be drawn from the content of this infographic? • What drew you to THIS infographic? Why did you choose this one? What do you like about it? Be specific.
Creative Thinking	• If you were to redesign this infographic poster, what would you do differently? Describe.

INFOGRAPHIC CREATIVE EXTENSION

Once students have become familiar with and comfortable creating infographic posters, they may look for opportunities to create more. Here are a few ways to work infographics into your classroom:

- Have students create an infographic poster in place of a book report.
- After a field trip, have students document their experiences in an infographic poster—complete with facts that they learned.
- Use an infographic poster to creatively depict the order of mathematical operations (also known as *pemdas*: parenthesis, exponents, multiplication, division, addition, and subtraction).
- When studying the planets, students can create an infographic poster for an individual planet or for the entire solar system.
- Be creative and ask your students to find even more ways to incorporate infographic posters.

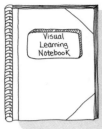

"Grab your visual learning notebook, turn to a blank page, and make a quick list of topics that could be depicted in an infographic poster format. Write words or phrases followed by a quick doodle that comes to mind. There are nearly endless possibilities when it comes to depicting data and information in an infographic poster!"

Moving On

Informational graphics are ubiquitous. Students encounter them every day, and yet it is rare that a curriculum includes specifics about how to decode or create these forms of visual communication. In this chapter we've looked at icons, maps, timelines, infographic posters, and more with instructions and activities for viewing, interpreting, and creating informational graphics at different grades and in different curricular areas. Next up, we'll discuss the personal side of visual learning with a look at journals.

Visual Journals

While many people may think of journaling as a private activity often used to express and work through one's innermost thoughts, journaling has a long history in the education field. For years, teachers have asked students to write down their thoughts on materials discussed in class or to record observations as they progress through a multitiered lesson—all in journal form. If you've never used journals with your students, this chapter will offer ways to introduce the concept and get students engaged in the process. We'll also look at how adding a visual component can aid in learning and comprehension. A journal that includes both images and text provides a unique multimodal representation of students' learning and experience helping them both show and tell what they know.

An individual's journal can take on a life of its own. Day after day, month after month, and year after year, observations, ideas, dreams, plans, and hopes get chronicled alongside little nuggets of wisdom, scraps of truths, and even painful memories. Our ruminations can create a picture in words and images of who we were, who we are, and who we are becoming. The process of journaling *can change* the journalist.

Let's look at two types of visual journals applied to classroom use: life notebooks and nature journals.

- **Life notebooks** are comprised of personal, school-related, and creative forms of expression and are a documentation of each student's day from his or her perspective.

- **Nature journals** are best described as part scientific observation and part personal observation combined as one reflects on and depicts what he or she sees in nature.

These two notebooks are unique in their form and purpose. The journal samples that follow can provide ideas about how to get kids journaling. As you read, keep in mind that you won't use all the ideas provided. Pick and choose ones that work best for your teaching style or that you think might be most effective for your curriculum.

Both of these journals can be used:

- as an outlet for personal expression
- as a place to record and reflect on experiences
- to capture thinking and personal growth over time
- to foster self-knowledge and self-reflection

- as a place to collect thoughts and ideas related to classroom learning
- as a go-to resource for creative expression

Life Notebooks as Visual Journals

Self-expression is often reserved for the arts, whether it be visual, performing, or creative writing. It isn't always something that one feels comfortable putting on display for the whole world to see. Life notebooks offer students a chance to discover a balance between their creative and academic sides that feels right to each individual.

Life notebooks are interactive and integrate visual and verbal expression. They are unique for each student and are used to both chronicle personal experiences and reflect on essential learning from the school day or school week. Creative writing and creative depicting prompts are also used to encourage and support the design of personal life notebooks. Teachers consistently report that this type of documentation and reflection has resulted in considerable increases in student motivation, retention, and engagement.

When I first began giving professional development workshops, I asked participants (teachers and administrators) to chronicle events from their days and to pay attention to their emerging visual work in the classroom. Despite some skepticism, the participants agreed.

After some time working with their life notebooks, participants became more introspective about, as well as more comfortable with, the entire visual journaling process. Subsequently, they also became more confident about asking their students to keep life notebooks in a similar way.

Once participants began using their life notebooks regularly, they stopped seeing the process as an assignment and recognized it as a method for exploring issues and ideas creatively and personally, in a way that was visually relevant to each individual. Journals capture thinking, feeling, and personal growth over time while fostering self-knowledge and self-reflection.

The educational benefits of life notebooks include helping students find their writing voices and providing opportunities for students to explore and experiment with different forms of images and illustrations. The notebooks give students daily opportunities to express themselves verbally and visually about numerous subjects, emotions, feelings, and observations in a way that isn't evaluated for "correctness." When used daily, this tool can help students connect with their own thoughts and communicate them on paper, be it with words, mixed media, images, doodles, or other forms of artifacts.

Students of all ages keep their notes, sketches, and inspirations in their life notebooks. Enthusiastic students often enjoy the freedom of crafting these blank books in a way that gives each one its own personality. On the other hand, students who are not as excited about doodling, drawing, or writing have found they can use collage, single words, or simple captions to provide some personalization to their life notebooks. Further, digital notebooks provide an opportunity to incorporate hand-rendered as well as digitally created materials.

Viewing and Interpreting Life Notebooks

As mentioned earlier, life notebooks are inherently unique—each one will be shaped by the student's individual experiences. The possibilities are limitless for students naturally driven to express themselves. Yet, they can cause anxiety for others who prefer structure to help them create. The following viewing and interpreting activity is a great way for students to learn about this form of journaling and see visual samples of various life notebooks done by students and teachers with a wide range of abilities.

ACTIVITY VIEWING LIFE NOTEBOOK SAMPLES

Learning Objectives
- Students will compare and contrast different samples of life notebooks.
- Students will distinguish key features of life notebook samples.

Visual Objectives
- Students will analyze the visual content of journal samples.
- Students will interpret the meaning of the visual and verbal content in the context of the life notebook.

Materials
- Samples of life notebook pages, created by you or prior students who gave permission for this use. If you have never used life notebooks before, you will need to create several samples of what pages might look like. Create samples that show a variety of doodles and designs, text, and memorabilia. Show a variety of styles and levels of detail. Design some elaborate pages, some simple pages, and some pages that seem incomplete or not well developed. These samples will provide content and design for students to discuss and compare before starting their own life notebooks.

Procedure
In this activity, students will view many samples of life notebooks. It is important to include samples that illustrate a wide range of artistic ability, ranges of creative expression—both visual and verbal and artistic style and media (realistic, abstract, drawing, painting, collage, and so on). Students will benefit from a visual reminder that you don't need to be an artist to express complex thoughts through simple drawings. These samples are from life notebooks of students of varying ages who depicted important aspects of their lives.

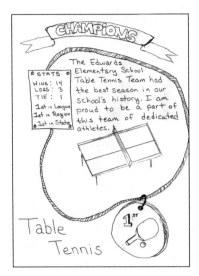

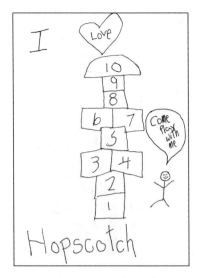

When reviewing the sample life notebook pages, have students consider the following:

- How does the student include both visual and verbal content in the life notebook?

- How do words and images fit together to create meaning on the page?

- How do the images illustrate a student's personal experiences?

There are no right or wrong answers to these questions. However, as students gain more and more experience reviewing and analyzing sample work, they will begin to expand their repertoire of ways to express their thinking, feeling, and learning. Subsequently, they may find new ways to chronicle and depict their experiences in their own life notebooks.

Life notebooks are kept by students for their own use, so they are not necessarily meant to be "read." Rather, they are a visual text that may be voluntarily "shared." When I provided my seventh- and eighth-grade students with blank books, I told them I would occasionally provide prompts, but the content of the notebooks was up to them. I had one requirement: they needed to fill at least one page each day. Every week or two, I would ask them to choose one or two pages to share with me. The students designated the pages I could look at with a sticky note, and I would respond with brief remarks also on sticky notes. I viewed the pages they wanted to share with me and responded with descriptive feedback.

It's important not to judge or evaluate the visuals critically. The most effective feedback will show the student how their entries impact other readers. For example, you might say, "David, your writing is particularly detailed on page 28 in the entry that explains the day your class spent replanting trees. You also meaningfully incorporate academic vocabulary throughout this entry. Thank you for sharing this with me." Or, "Emerson, by creating a detailed agenda of the day you spent planting trees, writing your personal reflections of the day, and including the photo of the sapling you planted, you've given me a vivid sense of how much attention and care went into your work that day."

Other students might have very brief or incomplete entries. In such cases, try feedback with specific recommendations for improvement. For example, you might say, "Ian, your entries are quite brief. Let's think about how you might elaborate a bit. Writing in more detail and providing a background or setting in your doodles would be two ways to expand upon your writing and images. Please see me if you'd like to discuss this," or "Lucy, you write beautifully and tell interesting stories. Please work on simple illustrations with your next entry. Come see me if you want to discuss ideas about how to approach this." Since life notebooks are personal expression, they are not graded, but students should receive feedback in a timely and individual way.

Creating a Life Notebook

You don't have to wait for the beginning of a new school year to introduce life notebooks to your students. Check the clearance racks after the back-to-school shopping frenzy, and you may be able to pick up enough blank journals for your entire class at a very reasonable cost. One of the teachers in our professional development group found simple blank books for just a dollar each. Some teachers have used simple composition books. Graph paper in comp books tends to work better than lined pages, since graph paper can stimulate visual expression.

ACTIVITY WELCOME TO YOUR LIFE NOTEBOOK

Learning Objectives
- Students will personalize their life notebooks.

Visual Objectives
- Students will construct the first entry of their life notebooks by reproducing the visual alphabet.
- Students will elaborate their first entry with text and illustrations about themselves.

Materials
- life notebooks, pencils and pens, "Visual Alphabet and Six Essential Design Elements" handout (see page 220)

Procedure
- Have students write their names (in pencil) on either the cover or inside cover of their journals. Encourage them to incorporate some visual design into their names (but to keep the names legible). Drawing and collage may be used to personalize life notebook covers.
- Tell students to leave the first page of the notebook blank. This serves as a privacy page if someone opens their journal looking for the owner's name.
- Have students copy both the visual alphabet and the six essential design elements on two facing pages (preferably pages 2 and 3). This will be a visual tool guide in the front and a built-in reference resource. It might look something like the following example.

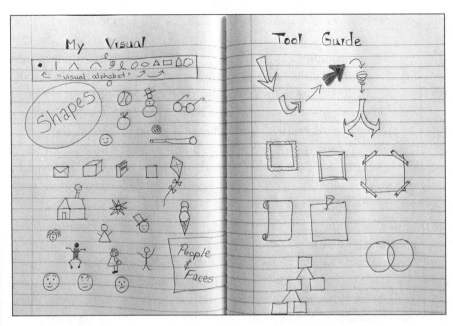

- Provide time for students to create a first entry about themselves. This could be in the form of a mind map or one pager (see chapter 5). Students can create a doodle or sketch of themselves and include: family, pets, hobbies, friends, favorites books or movies, and so forth. The following example packs in a lot of information about the student who created the entry.

To allow students to exercise their visual skills, it's important to set aside class time for them to journal. Anywhere between five and fifteen minutes is good, depending on what you hope they'll accomplish. Obviously, more complex prompts will require more time. Use your discretion. You can have a set assignment—for example, free doodling—or you can vary things by trying the following prompts on different days.

- **Cover Art:** Students design their covers with a title of their choosing. They can incorporate textures, colors, duct tape, or various media (collage). Making the notebook their own goes a long way toward owning the process and the product. Students may create their cover in a day or, more likely, work on the cover design over a period of days, weeks, or even months. In this way, the cover may be layered and represent a montage of the month/semester or even the academic year.

- **Morning Doodles:** Many teachers choose to start the day with a morning doodle. This can be handled a number of ways. One teacher I know puts on music and students write and doodle for ten minutes about any thoughts the music inspires. Another idea is to read a short passage (no more than a sentence or two) from a book and ask students to doodle about what comes next. In this next example, the student chose to doodle about what had happened in her day so far and what she had to do later.

- **My Day:** Encourage students to record experiences from their day. They can express their joy, frustration, excitement, or wonder about anything and everything that happened to and around them in a single day.

- **What I Learned Today:** Have students create an image and write a response to this prompt. Academic reflection consistently shows improvement in recall, analyses, and engagement.

- **Add an Adjective:** Sometimes, all it takes is a single word to get students started. Adjectives make great life notebook prompts. Students can elaborate on their verbal entries by making words more visually distinct with changes in color, size, and boldness. Using the six essential design elements, students can create frames to separate ideas and concepts, arrows to help show direction, or bullets to give a list more impact. Try the following words to prompt ideas for visual and verbal journaling:

> Amusing, Angry, Bashful, Brave, Calm, Challenging, Clever, Cozy, Cranky, Difficult, Dreadful, Embarrassed, Excited, Friendly, Fuzzy, Gentle, Hard, Heavy, Ingenious, Irritated, Kind, Long, Messy, Mischievous, Moody, Nice, Odd, Proud, Quiet, Running, Silly, Simple, Sleepy, Speedy, Spooky, Surprised, Tiny, Tough, Truthful, Ugly, Upset, Victorious, Wild, Wise, Wonderful, Yearning, Zany

In this example, a student chose a compare-and-contrast approach to depict the word *messy*.

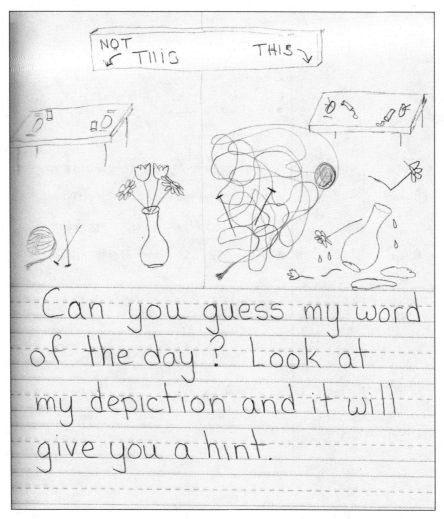

- **Miscellaneous Prompts:** Some students might need more than a single word to get them going. Try the prompts in **figure 6.1** to get students both doodling and writing. Writing prompts can get writers writing when they need a little direction. The following visual/verbal prompts can be catalysts to get students journaling.

FIG. 6.1 JOURNALING PROMPTS

Visual	Verbal
Doodle or depict anything that comes to mind	Write for 5 minutes without worrying about grammar or punctuation, just write whatever comes to mind and let your words flow
Create visual expressions of academic subjects	Write about essential concepts learned and areas of interest studied
Things you like	
Things you don't like	Write your life story in one sentence; illustrate it in one image
Your house	Your best qualities and strengths
Your favorite: • Quality • Friend • House • Place • Relative • Hobby • Food • Subject • Sport • Animal	Your favorite: • Quality • Friend • House • Place • Relative • Hobby • Food • Subject • Sport • Animal
The perfect pet	Something you might like to change about yourself
Your bedroom	Write everything you know about being human
Your family	A question you'd really like an answer to and why
Life at its fullest	What you might find at the end of the rainbow
What would you pack in a suitcase for a monthlong trip?	
Where would you go for a monthlong trip and what would you do?	
Change in your life	
An invention that accomplishes something that would improve your life	

In addition to the previous activities, a full curriculum unit that features life notebooks is in chapter 11.

"Life notebooks have become an essential part of our learning. The students and I doodle every day. We spend the first ten minutes each morning writing and illustrating about the goings-on in our lives. This could be as simple as 'What I had for dinner last night' to illustrating images of a favorite pet. These valuable notebooks provide a space for students to write and doodle—or draw—freely. I find this primes the pump for the day. By working in their own notebooks, students have a fair bit of autonomy, they are engaged, and it fires up both the visual and verbal learning systems for the day. If any of the students are stuck on what to write or doodle on any given day, I go back to the visual triad model and ask, 'What have you seen? What have you imagined? What would you like to depict?'"

Teachers find many creative ways to incorporate life notebooks into the school day. Some report that their students love to come in first thing in the morning and open their life notebooks to document everything they experienced the previous day. This is great because it gets students engaged from the start and also gets the creative energy flowing. Middle school teachers have commented that even though they may only have students for a short period each day, many students were ready, willing, and able to complete a page a day as self-imposed homework.

"Grab your visual learning notebook and depict one of the benefits of a life notebook. Take a look at the following list of benefits and choose a couple that you would like to cultivate in yourself and your students. Then illustrate what you value about keeping a life notebook."

A life notebook:

- develops a habit of self-expression
- communicates in words and images
- is a place for expressing feelings and thoughts
- is a place for an everyday doodle or a representational sketch
- documents significant life events
- fosters reflection
- chronicles experiences
- potentially helps solve problems
- is a place to take risks and be creative
- encourages self-understanding
- enhances personal insights
- accesses critical and creative thinking skills

Science Notebooks

Another type of journal is a science notebook. Science notebooks are meant to replicate the kind of journals that scientists keep to document a running record of their thinking. These notebooks are ubiquitous in schools and apply to many different topics within the science curriculum: anatomy, astronomy, biology, botany, earth science, and more.

Unlike life notebooks, science notebooks can be used to document and assess student learning and growth over time. They are a tool for students to visually and verbally record and reflect upon their various science learning experiences. While life notebooks aren't necessarily meant to be shared, science notebooks are meant to be accessible to others. Students can share them with each other and learn from each other's processes, content, and individual style. Students record their lessons, procedures, predictions, designs, experiments, observations, data, descriptions, explanations, thoughts, and questions using both illustrations and written entries.

There are four main goals for using science notebooks:

1. to build and illustrate student thinking about science lessons and studies

2. to replicate the work that scientists do

3. to integrate images and words to convey knowledge and show meaning

4. to explain students' processes and thinking about what they learn

These notebooks document students' responses to their academic learning and are unique to each student since they record both the content of their lessons and their reflections on these lessons. The notebooks can be used before, during, and after an investigation or instructional activity. Over the course of a year, teachers have found that science notebooks are useful in documenting knowledge acquisition, conceptual growth, and higher-order thinking skills.

Science Notebooks: Writing About Inquiry by Lori Fulton and Brian Campbell offers notes, guidelines, and examples to get students started on using science notebooks.

Nature Journals:
Closely Observing the World Around You

As children head outdoors to play, explore, relax, or work, they are constantly using their senses, imaginations, and critical thinking skills to develop hypotheses and explain their observations. Exploring and observing come naturally to children. However, the skills of interpreting and recording those observations need to be taught.

Often part of the science curriculum, nature journals can strengthen and refine students' critical thinking skills by helping them become more aware of what they observe around them. They are unique and distinct from science notebooks in that they focus on the natural world—whether students explore outdoors or observe natural artifacts brought into the classroom. They also allow for students to exercise skills in close observation that become detailed drawings.

Nature journals can be used successfully with students of all ages. Around eight years of age, children developmentally transition from drawing abstract symbols of what they observe to representational drawings that illustrate what they actually see. Once students make this transition, we can guide their focus to look closely at what they see and depict.

Yet, even while developing the ability to draw more accurately than abstractly, many people draw what they *think* they see rather than what is actually there. In other words, students may draw a generic representation of a mushroom, rather than observing and documenting the unique features of the actual mushroom they are observing. Nature journaling can foster growth in scientific thinking and can prompt students to become better observers. Students who participate in *field journaling*—nature journaling in the outdoors—become more aware of their surroundings, their communities, and their place in the world.

Some additional benefits of keeping a nature journal:

- Sketching in nature journals can support students who may struggle in other classes due to difficulties with language or writing skills.

- English language learners and many students with special needs prefer to demonstrate their knowledge and understanding through visuals first.

- Teachers can view a student's drawing and immediately determine the level of understanding that is represented.

Viewing and Interpreting Nature Journals

Introducing nature journals at the beginning of the school year starts a practice that can connect experiences throughout the entire year. At its most basic, a nature journal can record the seasons by documenting changes in plants and animals around the school (see the extension activity at the end of this chapter), weather patterns (the changes, the frequency, the intensity), and community events, such as when students in my area replanted trees after a fire in a local park. Nature journals may be started any time of year. Or, you might have your students keep nature journals for just a part of the school year, depending on curricular needs. Whenever you choose to introduce nature journals, you'll be engaging visual learning skills.

Before we ask students to create a nature journal, we need to show them what comprises a good one. The following viewing and interpreting activity will encourage students to put aside what they think they know about nature and see things from a different angle.

ACTIVITY VIEWING NATURE WITH A FRESH PERSPECTIVE

Learning Objectives

- Students will compare and contrast multiple examples of nature journals.

- Students will describe their observations of nature illustrations.

- Students will explain the purpose of nature journals.

- Students will discuss the attributes of well-developed nature journals.

- Students will compile a list of questions for further exploration that are based on the nature journal samples they view.

Visual Objectives

- Students will decode the visual content of the nature journals they view.

Materials

- images or samples of nature journal pages found online, access to nature or nature items

Procedure

Begin by curating an assortment of images of nature journal pages that show a wide range of skill, talent, and subject matter. You should be able to find a good selection online by searching for "nature journal pages." Choose a wide selection from modern times to very early examples. You might also share the following examples of student-created nature journal pages.

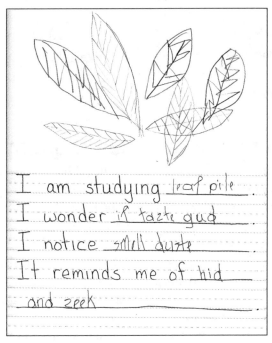

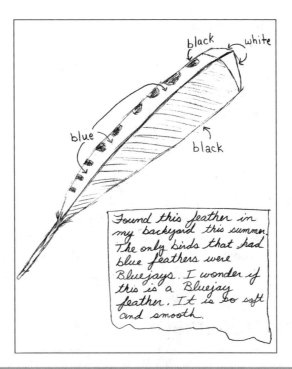

I recommend searching for examples of nature journals written by Charles Darwin or Lady Ann Fanshawe. Both are good, stark contrasts to how more modern nature journals look and they offer insight into different aesthetics that can be used.

Once students have had a chance to view the samples, use the following discussion questions to talk about what they're seeing:

Discussion Questions

1. Ask students to view a sample journal page and talk about their observations. The first instinct of many students might be to make aesthetic judgments: "It's pretty," "It's ugly." There are no right or wrong answers here. You're simply asking them to make observations.

2. While sharing observations, students should be encouraged to observe, question, and discuss. "I wonder . . ." is a powerful prompt to scaffold higher-order thinking in the form of analysis, compare and contrast, and hypothesizing. Some questions, depending on what they're observing, might include:

   I wonder . . .

   Why is the end of a pinecone scale pointy and sharp? How would that help the pinecone?

   Why do roses have thorns?

   Why do butterflies look like they have eyes on their wings?

   Why do snakes shed their skin?

   Why are there so many weeds in the garden?

   Make sure students know that their questions don't necessarily need to be answered immediately. Record their questions and use them as starting points for later investigation. If you incorporate this approach regularly, the art of questioning can steadily improve, and it will encourage the development of curiosity in your students.

3. Ask your students what other thoughts come from their observations. Try to come up with as many associations as possible:
   - Does this remind you of something you've seen before?
   - Can you make a comparison that connects this to something new or different?

Linking new observations to familiar objects or ideas strengthens the connection of the new knowledge to previously known facts. Making these connections may also lead back around to closer observations and more questions. Encourage students to say, "This reminds me of ..." This prompt scaffolds analysis as well as metaphors and similes. Students think critically and creatively while working with real-world specimens.

Creating Nature Journals

Creating and keeping nature journals reinforces higher-order thinking skills through observation, questioning, analyzing, and documentation. Learning to look deeply and see details requires practicing these skills regularly. Students engage in analysis, comparison, and synthesis by completing analogies. They also make connections to prior knowledge by responding to the following three prompts:

- I notice ...
- I wonder ...
- It reminds me of ...

As we've established, drawing helps students convey what they see and understand. This process is especially effective when drawing things they have not seen before. Asking students to record faithfully what they see—to sketch in detail what is in front of them rather than an outline that represents the object—will encourage deep observation. It is a different way of seeing and representing what we know.

Students will understand and have evidence of what they see and depict—as differentiated from other students' representations—when they can discuss their drawings and the accompanying text in one of their nature journal entries.

Exploring Nature in Urban Terrain

Rural schools may find access to nature easy. If you are located in an urban setting, it might take more than a casual glance to find adequate examples of nature to record. Don't dismiss certain types of vegetation as "weeds"; they're part of nature and just as worthy of study as any plant. In *The Curious Nature Guide: Explore the Natural Wonders All Around You*, Clare Walker Leslie illustrates these resilient plants in the abandoned lot in her city neighborhood.

ACTIVITY SEEING DEEPLY WITH NATURE JOURNALS

Learning Objectives

- Students will select objects from nature to depict in their nature journals.

Visual Objectives

- Students will draw nature specimens of their choosing in their nature journals.
- Students will write a description of the visual features of their specimens.
- Students will discuss the features of their drawings with classmates.

Materials

- access to nature (either by going outdoors or curating a selection of items to bring into the classroom), unlined journal notebook, copy paper stapled into a booklet, pencils, pens, colored pencils, magnifying glass, field guides

Procedure

If you can go outdoors, you'll most likely have a variety of items to choose from. If you will be indoors, you'll want to have gathered some natural materials. Consider stones, blades of grass, leaves, pinecones, or anything else you can easily bring indoors.

Based on your environment, choose one of the following activities to begin:

- **Pick One:** In this activity, each student selects one natural item: a twig, a leaf, a petal, a blade of grass, a pinecone, a pebble, or even a pill bug or an earthworm. Students draw their items and add descriptive, identifying details in their nature journals. Have students answer one of the following three prompts:

  - I notice . . .
  - I wonder . . .
  - It reminds me of . . .

  When finished, have students pair up to share their sketches and observations.

- **Who Am I?** In this activity, students take five minutes to record and depict careful observations of a particular plant or other specimen. Once time is up, the specimen is put out of sight, and students answer one of the following three prompts:

  - I notice . . .
  - I wonder . . .
  - It reminds me of . . .

Then have students use field guides and other resources to attempt to identify their specimen. Once students have identified the specimen, the sketches and findings may then be shared with the whole group.

- **Class Field Guide:** When taking an outdoor field trip, assign each student a different plant, animal, or mineral to study. Give students adequate time to observe and depict their specimen, making sure they identify and neatly label their specimen. Once back in class, students can create an illustration and a description on white paper. Have students record their findings. When everyone is done recording, put all pages together into a class field guide. Students might even find photos online to accompany their hand-drawn depictions. These can also be included in the guide.

In addition to the previous activity, chapter 10 provides another unit that features nature journals.

CREATIVE EXTENSION

Ask students to set aside four pages in their nature journals so they can document changes to nearby trees. Each page should be named for a season: Trees in the Fall, Trees in the Winter, Trees in the Spring, Trees in the Summer. When school starts in the fall, ask them to record their observations: Are leaves falling from certain trees? Are pine needles thinning on others? These observations should include text and depictions of how the trees look. Over the course of the following few months as they observe the same trees, students will most likely see the skeletal outlines of branches and twigs against the winter sky, absent of leaves and devoid of color or perhaps covered in a frosting of snow. Their depictions of the same trees might be drastically different depending on the type of tree.

As the months continue to pass and the warm weather returns, ask students to observe the small telltale signs of spring: petite buds may break the surface of the branches and then eventually burst out as fresh new leaves or flowers. Students can add color and details to their page titled Trees in the Spring. And, whereas most schools are out for the summer, for the final entry of seasonal observations of the trees, students can imagine and depict what the trees will look like in the height of summer.

Providing timely and detailed feedback for students will help them develop strong visual observation and depiction skills. One caution: Avoid commenting on the level of artistic rendering. We don't want to say, "That's a very pretty flower," or "You are a talented artist." The emphasis should be on the observational process not on the ability to draw. For example, we might comment to a student, "You've used writing and drawing to describe this pine cone very well," or "This drawing shows the surroundings of the robin's nest with very good detail. That's an excellent observation."

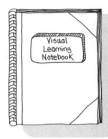

"Grab your visual learning notebook and practice nature journaling. Take a moment to go outside (at the very least, you will need to look outside) and just breathe and observe. On a blank page, chronicle and depict your trip outside. Take your time and render what you observed with all your senses. Try to use several of the visual tools in your toolbox."

Susan

Moving On

Working with teachers who use life notebooks or nature journals—or both—has been gratifying. The samples from their students' journals that they bring to our follow-up professional development meetings show how well students respond to integrating visuals and text into their work. Teachers often report that students retain more knowledge, as evidenced on quizzes and tests. Students also write more and with better quality when they have used visual learning strategies during their studies. Overall, journals can be a great way for students to exercise their creative and critical skills all at once.

Image as Story

For many children, their first introduction to visual texts comes in the form of picture books. Filled with bright and fun images, picture books are a natural attraction for developing minds.

Young children are eager to explore and "read" picture books. Making illustrated stories part of a child's life can help them gain both pre-reading and early literacy skills. Often, children can figure out the story just from looking at the illustrations, whether or not the book includes text.

Older students can also benefit from studying and creating picture books, developing both critical and creative thinking skills in the process. In this chapter, we'll look at picture books with an eye toward understanding the illustrations—with and without text—that make these books so compelling.

> To delve into the wide variety of visual texts available to students would require a whole other book. We'll focus on picture books, but keep in mind that comics, anime, and graphic novels are being used more and more in fourth- through twelfth-grade English language arts (ELA) curriculum. Resources for teaching and creating cartoons, comics, and graphic novels are at the end of the chapter. I recommend exploring these types of texts to supplement your visual teaching.

Reading the Pictures in Books: Where It All Begins

I once had the opportunity to visit a school library during community story time, a monthly multigenerational event during which grandparents and other caregivers came to the school to choose books and read with students. The visitors and their students—mostly kindergartners and first graders—would browse the stacks and choose one or two books to read together. Inevitably, these young readers and pre-readers would be drawn in by the visuals. "Ooooh look at this picture!" and "This book is all about a snail. Isn't that kind of silly? But, he's so cute!"

One of the many wonders and joys of picture books for young children is that they can "read" them to others, whether the children are readers of text or not. Viewing the book a page at a time allows readers of any age to tell the story by reading the pictures. I noticed that oftentimes the reading of picture books began with a thoughtful look at the front and back covers. "What do you see?" "Who do you see?" the children are asked.

"What do you think this story might be about?" This of course, is a great way to encourage higher-order thinking skills—like prediction—at a young age.

As I continued to observe the community story time, I witnessed the same scene over and over. The children got very excited when the first page was revealed while the text (if there was any) was read aloud. Every page—right up to the last one—held their attention with new revelations of images and words. The closing of the book and the speaking of those last words, "The End," was frequently met with, "Oh, read it again. Read it again." It was evident from these moments that young children often seek repetition. They love gaining a better understanding and remembrance of the story. It's how they begin the process of gaining visual and verbal literacy.

Children immerse themselves in the reading of picture books and, when they do, they decode images and text. Picture books are ubiquitous in primary grade classrooms. But, using picture books in the classroom is often short lived as children move on to reading chapter books by third or fourth grade. This is an important progression of verbal literacy, but I would advocate for keeping illustrated texts, especially picture books, in the ELA curriculum to support the progression of visual literacy.

While some picture books are clearly designed for a younger audience, many picture books are quite sophisticated in their narrative and visual presentation and have applications for more mature learners. Like graphic novels, wordless picture books have been gaining in popularity with older students and their teachers. The elaborate illustrations in these books can engage even middle and high school students in analysis and creative interpretation of the story.

BENEFITS OF WORDLESS PICTURE BOOKS

The adage "A picture is worth a thousand words" perfectly describes the rich visual environment of wordless picture books. Different from typical picture books and even from most graphic novels, wordless picture books tell the story entirely through illustration.

Traditionally the domain of young readers, wordless picture books are in fact visual narratives that have application far beyond early childhood. Their appeal is derived from the absence of words, enabling students to craft the story on their own by immersing themselves in the rich imagery.

There are no right or wrong ways to interpret a wordless picture book and readers are free to create their own story. Although the cover, the title, and, in some instances, words hidden within the illustrations may provide clues to the illustrator's intent, the actual narrative is developed through analysis of the pictures. Each page presents rich literary dialogue where the student's imagination takes the lead.

Sharing wordless picture books with students provides teaching opportunities where the story is not limited by printed words or the cue to turn the page. Without these verbal cues, educators can explore deeper questions like:

- How does the picture show what the character might be thinking right now?
- How does the picture show how the character might be feeling?
- What do you think will happen next and why?
- What clues have you gotten from the pictures?
- How does the color and style of the illustrations set the tone for the story?

Each story is open to individual interpretation, and students benefit from hearing and discussing their classmates' differing perspectives.

Wordless picture books encourage:
- imagination and creativity
- deductive reasoning
- interpretation
- critical thinking
- sequencing
- predicting
- vocabulary
- speaking and listening
- role-playing
- supporting opinions with visual evidence

Providing a place for wordless picture books in your classroom not only provides students with the opportunity to enjoy an extensive visual narrative, it also helps students understand how to interpret, negotiate, and derive meaning from complex visual information—all essential skills for enhancing verbal and visual literacy.

PICTURE BOOKS IN THE K–8 CLASSROOM

So, how can we justify the curricular decision to bring picture books into the upper-elementary classrooms and beyond? Let's look at the benefits of picture books in K–8 classes:
- They introduce young children to stories.
- They support the development of pre-reading and early literacy skills.
- They help older kids with verbal comprehension and prompt them to read critically.
- They help teach students how to predict what's going to happen next.
- Illustrations and images can teach students to watch, look, and listen for clues, warning signs, and exciting things they might otherwise miss.
- As readers gain more experience, they can learn inference—how to "read between the lines" by cross-referencing the text and pictures.
- Picture books without text can be used to prompt interpretation and storytelling activities.

Viewing and Interpreting Picture Books

To prepare students to view and interpret picture books, it's good to begin with discussing storytelling concepts, a plot model, and related vocabulary. Understanding the elements that go into making a story—visual or textual—will help students make correlations between existing stories and ones they want to tell.

Here are some important storytelling concepts to review:
- Character: person, animal, or other being who is a central figure in a story or book
- Setting: the surrounding environment in a story
- Story: an account of events or experiences—real or imagined—as told in visual and verbal narrative
- Plot: the sequence in a story ("This happened, which made this happen, which made this happen . . .")

Students often have ideas for the characters, setting, and story they want to tell. Planning the plot is often more challenging. A go-to resource for helping students understand and plan the plot structure—the plan of action for the story—is the Freytag plot pyramid. When introducing your picture book unit or project to your class, begin with the Freytag pyramid to look at the parts of the picture books that you and your class will read—both together and individually.

FREYTAG PLOT PYRAMID

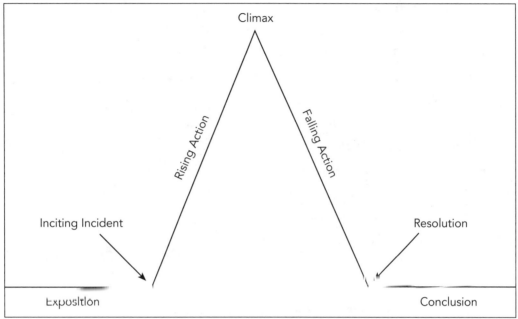

Plot Vocabulary

When viewing and discussing plot structure, it is helpful to have a common understanding of related plot vocabulary. You and your students should use the following language to discuss the plot sequence of the stories you read in class and of the stories you and the students create.

- Exposition: Who are the characters and where are they?
- Inciting incident (or conflict): This is what gets the story moving and gives the characters something to do/achieve.
- Rising action: This is what the characters do to try to succeed. They might fail, but they keep trying.
- Climax: This is the final action taken by the characters in an attempt to achieve their goal.
- Falling action/resolution: This is what happens after the character has achieved the goal.
- Conclusion: This brings the story to a close.

It's important to have a good selection of picture books on hand as you teach students how to view and interpret them. If you don't have any in your personal collection, you'll find what you need at a library. Choose a diverse array of authors, illustrators, and art styles. Here's a list of recommended books to get you started.

Recommended Children's Picture Books (with words)

- *Why Mosquitoes Buzz in People's Ears* by Verna Aardema, Leo Dillon, and Diane Dillon
- *Goodnight Moon* by Margaret Wise Brown and Clement Hurd
- *The Name Jar* by Yangsook Choi
- *Firebird* by Misty Copeland and Christopher Myers
- *Abuela* by Arthur Dorros and Elisa Kleven
- *Whoever You Are* by Mem Fox and Leslie Staub
- *The Snowy Day* by Ezra Jack Keats
- *Sleep Like a Tiger* by Mary Logue and Pamela Zagarenski
- *It's Okay to Be Different* by Todd Parr
- *Ish* by Peter H. Reynolds
- *The Dot* by Peter H. Reynolds
- *And Tango Makes Three* by Justin Richardson, Peter Parnell, and Henry Cole
- *Green Eggs and Ham* by Dr. Seuss
- *No, David!* by David Shannon
- *Mufaro's Beautiful Daughters* by John Steptoe
- *I Love My Hair!* by Natasha Anastasia Tarpley and E. B. Lewis
- *Mr. Wuffles!* by David Wiesner

Recommended Children's Picture Books (without words)

- *Anno's Journey* by Mitsumasa Anno
- *Zoom* by Istvan Banyai
- *Journey* by Aaron Becker
- *Quest* by Aaron Becker
- *Flashlight* by Lizi Boyd
- *Inside Outside* by Lizi Boyd
- *Good Dog, Carl* by Alexandra Day
- *Hank Finds an Egg* by Rebecca Dudley
- *Wave* by Suzy Lee
- *Museum Trip* by Barbara Lehman
- *A Ball for Daisy* by Chris Raschka
- *Where's Walrus?* by Stephen Savage
- *Chalk* by Bill Thomson
- *Flotsam* by David Wiesner
- *Tuesday* by David Wiesner

ACTIVITY DIGGING A BIT DEEPER: ANALYZING PICTURES IN GREATER DETAIL

Learning Objectives

- Students will read a wide variety of picture books—with and without text—to build an understanding of different texts, of themselves, and for personal fulfillment.

Visual Objectives

- Students will apply visual and verbal decoding strategies to comprehend, interpret, evaluate, and appreciate picture books.

Materials

- picture books with and without text (see previous suggestions)

Procedure

For this activity, select a picture book to read to the whole class. Before you start, share the following list of discussion questions with students so they know what to look for as you progress through the book. Read in such a way that all students may view the illustrations (using a document camera to project the pages, if possible). If the book you've chosen has no text, leave each image up for ten to twenty seconds in silence. Don't describe the image; this could influence the students' own interpretations. After reading the book to the class, use the following discussion questions as a guide. These questions focus on the illustrations and lead students through a discussion of character, illustrations, setting, and plot. Of course, you may want to discuss the text and images at the same time if reading a book that has both.

Discussion Questions

Characters and Illustrations

- Consider the cover of the picture book as its first illustration. Sometimes a cover illustration is indicative of something important to the story. Sometimes it just shows the main character. Sometimes it is about establishing mood. What does this cover say to you?
- How many illustrations included characters?
- How many illustrations included close-ups of characters' faces? What impact does this have?
- How did the close-up illustrations help you understand the character?

Setting

- Where does the story take place?
- What parts of the illustrations showed the setting?

Inciting Incident, Rising Action, and Climax

- How do the images illustrate the challenge or problem the main character faced?
- How do the images illustrate the actions that happened after this challenge or problem?

- What part of the story had the most intense action? Or, what part of the story is where the climax occurred? How is this depicted in the illustrations?

Resolution and Conclusion
- How do the images illustrate how the actions come together toward the end of the story?
- How do the images illustrate the resolution of the challenge?
- How does the book end? How do the images illustrate the conclusion?

Text
- If there is text: Would the story work without words?
- If there is no text: How do the pictures tell the story? Would the story work if words were added?

This viewing activity and the subsequent discussion can be repeated with several different picture books—both with and without text—to show students a wide range of styles.

ACTIVITY PICTURE BOOK DISCUSSIONS ROUND 2

Learning Objectives
- Every student will select a favorite picture book to study in depth.

Visual Objectives
- Students will apply visual and verbal decoding strategies to analyze character, setting, and plot.

Materials
- student's favorite illustrated book from home or the library, picture books with and without text, pencils or pens, and copies of "Character Portrait," "Setting," and "Illustrated Plot Pyramid" handouts (see pages 239, 240, and 241)

Procedure
Ask students to bring in their favorite illustrated children's books from home or the library. Have several additional illustrated children's books on hand for those who need them.

1. Have the students read their picture book silently to themselves.
2. When everyone is finished, walk students through completing the following three handouts.

Character Analysis: Use the "Character Portrait" handout to help students analyze the book's main characters.
- Instruct students to write the main character's name and draw a small portrait of what that character looks like.
- Ask students to write responses to the following three prompts:

- Describe the character.
- How does the character act?
- How does the character relate to other characters in the story?

See the following student example. Once completed, students can set their templates aside for use later in the activity.

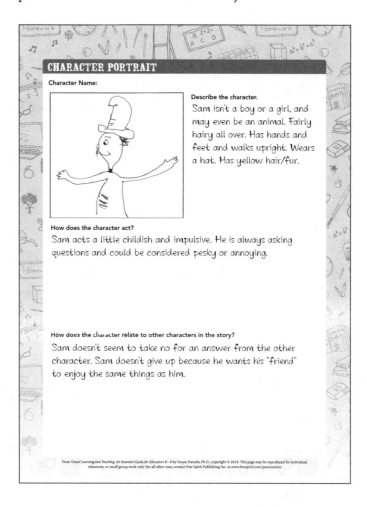

Setting Analysis: Use the "Setting" handout to discuss the book's setting and atmosphere.

- Instruct students to create a sketch of the setting. If the book shows more than one setting, ask students to pick their favorite.
- Ask students to write a response to the following prompt:
  - Describe the setting. Make sure you include specific details.

See the student example on the next page. Once completed, students can set their templates aside for use later in the activity.

Plot Analysis: Students will use the "Illustrated Plot Pyramid" to illustrate the exposition, rising action, climax, falling action, resolution, and conclusion of their chosen picture book. Each part of the plot structure has a box for creating a simple illustration.

- Arrange students into small groups and have students take turns reading their books aloud while showing the images to the group.

- Once a student has finished reading his or her book, the other students in the group should go around and share three reasons why they did or did not like the book. Do this until everyone has read their book aloud.

- Students can then discuss how each book was designed and structured in terms of the characters, setting, and plot, using their completed handouts.

- Hold a whole-class discussion and ask everyone to share their impressions of and discuss their findings about the elements of picture books.

These book viewing and discussion activities can easily be extended and continued over several class periods. The images and words can ignite lively discussions as students view, read, and respond to their chosen stories. Facilitated discussion will channel student thinking through analysis, interpretation, and critique. Students will have a stronger idea of what they like in a picture book as well as what makes for an engaging and compelling picture book presentation. This will prepare them for creating their own picture books.

Creating Picture Books

As soon as children begin making marks with meaning, many quickly become authors and illustrators of their very own picture books. From a few meaningful circles, lines, and shapes, children craft playgrounds, bedrooms, houses, dancing people, and forests without even understanding the definitions of a noun, a verb, or an adjective. They do this instinctively. Similarly, when prompted, "Tell me a little about it," they often quickly rattle off the setting, main character, and plot, all without fully understanding those parts of a story.

> ## Resources for K–2
> The stories that children create may be based in experience or completely invented from their imaginations. Two resources that help guide early writers and illustrators through the process of writing and illustrating different forms of stories and books are:
>
> *Special Memories* by Rozanne Lanczak Williams and C. A. Nobens
>
> *My Picture Story* by Rozanne Lanczak Williams and Benton Mahan

The ability of students to translate what their imagination is building onto a page using simple yet meaningful marks is the beginning of visual and verbal communication. The sharing of their story with a peer, parent, or teacher helps them put words to their story and give their imagination a voice. The ability and desire to share one's imagination doesn't disappear as the years pass, although it may wane as their education moves away from reading picture books regularly. Activities that are structured around visual creation, like creating their own picture books, offer students opportunities to share their imagination and give it a voice well into their upper-elementary years and beyond.

In the following activity, students will plan, write, illustrate, and "publish" their own picture books. We incorporate the use of graphic organizers so students can brainstorm ideas for the characters, settings, and plots of their stories. Students will create story-boards to plan the relationship between the illustrations and text. Finally, students will create, bind, and "publish" their books in an attractive manner and present their books to their peers.

This project is multifaceted and will require several class periods. Exactly how much time you dedicate will depend on your class, your grade, and the time you have. My experience with classroom teachers is that a picture book cannot be thoughtfully designed and created in less than five class sessions. The creation of picture books is often more about the creative process than the final product. Students with perfectionistic tendencies may find creating a whole book intimidating but stressing the process over the product is helpful.

If possible, have examples of student-made books from prior classes on hand to show alongside those that have been professionally created. It is always good to show students a variety of completed projects so they can set realistic goals for themselves. Finally, make sure to have fun. Remember, this process is about sharpening visual literacy skills and students sharing their imaginations through images and text.

Guidelines for Writing and Illustrating a Children's Picture Book

Creating picture books can create excitement in the classroom. While some students might need a little more encouragement than others, many students are eager to start their books. When planning this project, keep in mind that creating a picture book without text also can be a very good option. You can offer this option to all students but particularly to young students who are still struggling with writing. In the early grades, you might also have students create their images and dictate the text to you to record for them. The following are general guidelines for creating a picture book. As always, please modify these as needed for your students, classroom, and curricular needs.

Children's picture books typically present a simple story in about thirty or so pages. A common format is to create fourteen or so two-page spreads. (A spread is two pages of a book, with both pages visible when the book is open.) Keep in mind, however, that younger students might struggle to fill three spreads while some students may stretch beyond sixteen spreads. Again, adjust the expectations and requirements for your class, your grade, and the time you have available.

A good warm-up and prewriting activity is to review what the students learned from the viewing and interpreting activities. Ask the class:

1. What have you learned about picture books?
   - Characters?
   - Setting?
   - Plot?
   - Illustrations?
2. What have you learned about how words and pictures work together in picture books?
3. What did you like about the stories you read in class?
4. If you were to create a picture book of your own, what kind of story would you want to show and tell about?
   - Would it include people? Real or imagined? Friends? Family? Animals? What kind?
   - Where would the story take place?
   - Would the story be based on something from your life or come completely from your imagination?
   - What is the main character trying to do? Take a journey? Solve a problem? Find something important?
   - What would be the climax? What would be the action that helps the characters achieve their goal?
   - How would your book end?

ACTIVITY CREATING STUDENT PICTURE BOOKS

Learning Objectives
- Students will create a story to develop into a picture book.
- Students will plan their main characters, setting, and basic plot structure.
- Students will design illustrations.

- Students will write text that tells the story and supports the illustrations.
- Students will construct their physical books.

Materials
white paper, pencils, black pens, colored pencils, cardstock, "Two-Page Spread Layout" and "How to Create Your Picture Book" handouts (see pages 242 and 243), stapler

Procedures
1. Introduce creating picture books.
2. Review the following text, illustration, and character guidelines.
3. Have students create a rough draft of their pictures and text.
4. Distribute "Two-Page Spread Layout" and "How to Create Your Picture Book" handouts.
5. Read through the directions with the class.
6. Allocate several class periods for writing, illustrating, and constructing the picture books.
7. Have young authors read their books aloud after they are finished.

Consider the following text, illustration, and character guidelines as you prepare to teach students how to write and illustrate picture books.

Text Guidelines
- The text of a picture book should consist of simple sentences and short paragraphs.
- Active verbs help keep the story lively and dynamic. "Crinkle the cat **bounded** across the room and **pounced** on Adriana's lap" uses two active verbs. This sentence is more dynamic than, "Crinkle walked across the room to see Adriana."

Illustration Guidelines
- Illustrations should be the centerpiece of a picture book. In fact, some picture books are only illustrations.
- Illustrations both "show" and complement the text. Most often, text is written before illustrations are designed.
- While illustrating, keep in mind that details can convey unique aspects of character, setting, and action. However, too many redundant details in the text can be distracting. For example, a vivid and detailed illustration would not require companion text such as, "Once upon a time, there was a red-haired girl named Marla who wore a green dress and a yellow hat and had freckles and bangs." The illustration can show us this information so the text is redundant. Discuss this with students. Ask them to give examples and their opinions.
- When deciding how to illustrate a book, it can be helpful for students to consider the responses to these questions.
  - Who is this character?
  - Where is the character?

- ○ When is the action happening?
- ○ What are the characters doing or saying?
- ○ Why? What is their motivation?
- ○ What is the focus of the story?
- ○ What makes us interested and holds our interest in this story?

Character Guidelines

- The main character should be easily recognized through one or two strong and distinguishing traits or attributes. This might include: size, personality, age, gender, occupation, role, and species. Brainstorm with students about different aspects of these characteristics that might shape the personality and look of the characters in their books.

- These distinguishing traits can be presented through both text and illustrations. Drawing sample character sketches with slightly different features is a good warm-up activity and helps students make decisions about the features of their characters.

This sample spread shows how the plan for text and illustrations facing each other across a two-page spread might look.

TWO-PAGE SPREAD LAYOUT

Little Red was a happy young girl, happy to live in her lovely cottage, happy to have a lovely red cloak, and happy that she would visit her lovely grandmother today.

Page __2__   Page __3__

Little Red was also happy to help deliver some soup and lovely flowers to her grandmother.

Page __4__   Page __5__

Page _____   Page _____

As books are completed, offer up the appropriate fanfare as they come "hot off the press," and congratulate each new author for officially translating their initial story idea into a finished picture book.

Have students read their completed books to the class as a form of celebration. This can also be a source of inspiration for those students who are still writing and illustrating.

Discussion and Extension

Lead a discussion about picture books—either professionally published or by the students—to get kids thinking about the varied approaches to storytelling.

PICTURE BOOK DISCUSSION QUESTIONS

Thinking/Skills	Discussion Questions
Knowledge and Understanding	• Who were the main characters? • What was the basic story?
Application	• If you were to interview the main characters, what questions would you ask?
Analysis	• How is the setting related to the characters and the plot? • Did the illustrations match well with the story? Why or why not?
Evaluation	• What did you like about this picture book? • Were the pictures effective in illustrating the story? • Would it have made the book better to have illustrations that were more or less colorful?
Creative Thinking	• If you were to retell the story, how would you do so? • If you were to illustrate the story differently, what would you do?

"My students get very excited about the picture book project. They often ask for more time to work on their stories and illustrations. What I like about the picture book project is that it is open-ended. I have students creating graphic novel/comic book formats. I have one student working on a novel as her book that uses an occasional illustration. I have one student who is a poet, and he has a visual and a poem on each two-page spread. The visual responses to this project are so varied. Each student gets to create their own book in a way that is meaningful to them."

Jenna

CREATIVE EXTENSION

Once the ink is dry on the published book, your students may want more ways to share their stories. Here are several options to extend their learning out into the school and into the community.

- **Book Fair:** Display students' books in the school library or media center. Create "About the Author Cards" to place next to the books with a photo and short bio. Arrange book readings by the author during which classes may schedule time to hear a particular story.

- **Visiting Authors:** Send your young authors on "book tours" after their books are published. Arrange to have your students read their books to another class. These book tours can be as simple or as elaborate as you'd like. Some enthusiastic and animated authors may choose to include props and costumes for their book readings, while others may be content to read their book and then entertain a short Q & A afterward.

- For younger students, especially kindergarten students, it may be better to have another class visit so your students are in the comfort of their own classroom while reading. Also, younger students often prefer to read to a "book buddy" rather than to an entire class.

STORYTELLING WITH PICTURES FOR OLDER STUDENTS

Illustrated storytelling can appeal to all ages. As we get older, we can apply our appreciation for picture books to other visual texts. Such as:

Cartoons & Comic Strips: A cartoon is a sketch or drawing, usually humorous, in a newspaper or magazine that symbolizes, satirizes, or provides a caricature of a subject or person of popular interest. Cartoons can range from a single image to several panels. When displayed in a series of panels, it oftentimes is referred to as a comic strip. Cartoons and comic strips represent minimalized storytelling, conveying an idea with very little imagery and narration.

Students see cartoons and comic strips all the time, but when teaching visual literacy, we want them to view these texts with greater discernment. Studying cartoons and comics can help students better understand storytelling fundamentals and how illustration can show emotion and the passage of time. All students can benefit from having cartoons and comic strips in their curriculum. With more exposure to these visual texts, students can develop an eye for interpreting the stories these images are depicting.

Comic Books & Graphic Novels: As teachers, it's important to view comic books and graphic novels from a visual literacy perspective. They are chock full of images, shapes, symbols, colors, and line weights. These long-form illustrated stories can weave a complete, multifaceted story. Comic books and graphic novels have the length needed to tell several storylines and hold a reader captive.

Comic books are frequently (but not always) serialized and tell a story over several issues. Graphic novels are more like text-based novels and tell a complete story. Comic books and graphic novels can speak to nearly everyone because they combine bold visuals with well-chosen and well-crafted words to complete the story.

While there's a logical progression to including illustrated texts in a student's education (picture books for preK and early elementary, cartoons and comic strips for upper elementary, comic books and graphic novels for middle and high school), it's never too late to introduce these texts. In short, if middle school students don't have a grounding in picture books, you can still start them with a graphic novel. Check out the following resources to learn more about these other visual texts.

Resources for Studying and Creating Comics and Graphic Novels*

Books

Building Literacy Connections with Graphic Novels: Page by Page, Panel by Panel (2007) edited by James Bucky Carter. This volume showcases an impressive range of ideas on how educators can link traditional texts with graphic novels in the classroom.

Drawing Words and Writing Pictures: Making Comics: Manga, Graphic Novels, and Beyond (2008) by Jessica Abel and Matt Madden. Abel and Madden are a husband-and-wife team known for their artwork and educational initiatives. This is an excellent primer for aspiring comic creators.

Faster Than a Speeding Bullet: The Rise of the Graphic Novel (2012) by Stephen Weiner is an excellent book for teachers wanting to learn the evolution of comics into today's popular graphic novels.

Teaching Graphic Novels: Practical Strategies for the Secondary ELA Classroom (2010) and *Teaching Early Reader Comics and Graphic Novels* (2011) by Katie Monnin. These texts offer teachers a rationale for using graphic novels in the classroom as stand-alone curriculum and as bridges to traditional curriculum. Loaded with graphic organizers and resource suggestions, these are essential books for those interested in making their practice "graphic."

The TOON Treasury of Classic Children's Comics (2009) edited by Art Spiegelman and Françoise Mouly. While written for emerging readers, this anthology of short, familiar stories is an excellent resource for teachers who are interested in short, artistically complex comics for student exploration.

Understanding Comics: The Invisible Art (1994) *and Making Comics: Storytelling Secrets of Comics, Manga, and Graphic Novels* (2006) by Scott McCloud. The former book is a canonical exploration of the language, history, and theory behind comics, and the latter emphasizes the how-to of a comic's creation.

Websites

The Comic Book Project (comicbookproject.org) is an international nonprofit that works with educational organizations serving K–12 students to create comics for publication.

The Comics Workshop (marekbennett.com/comicsworkshop) is a site about Marek Bennet's comic education projects. The site includes videos, teacher resources, samples of student work, and links to Bennett's personal comics about teaching the art form to young people all over the world.

The Drawing Words and Writing Pictures Blog (dw-wp.com) is the comics education site maintained by author-artists and teachers Jessica Abel and Matt Madden. The site has features that speak to the novice artist as well as the seasoned professional.

EN/SANE (English Education and Sequential Art Narratives in Education) Word Blog (ensanworld.blogspot.com) by James Bucky Carter explores academic, commercial, and pedagogical issues surrounding the use of comics in the classroom.

The "Graphic Novel Group" at Making Curriculum Pop (mcpopmb.ning.com /group/graphicnovelcomics) is perhaps the most vibrant of the social networks at the site. The forum counts many top comic artists and educators as members. For that reason, it is an excellent place to find resources and ask questions about integrating comics into the classroom.

The Graphic Novel Reporter (graphicnovelreporter.com) is an online magazine for teachers and librarians interested in reviews of the latest graphic novels and interviews with their creators.

Graphic Novel Resources Blog (graphicnovelresources.blogspot.com) is a site maintained by University of Tennessee education professor Stergios Botzakis where he shares weekly reviews of graphic novels for young adults across every discipline.

Make Beliefs Comix (makebeliefscomix.com) is an educational comics creator where kids can create their own comics using stock artwork. Additionally, the site's creator Bill Zimmerman maintains a rich library of printable comics built around themes, allowing students to add the frames and dialogue.

Toon Books (toon-books.com) publishes comics for emerging readers using top-notch comic artists. This publishing house was created by *The New Yorker* cover editor Françoise Mouly and is designed to engage early readers.

The ToonSeum (toonseum.org) in Pittsburgh, Pennsylvania, is a small museum dedicated to comic and cartoon arts.

Excerpted from Goble, P., and Goble, R. R. (2016) Making Curriculum Pop: Developing Literacies in All Content Areas. Minneapolis, MN: Free Spirit Publishing. Used with permission.

"Grab your visual learning notebook and doodle or depict the process of creating a picture book. You may wish to depict the actual bookmaking process, or depict the process from the author's perspective."

Susan

Moving On

Picture books and graphic novels are powerful learning and teaching materials that may be incorporated into curriculum across subject areas and grade levels. They can help build language skills, support literacy and learning in language arts, inspire visual thinking, and increase engagement. As you contemplate curriculum development, differentiation, and design, keep these types of texts in mind as rich learning tools and adaptable materials for visual and verbal teaching and learning as applied at your grade level and in your setting.

CHAPTER 8

Visual Learning Portfolios and Reflective Practice

Now that we have a full complement of tools in our visual toolbox to get students thinking and acting visually, we should discuss the various ways of documenting and reflecting on student growth as it pertains to visual learning and acquiring visual literacy skills.

Most completed assignments end up in the "backpack black hole": finished, forgotten, and never to be seen again. But, as your students start to produce more visually based projects, both you and they may find it helpful to retain their work in a visual learning portfolio. Let's look at the benefits of visual learning portfolios and reflective practice.

Visual Learning Portfolios: More Than a Storage Solution

Students are so much more than their last test score. Nowhere is this more evident than when we're able to watch them grow and develop as they make connections between what we teach and the world around them. In the context of visual learning, an excellent way to monitor a student's progress is with a visual learning portfolio.

A well-kept visual learning portfolio is an easy way to collect visual learning assignments. A portfolio can also serve as a tool to give students and parents a "big picture" view of students' progress and learning.

In this section, we will define several types of portfolios and focus on one that is specific to visual learning. We will address the benefits and importance of visual learning portfolios and provide a framework for curating appropriate material.

Defining Portfolios and Choosing One for Visual Learning

While there are several types of portfolios, the one you'll find most useful for documenting a student's visual learning and mastery over time is called a growth portfolio. Growth portfolios are designed to:

- show growth over time
- develop skills of self-reflection and goal setting
- showcase skill strengths while identifying skills or activities that need improvement
- collect product samples and drafts along the way
- track the development of one or more products

Other Types of Portfolios

Two other types of portfolios are showcase portfolios and evaluation portfolios. **Showcase portfolios** typically display year-end accomplishments. These could be sent along with the student to his or her teacher the following year to demonstrate the student's current abilities.

Evaluation portfolios document a student's achievement for grading purposes. They can be used to show each step of progress toward satisfying standards. And, in some cases, the information might be used to find a student an appropriate placement in a class or program.

For more information about showcase and evaluation portfolios, check out Jon Mueller's Authentic Assessment Toolbox at jfmueller.faculty.noctrl.edu /toolbox. Jon is a professor of psychology and education who specializes in authentic assessment and the use of self-reflection in portfolios. Jon's work has informed my practices when using portfolios with K–8 teachers and classrooms.

But the thought of collecting *yet another* stack of papers for a portfolio—a stack that sits around all year—probably isn't appealing to most. In truth, a visual learning portfolio can actually cut down the stacks of finished projects, completed worksheets, quizzes, and tests. These portfolios are carefully curated to avoid extraneous work. Not every project is included. Selecting the assignments that make the cut is an important part of building a visual learning portfolio.

You have a lot of flexibility and many options when deciding on a portfolio format. You'll want to choose one that best fits your work style and classroom space. A visual learning portfolio can be created in several different formats. **Figure 8.1** gives a few examples:

FIG. 8.1 PORTFOLIO GUIDE

Type	Pro	Con
File folder—This can be a simple manila folder or even an inexpensive two-pocket folder.	The advantage of housing a portfolio in a folder is that it is simple, accessible, and cost effective.	Care must be taken to file items in chronological order, otherwise it can be time consuming to look through. Also, it's easy for papers to fall out.
Binder—A good three-ring binder with plastic protector sheets.	This option enables students to review past assignments quickly and swap out older entries for newer ones. (More on this in the discussion on self-reflection later in the chapter.) You can also easily add dividers for different assignments, subjects, or projects.	They can be bulky. Because you'll need one for every student, they can take up lots of space.

CONTINUED ▷

FIG. 8.1 PORTFOLIO GUIDE, CONTINUED

Type	Pro	Con
Digital—Assignments can be scanned and stored on any computer (classroom desktop or student laptop) or flash drive.	A digital portfolio creates a fairly permanent record. It's easy to transfer, make copies, and forward to a new teacher. Scanning and using digital apps for organizing graphic files is perhaps the most efficient way to maintain students' portfolios over the years. This preserves content for review in school while allowing students to take home original documents.	Scanning and cataloging documents can be very time consuming.

One or a combination of these formats may work best for you and your classroom. The process of maintaining a visual learning portfolio needs to integrate into your day and not cause friction. Start with whatever is simplest and expand as you figure out how much time you have to devote to maintenance.

Benefits of Visual Learning Portfolios

Visual learning portfolios

- link teaching, assessment, and reflection of learning
- present a student's visual learning samples
- allow for assessment of both process and product
- represent a student's growth in design and construction of visual representations—gathered over time
- address improvement and effort in gaining skills of visual communication
- present an interactive approach to performance assessment (What has gone well? What should I do next?)
- emphasize what students can do rather than what they cannot do
- present a visual demonstration of a student's performance across curricular areas
- engage students in establishing their own learning goals and assessing their progress toward those goals
- document each individual student's visual abilities and achievements while allowing for the individual differences between students in a class
- value self-reflection along with self-assessment

Planning the design and contents of a visual learning portfolio works best when students collaborate with teachers to select work samples, establish assessment criteria, and set goals. To do this, many teachers schedule portfolio planning meetings with each individual student. During these meetings, the teacher and student can discuss the products that should be included in the visual learning portfolio. Together, they both identify strengths to be represented and skills still to be developed. And, in some cases, visual learning portfolios give students the opportunity to select the work that they feel best illustrates and documents their strengths and their interests. When students can clearly see and value their abilities, they are often more engaged in their learning and its assessment. We'll discuss student-inclusive assessment later in the chapter.

Developing Visual Learning Portfolios to Document Growth

Let's say you are on a roll and have been assigning strong visual learning projects like there's no tomorrow. Your students have amassed an impressive collection of visually rich assignments. But, at the end of the day, not all projects belong in a portfolio. Some might be early, rough attempts. Some might include mistakes. Or some might be great but there might be better examples of the same skill set. How do you decide what should and shouldn't go in a visual learning portfolio?

When creating visual learning portfolios, consider three critical aspects: purpose, audience, and content.

Purpose: Ask yourself, "What is the purpose of the visual learning portfolio as it relates to the lesson(s) being taught?" Likely, the main purpose of a visual learning portfolio will be to document student use of visual tools and forms of visual communication with work samples. Examples of work samples that could be placed in a visual learning portfolio are included in **figure 8.2**.

Audience: Ask yourself, "For what audience(s) will the visual learning portfolio be created?" Most often it will be for the student, the teacher, fellow classmates, and parents. Teachers typically will present and discuss a child's visual learning portfolio at parent conferences. If the child is present, he or she can present his or her own visual learning portfolio. The visual learning portfolio's audience may include next year's teacher to communicate the student's learning and growth in the prior year. Keep in mind that the intended audience might include diverse subgroups. You won't be able to satisfy the needs/expectations of each subgroup. So, it may be necessary to designate a primary audience and tailor the content to that group's needs/expectations.

Content: Many teachers ask: "What samples of student work should be included?" and "What visual products and projects should be assessed?" The content included in the visual learning portfolio will vary greatly by grade, class, and curriculum. Figure 8.2 lists examples of recommended portfolio content for several different purposes. Use as many purposes as you feel are necessary.

FIG. 8.2 VISUAL LEARNING PORTFOLIOS AS GROWTH PORTFOLIOS*

Purpose	Possible Items to Include
To show growth or change over time	• early and later pieces of work • rough drafts and final copy • self-reflections on growth • goal-setting sheets • reflections on progress toward goal(s)

CONTINUED ▷

FIG. 8.2 VISUAL LEARNING PORTFOLIOS AS GROWTH PORTFOLIOS, CONTINUED

Purpose	Possible Items to Include
To show the development of process skills	• samples that show development of seeing, imagining, and depicting skills • self-reflection sheets accompanying samples of work • reflection sheets from teacher • identification of strengths and challenges • goal-setting sheets • reflections on progress toward goal(s)
To show strengths and challenges	• samples of work reflecting specifically identified strengths and challenges • reflections on strengths and challenges of work samples • goal-setting sheets • reflection on progress toward goal(s)
To follow the development of one or more products or performances	• multiple drafts of product or performance • self-reflections on drafts • reflection sheets from teacher

*Adapted from Jon Mueller, jfmueller.faculty.noctrl.edu/toolbox/portfolios.htm. Used with permission.

Visual learning portfolios may also be used to document new instructional approaches to track the student's ability to construct meaning and highlight the teacher's role in providing visually integrated lessons. For example, a visual learning portfolio may include everything from early encounters with the visual alphabet and basic doodling, to using graphs and diagrams to represent data, to a scanned copy of a student's completed picture book.

Curating with the Visual Learning Portfolio in Mind

Once you've decided to use visual learning portfolios in your classroom and you've identified the purpose, audience, and content, you can start curating items for the portfolio. Place visual learning items into the portfolio in chronological order with the newest items on top. The visual learning portfolios—folders, binders, or digital folders—should be accessible to students so they can add representative samples from their ongoing learning during the year. In the beginning, don't worry about having too much in the portfolio. Once students are given the opportunity for self-reflection, they will be more selective and remove less relevant material. This keeps the visual learning portfolios manageable.

"At the beginning of each new school year, I am handed my class list and then proceed to the office to learn more about my students and their needs by examining their individual cumulative folders. This past year, in addition to their cumulative folders, I was given access to the visual learning portfolios of several students. I felt as though I was given a gift. With both of these pieces, I felt that I had a clearer picture of my new students and more insight into their learning styles, strengths, and preferences."

Martin

Visual Learning Portfolios: An Opportunity for Self-Reflection and Assessment

Creating the portfolio is a rich visual learning experience. Originally, portfolios were modeled after the visual and performing arts format of showcasing accomplishments, but today, portfolios are used as highly flexible instructional and assessment tools in the classroom. They can be adapted to accommodate diverse curricula and classrooms, and students of all ages and grade levels.

Ideally, the student will participate in the selection of visual learning portfolio content and the development of self-assessment criteria and self-reflection goals. Portfolio design and management becomes a collaborative process between teachers and students using regular review and feedback. As mentioned earlier, teachers can schedule portfolio planning or portfolio review meetings with each student on a regular basis throughout the year to collaborate and curate the contents of the visual learning portfolio together. This requires teaching students how to carefully assess their own work and how it best fits in the portfolio. Let's take a closer look at self-reflection and assessment as they pertain to visual learning portfolios.

The Importance of Self-Reflection

When visual teaching and learning takes place, the learning doesn't end when the teacher grades or evaluates the assignment. Student understanding and self-reflection is perhaps the most impactful aspect of the learning process.

A Closer Look at Reflection*

Reflection enhances the process of skill development and virtually all learning in innumerable settings. For example, it can be beneficial for educators to frequently reflect upon what is working or not working in their teaching, how they can improve what they're doing, how they can help students make connections to the learning, and much more. Reflection occurs naturally and organically as we observe students working, evaluate and guide their work in progress, and assess their finished projects or assignments.

Students also need to learn to effectively reflect upon their learning and growth. As a skill, reflection is not something that can be mastered after one or two attempts. Developing good reflective skills requires instruction and modeling, lots of practice, feedback, and more reflection.

*Adapted from Jon Mueller, jfmueller.faculty.noctrl.edu/toolbox/portfolios.htm. Used with permission.

So, how can we help students learn the skill of self-reflection? In this section, we will address incorporating self-reflection into the classroom environment without it becoming "yet one more thing" to do.

When students are asked to respond to prompts such as "I selected this piece because...," they may respond with "I think it is nice," or "I like it." We'd like them to elaborate on that response. Tentative responses aren't necessarily resistance or reluctance. Students need to be taught how to respond to such prompts. They need to be taught how to identify their strengths and weaknesses and to set appropriate goals for themselves and their work.

Students often rely upon adults, especially teachers, to evaluate their work. How many times have your students come to you with an assignment or a project and asked, "What do you think of this?" or "How does this look to you?" These are both valid but general questions. A more specific prompt can garner a more specific response.

Ideally, the goal of self-reflection is more thoughtful discussion like: "I wanted to express sadness so I used more cool colors in this piece, how does it look?" Or, "I think I captured the differences and similarities of Disney princesses accurately in this Venn diagram. What do you think?"

Students need to learn both self-assessment (according to criteria and goals of the particular assignment) and self-reflection (which is usually subjective, qualitative, and in the form of open-ended questions). It can be helpful for students to learn the nature of self-assessment and self-reflection and to practice both in a safe and nurturing environment. The "Visual Learning Portfolio Self-Assessment" form (see page 244) allows students to practice these skills. The content can be modified to fit the requirements for different assignments.

Self-assessment typically is implemented with a rubric that includes several predetermined criteria established by the educator. The form has some basic criteria already filled out along with space for students to add criteria specific to their needs. Collaborate with your students to create criteria that relates to their work and that addresses qualities important to the students. Feel free to swap out any questions you don't feel are perti-nent. Students can assess their individual products or projects and rate themselves using your criteria and their self-created criteria. This insight into how students perceive their efforts can help teachers adapt the level of instruction and challenge to keep students engaged.

The reflection phase of the visual learning portfolio process should be ongoing as students learn how to select pieces to include in their portfolios. Students need to engage in multiple reflective activities. Goal setting is part of their reflection that looks at self-assessment and identifies skills to work on. Student reflection on the work and products in their visual learning portfolios helps identify students' strengths and weaknesses, evidence of progress, and specific strategies for continued improvement. The visual learning portfolio process will be most meaningful and purposeful when students are focused on specific goals, especially self-chosen goals.

This example shows a student's filled in Visual Learning Portfolio Self-Assessment.

Once opportunities for reflection (practice) take place, feedback to students and further reflection can be provided through conversations with others. Peer editing is one way for students to practice presenting their work to someone else. They can also

VISUAL LEARNING PORTFOLIO SELF-ASSESSMENT

Name: Jessica Lin   Date: 9-17-17

Self-Created Goals Growth/Progress	Attempting/ Beginning	Strong Effort	Meeting Self-Expectations	Exceeding Self-Expectations
Depictions match the image in my mind			X especially Keiko	
I want to become comfortable using the visual alphabet			X used all of it	
My work balances visual depictions and verbal phrases			X	
My visuals convey meaning and help me remember			X	
My images show thoughtful design			X	
I want to learn how to give and take clear feedback		X		

Self-Reflection: (May be chosen from list provided or self-created.)

1. Do I feel comfortable using doodling and other types of drawings?
   Yes! I love it. Fun and helps me learn.

2. What are my goals for the design and writing in my Life Notebook?
   Add variety to the designs and writing on my pages.

3. What are my future goals for my visual portfolio?
   Demonstrate visual learning in different subjects.

receive feedback and reflection through conferencing. Parents may meet with teachers to review their child's visual learning portfolio, or the student may participate in the conference as well.

The following prompts can help guide the student through the self-reflection process. Answers can be entered in the self-reflection section of the self-assessment form. Please note that different prompts relate to some assignments more than others. So, it is not necessary to use all of the prompts. Also, you may have some questions about your own curriculum that you want to incorporate.

PROMPTS FOR SELF-REFLECTION IN THE VISUAL LEARNING PORTFOLIO

- What have I learned from using the visual alphabet?
- What are my visual strengths?
- What are my visual challenges?
- How would I describe my visual, doodle-drawing style?
- What forms of visual texts do I regularly read?
- Am I aware of the visuals in my environment?
- What are my goals for increasing my ability to read visuals in my environment?
- Do I feel comfortable and confident using doodling and other types of drawings?
- Do my doodles, depictions, and illustrations clearly communicate what I know?
- Do I use visuals and text together to better show and tell what I want to communicate?
- Am I comfortable reading and creating various forms of graphics?
- What are my goals for my visual journal?
- Who can I ask to help edit my work and give me feedback?
- Who should I ask for help?
- What are my future goals for developing my visual learning portfolio?

Toni

"My students benefit in so many ways from keeping their visual learning portfolios. Even reluctant doodlers are gratified to see their progress over time. It means so much to be able to give detailed feedback to my students. Using visual learning portfolios and rubrics keeps the emphasis on completeness, accuracy, neatness, and growth and not on artistic ability. Meanwhile, students gain the understanding that even simple doodles or drawings can show what they know, and they learn more about themselves as they practice setting goals and then reflecting upon their growth and progress toward those goals. Their work shows both of us how they have processed and depicted our classroom studies. This tells and shows so much more than any test score could."

Visual Learning Portfolios as Formative and Summative Assessments

Portfolios are often embraced as an assessment tool. As representations of classroom-based performance, they can be fully integrated into most curricula. Unlike quizzes, tests, or other quantitative measures that take additional time to create and administer, portfolios integrate with and supplement—rather than take time away from—instruction. The inclusion of student work is not an "extra" to be done; it is a natural part of the learning process.

For our purposes, we'll continue to use the growth portfolio format for our visual learning portfolios since it documents development over time and includes selected showcase pieces. In this way, both formative and summative aspects of assessment can occur within one visual learning portfolio.

Formative assessments are used to provide ongoing feedback regarding student learning. They help teachers plan for instruction and help students better understand their learning. They can also identify students who need more help or concepts that need reteaching. This assists teachers in determining the effectiveness of specific instructional strategies. For visual learning assessment, we look for student images that convey meaning and that have clear features and details in design. If images are not well-developed or seem incomplete, a conference is scheduled with the student to develop visual learning goals for future assignments.

Summative assessments are planned in advance; they include predetermined criteria, often associated with academic standards, and are used to evaluate learning at the end of a lesson or unit of study.

The "Visual Learning Portfolio Assessment Rubric" form (see page 245) can be used to assess a student's visual products. This feedback can be shared with students and parents in the intermediate and middle school grades. However, for grades K–1, this feedback is too advanced. I suggest only sharing the rubric at parent conferences.

The rubric does not include criteria to rate artistic ability. As emphasized earlier in the book, it's best to refrain from offering feedback that relates to artistic ability. Visual learning can be encouraged by talking about design aspects that don't require particular artistic ability, such as line weight, spacing, layout, and integration of text and images.

Offer suggestions like this:

- You have excellent content. Your title gets a bit lost, though. Remember, you want your page title to stand out. You could try making the letters bigger or darker.

- You work so well in black and white. Why don't you try some color in your next one pager and see how that feels? If you don't like it, you can always go back to black and white.

- I see that you used the suggestions from our last meeting. How do you think that impacted the design of this poster?

- Placing the tiger in the center is very effective. What are your thoughts about how to use the rest of the page?

Not this:

- That looks just like a Bengal tiger! Perfect. What will you do next?

- What is that supposed to be? Oh, I can't tell. I think you better draw it again.

- Perfect! This is the best I have ever seen!

The following example is of an assessment rubric for a young student's visual vocabulary flash cards, along with several examples of the student's sight word flash cards.

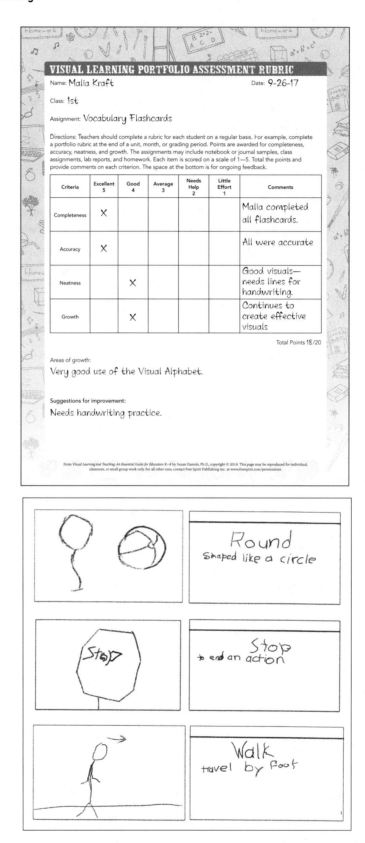

VISUAL LEARNING PORTFOLIO ASSESSMENT RUBRIC

Name: Malia Kraft

Date: 9-26-17

Class: 1st

Assignment: Vocabulary Flashcards

Directions: Teachers should complete a rubric for each student on a regular basis. For example, complete a portfolio rubric at the end of a unit, month, or grading period. Points are awarded for completeness, accuracy, neatness, and growth. The assignments may include notebook or journal samples, class assignments, lab reports, and homework. Each item is scored on a scale of 1—5. Total the points and provide comments on each criterion. The space at the bottom is for ongoing feedback.

Criteria	Excellent 5	Good 4	Average 3	Needs Help 2	Little Effort 1	Comments
Completeness	X					Malia completed all flashcards.
Accuracy	X					All were accurate
Neatness		X				Good visuals— needs lines for handwriting.
Growth		X				Continues to create effective visuals

Total Points 18/20

Areas of growth:

Very good use of the Visual Alphabet.

Suggestions for improvement:

Needs handwriting practice.

This assessment rubric enables teachers to evaluate and assess all levels of visual products regardless of their level of complexity. Whether the student has created an infographic or they've depicted a lesson in their visual learning notebook, this assessment form can be used to document their growth in visual skills as well as the strengths of the piece the student has just completed. Though all students have participated in the same learning, the work reflected in the student's visual learning portfolio uniquely represents his or her individual contribution. This assessment form tailors evaluation and feedback to the individual.

Along the way, you have created samples of visual tools and texts in your visual learning notebook. Keeping a visual learning portfolio for yourself makes sure your work doesn't "slip away." Save your examples to refer back to and to use again, to show your own growth over the course of your first year of implementing visually integrated teaching and learning, and to share with future classes and colleagues. This may sound like one more thing to do, but this is not busy work. A visual learning portfolio is evidence of your visual classroom instruction and a tangible reminder of your continued professional development.

Your students may enjoy viewing your early attempts at the visual alphabet as they are making their own first attempts. And, just as your visual learning portfolio will show examples of your progress over the course of the year, students will also be able to see their own growth as they learn about and create the wide range of visual texts you've introduced them to.

Moving On

Visual learning portfolios are a holistic way to collaborate with students, set goals, and assess students' progress over time. Further, they enable students and teachers to reflect together and discuss learning in a meaningful way. As you implement the use of visual learning portfolios, revisit the purpose you established for your class's portfolios. While you teach students about visual learning portfolios, the purpose you set will guide what is included and what is not in the students' portfolios. This clarity will help make portfolios more manageable for you and your students.

PART THREE

Incorporating Visual Tools AND Texts INTO Subject Area Lesson Plans AND Curriculum

Designing Visually Integrated Curriculum

As educators, it's important to make sure the way we teach fits with curriculum development and content standards. Because visual learning is just coming into its own, many school districts may not yet understand the value of implementing these strategies. It will be important to justify letting students imagine, create, doodle, watch video clips, and stare at blades of grass. You may need to demonstrate how colors find a logical and intentional place in math, literature, or reading comprehension. The easiest solution is to show how visual learning links with required academic skills and competencies. Fortunately, visual thinking skills are now included in many state and organizational standards. Most prominently, they are included in Common Core State Standards (CCSS) and the Next Generation Science Standards.

Whether or not you are actively using the CCSS or the Next Generation Science Standards, it's significant to note that visual learning and literacy are integrated in these standards. This represents a shift from the text-only emphasis used in the past. Not long ago, you couldn't locate visual content or skills in a standards document, aside from map and graph reading. Now we know that visual and verbal learning together significantly increase understanding and retention. With this book, teachers have access to tools that integrate meaningful visual learning across the curriculum, that actively engage students, and that optimize students' multimodal learning capacities.

Visual Learning and Content Standards

The Common Core State Standards, adopted by 45 states, include mandates that link to visual skills and texts. The anchor standards, for example, call for students to do the following:

- Integrate and evaluate content . . . visually and quantitatively, as well as in words (Reading).

- Make strategic use of . . . visual displays of data to express information and enhance understanding of presentations (Speaking and Listening).

- Apply the reading anchor standards to texts that include information displayed in graphs, charts, or maps (Range, Quality, and Complexity of Text).

Examples of Common Core State Standards that Address Visual Learning in Specific Content Areas

It doesn't take much work to pair existing standards with visual learning strategies. The following figures show a few examples of how the techniques we've discussed can be used to meet CCSS.

FIG. 9.1 ENGLISH LANGUAGE ARTS—COMMON CORE STATE STANDARDS

Standards	Visual Strategies in This Book
CCSS.ELA-Literacy.CCRA.R.7: Integrate and evaluate content presented in diverse media and formats, including visually and quantitatively, as well as in words.	Infographics, One Pagers, Graphs, Diagrams, Illustrated Timelines
CCSS.ELA-Literacy.CCRA.R.6: Assess how point of view or purpose shapes the content and style of a text.	Viewing & Analyzing Icons, Graphs, Diagrams, Infographics, Picture Books, Graphic Novels
CCSS.ELA-Literacy.CCRA.SL.5: Make strategic use of digital media and visual displays of data to express information and enhance understanding of presentations.	Reading & Creating Infographics

FIG. 9.2 READING: LITERATURE—COMMON CORE STATE STANDARDS

Standards	Visual Strategies in This Book
CCSS.ELA-Literacy.RL.K.7: With prompting and support, describe the relationship between illustrations and the story in which they appear (e.g., what moment in a story an illustration depicts).	Reading & Analyzing Picture Books, Cartoons, Comics, Graphic Novels, Storyboards
CCSS.ELA-Literacy.RL.1.7: Use illustrations and details in a story to describe its characters, setting, or events.	Reading & Analyzing Picture Books, Cartoons, Comics, Graphic Novels, Storyboards
CCSS.ELA-Literacy.RL.3.7: Explain how specific aspects of a text's illustrations contribute to what is conveyed by the words in a story (e.g., create mood, emphasize aspects of a character or setting).	Reading & Analyzing Picture Books, Cartoons, Comics, Graphic Novels, Storyboards

FIG. 9.3 READING: INFORMATIONAL TEXT—COMMON CORE STATE STANDARDS

Standards	Visual Strategies in This Book
CCSS.ELA-Literacy.RI.1.7: Use the illustrations and details in a text to describe its key ideas.	Reading & Analyzing Infographics, Diagrams, Charts, Graphs, Maps, Mind Maps, Photographs, Illustrated Timelines, Storyboards
CCSS.ELA-Literacy.RI.3.7: Use information gained from illustrations (e.g., maps, photographs) and the words in a text to demonstrate understanding of the text (e.g., where, when, why, and how key events occur).	Reading & Analyzing Infographics, Diagrams, Charts, Graphs, Maps, Mind Maps, Photographs, Illustrated Timelines, Flash Cards, Visual Vocabulary Cards, Visual Vocabulary Charts

CONTINUED ▷

FIG. 9.3 READING: INFORMATIONAL TEXT—COMMON CORE STATE STANDARDS, CONTINUED

Standards	Visual Strategies in This Book
CCSS.ELA-Literacy.RI.6.7: Integrate information presented in different media or formats (e.g., visually, quantitatively) as well as in words to develop a coherent understanding of a topic or issue.	Reading & Analyzing Infographics, Diagrams, Charts, Graphs, Maps, Mind Maps, Illustrated Timelines, One Pagers, Storyboards

FIG. 9.4 SPEAKING & LISTENING—COMMON CORE STATE STANDARDS

Standards	Visual Strategies in This Book
CCSS.ELA-Literacy.SL.K.5: Add drawings or other visual displays to descriptions as desired to provide additional detail.	Visual Vocabulary Cards, Visual Vocabulary Charts, Visual Note-Taking, Storyboards, Science Notebooks, Life Notebooks, Nature Journals
CCSS.ELA-Literacy.SL.1.5: Add drawings or other visual displays to descriptions when appropriate to clarify ideas, thoughts, and feelings.	Science Notebooks, Life Notebooks, Nature Journals, Visual Note-Taking, Mind Maps, One Pagers, Infographics
CCSS.ELA-Literacy.SL.3.2: Determine the main ideas and supporting details of a text read aloud or information presented in diverse media and formats, including visually, quantitatively, and orally.	See-Hear Graphic Organizers, Maps, Visual Note-Taking
CCSS.ELA-Literacy.SL.7.5: Include multimedia components and visual displays in presentations to clarify claims and findings and emphasize salient points.	Infographics, Graphs, Charts, Diagrams, Maps, Floor Plans

FIG. 9.5 SCIENCE & TECHNICAL SUBJECTS—COMMON CORE STATE STANDARDS

Standards	Visual Strategies in This Book
CCSS.ELA-Literacy.RST.6–8.4: Determine the meaning of symbols, key terms, and other domain-specific words and phrases as they are used in a specific scientific or technical context relevant to grades 6–8 texts and topics.	Viewing & Analyzing Maps, Diagrams, Mind Maps, Flow Charts, Graphs, Charts, Icons, Exploded Diagrams, Cross-Sections, Cutaways
CCSS.ELA-Literacy.RST.6–8.5: Analyze the structure an author uses to organize a text, including how the major sections contribute to the whole and to an understanding of the topic.	Storyboards, Mind Maps, Visual Note-Taking
CCSS.ELA-Literacy.RST.6–8.7: Integrate quantitative or technical information expressed in words in a text with a version of that information expressed visually (e.g., in a flowchart, diagram, model, graph, or table).	Science Notebooks, Visual Note-Taking, Creating Maps, Diagrams, Mind Maps, Flow Charts, Graphs, Charts, Icons, Exploded Diagrams, Cross-Sections, Cutaways

FIG. 9.6 NEXT GENERATION SCIENCE STANDARDS

Standards	Grades	Visual Strategies
K-2-ETS1-2 Engineering Design Develop a simple sketch, drawing, or physical model to illustrate how the shape of an object helps it function as needed to solve problems.	K–2	Science Notebooks, Exploded Diagrams, Cutaways, Cross-Sections
Earth's Place in the Universe Represent data in graphical displays to reveal patterns of daily changes in length and direction of shadows, day and night, and the seasonal appearance of some stars in the night sky.	3–5	Science Notebooks, Nature Journals, Infographics
Molecules, Organisms: Structures and Processes Develop and use a model to describe the function of a cell as a whole and ways parts of cells contribute to the function.	6–8	Diagrams, Illustrated Cross-Sections

These lists of standards are in no way exhaustive. For a more complete list of Common Core State Standards and Next Generation Science Standards, please see corestandards.org and nextgenscience.org.

Developing Visually Integrated Curriculum with Curriculum Maps

While working with my group of K–8 teachers to develop visually integrated curriculum units, we decided not to reinvent the wheel, so we built upon the curriculum map template from Diane Heacox's *Differentiating Instruction in the Regular Classroom: How to Reach and Teach All Learners.*[18] This is the same curriculum map introduced in chapter 3, see page 38.

Heacox's curriculum map begins each unit with essential questions and unit questions. To review, essential questions are big picture questions that help define the breadth and depth of the curriculum. For example, an essential question might be, "Do all stories have heroes and villains and a moral?" Unit questions are more specific to the current topic of study. A unit question might be, "Is Little Red Riding Hood a hero?" The essential and unit questions are followed by unit content presented in columns that identify:

- Common Core State Standards and/or State or Provincial Content Standards
- Content/Topics
- Skills
- Projects/Products

To separate the visual skills from the general skills, I modified the format of the curriculum map to include a fifth column for visual skills (see pages 246–247). The Common Core State Standards that explicitly address visual learning are listed in the map and in the lesson plans in chapters 10 and 11. Further, visual learning objectives are explicitly identified as well.

Figure 9.7 lists a range of projects and products you may wish to incorporate in your own curriculum development. You can add as many of these as might be pertinent to the visual skills column of your curriculum map. Bear in mind, you don't necessarily need to make each product you list in the column. But listing several products will give you options when the time comes to implement the lesson.

FIG. 9.7 IDEAS FOR VISUAL PRODUCTS

Doodles	Creating a computer slide presentation
Drawing, sketching, or painting	Making a mobile
Illustrating	Taking a photo and/or photoshopping an image
Building a prototype	Designing a structure
Designing a web page	Making a diagram, graph, or timeline
Creating a cartoon or comic strip	Planning advertising graphics
Making a clay sculpture	Making a collage
Writing and illustrating a graphic novel	Creating a digital montage of images and music
Designing a logo	Constructing a display of a collection
Making a map	Designing a photo essay
Making a poster	Creating a board game
Making a mural	Designing a pamphlet or brochure
Making visual aids for a presentation	Designing sets for a play
Creating a game or an app	Designing a greeting card
Constructing a scrapbook	Creating a blueprint
Mapping ideas	Storyboarding
Designing a postcard	Constructing a model
Creating a video	

Visually Integrated Curriculum Maps: The How-Tos

Whether you're new to creating curriculum maps or you've had experience, it may be beneficial to walk through the making of a map to see how we can tie the format to a visually integrated curriculum. We'll create a curriculum map for a unit on student identity.

STEPS TO DESIGNING VISUALLY INTEGRATED CURRICULUM

- Enter the subject or part of the curriculum under which this unit falls (for example, "Sixth-grade science").
- Write the theme or title of the unit you are mapping (for example, "Exploring Identity: 'Who Am I?'").
- List the essential questions of your curriculum (for example, "What is *heritage*?").
- List the unit questions (for example: "Who am I and where do I come from?").

- List the Common Core State Standards or state/provincial standards that relate to the unit in the appropriate column. Be sure also to include those standards that emphasize visual thinking and learning.

- List content or topics that are part of the unit in the appropriate column (for example, family history, artifacts, and autobiography).

- List the general skills you'll be focusing on in this unit in the appropriate column (for example, identifying relationships, comparing and contrasting, and interviewing).

- List the visual skills you'll be focusing on in this unit (for example, illustrating, doodling, collage, storyboards).

- List the projects or products that are options for students in this curriculum unit in the appropriate column. How will students demonstrate their learning? Choose tangible products and observable performances that require more than a quick daily instructional task (for example, a model of outdoor spaces, a blueprint, a heritage museum, an illustrated autobiography).

> "After learning the visual alphabet and the six essential design elements, and after working with visual tools and walking through the curriculum map process, I feel confident in how to meaningfully integrate visual teaching and learning across the curriculum. I keep a copy of the curriculum map on my desk as well as a copy of the ideas for visual products, insuring that I continue to approach curriculum design with an eye to the visual. My curriculum map is thorough, and the visual aspect is not an add-on. It is an essential component of my students' learning experience."

Carol

Moving On

You may be wondering exactly how this will all look in an actual lesson. How will all the tools and texts translate from the pages into the classroom? The best way to see how this works in a classroom—other than trying it yourself—is to examine how other visual teachers have put it into practice in their classrooms. While working on this book, I fine-tuned this curriculum map template with teachers I've trained over the years for their own use in grades K–8. Chapters 10 and 11 present four visually integrated curriculum units designed by these teachers.

Though these units were developed with specific grades in mind, they are all worth a read whatever grade you teach. Elements of each—most especially the visual skills and visual learning objectives—are readily adaptable across grade levels and subject matter. Every unit includes rich visual products and projects as well.

Visually Integrated Curriculum Grades K-3

As I mentioned in the previous chapter, the best way to really see how visually integrated curriculum works in an actual classroom environment is to examine how other visual teachers have put it into practice in their classrooms. Let's take a look at how the teachers I've worked with provided visual learning opportunities for all students by creating visually integrated curricula.

Curriculum Map Review

You will see examples of actual units of study, each with a completed curriculum map and two sample lesson plans, in the following two chapters. The curriculum maps have been filled in with all the pertinent information needed.

As you explore these visually integrated curriculum maps, take note that the units and lessons were not all created from scratch. Many of them were created years ago without a visual component. They've subsequently been adapted to include this aspect. You can use this curriculum directly as written here, or you can let this work inspire you to modify or adapt your existing lessons to include more visual products and projects.

A Note on Assessment

The following units suggest formative and summative assessment criteria, based both on content and visual curriculum. Most of the assessment and evaluation pieces in these lessons are open-ended and provide only broad criteria for assessment. Feel free to adapt these criteria into assessments that make the most sense for your classroom, your students, and your school.

Botany and Gardening in Own Backyard: Grades K–3 Science

In this unit, we'll be taking a closer look outside, focusing on the nature that surrounds us. Students will become familiar with incorporating visual products and projects within the early elementary science curriculum.

Unit Narrative

Nature is everywhere around us. From the smallest ant to the giant sequoia, nature enhances our lives and connects us to the earth. Over thousands of years, humans have sought to understand their world by observing and documenting growth and change through words, symbols, and images. Journaling has been a time-tested practice for recording and heightening our awareness of nature.

In this unit, students will be doing hands-on gardening and studying nature indoors or outdoors. Looking at nature like a scientist will help students develop important skills like describing observations, labeling sketches, noticing subtle changes in plant growth and decline over time, and reflecting on these documentation activities and students' observations. It will teach children to journal on their own time, where they choose, and how they want.

Curriculum Map

Subject: Science Grades K–3

Unit/Theme: Botany & Gardening in Own Backyard

Essential Questions
1. What is a garden?
2. How do plants cultivate and support life?
3. How does a garden contribute to our lives?
4. How does the earth support and sustain plant life?

Common Core State Standards and/or State or Provincial Content Standards	Content Topics
CCSS.ELA-Literacy.CCRA.SL.1 CCSS.ELA-Literacy.RI.1.5 CCSS.ELA-Literacy.RI.1.6 CCSS.ELA-Literacy.SL.K.5 CCSS.ELA-Literacy.SL.1.5 CCSS.ELA-Literacy.RI.2.7 CCSS.ELA-Literacy.RI.3.5 CCSS.ELA-Literacy.RI.3.7 Next Generation Science Standards LS1.A: Structure and Function LS1.B: Growth and Development of Organisms LS3.A: Inheritance of Traits LS3.B: Variation of Traits	Environment Botany Gardening Scientific method Technical writing and illustration

Unit Questions
1. What is a plant?
2. Why do we grow plants?
3. How does the earth support and sustain plant life?

Skills	Visual Skills	Potential Projects/Products
Identifying attributes	Inspecting, examining, studying, documenting	Documentation of observations using one or more of the following strategies: doodling, sketching, watercolor, colored pencils, pen/ink, and labeling
Determining cause and effect		
Classifying	Fine motor skills, observing, color analysis and manipulating	
Comparing/contrasting		
Identifying relationships		Nature journaling, photographs, drawing, written documentation
Drawing conclusions	Observational drawing, multimedia illustration	
Experimentation		Extension: Design Your Own Garden
Writing	Mapmaking	
Documentation		
Measurement	Measuring, designing	

LESSON 1 LOOKING CLOSELY AT ITEMS FROM NATURE

Subject: Science, Botany/Gardening Grades K–3

Duration: 1 hour and ongoing throughout the year

Materials Required
plants, insects, rocks, and other nature specimens, magnifying glasses, pencils, colored pencils, "Visual Alphabet and Six Essential Design Elements" handout (see page 220) for each student, writing paper or nature journals

Key Vocabulary
specimen, magnifying lens, loupe, observation, examine

Description
To promote thinking and analytical skills through interdisciplinary studies, students examine items from nature using hands-on tools. This promotes and cultivates higher-order thinking skills with a scientific emphasis. Students are asked to further their visual literacy by applying their observations and building connections to similar objects in the world around them.

Learning Objectives
- Students will learn to observe, draw, and reflect on a self-selected item from nature and/or an object from the classroom collection of nature artifacts.

Visual Objectives

- Students will analyze the features of an object from nature.

- Students will illustrate the chosen object.

- Students will create metaphors using the prompts: "What does this look like?" and "What does it remind me of?"

For additional activities, I recommend *The Private Eye (5X) Looking/Thinking by Analogy: A Guide to Developing the Interdisciplinary Mind* by Kerry Ruef. It contains over 200 activities that encourage students to use jeweler's loupes or magnifying glasses to observe, analyze, and make creative connections about objects in nature.

Lesson Introduction

Show the class an object from nature—a pinecone, daisy, seashell, rock, or something similar. Ask students what they notice about the item. Share ideas and create a graphic organizer (for example, a mind map) on the whiteboard or on chart paper to organize information. Tell students that they will learn more about nature by doing an in-depth study using observation and documentation. Explain that they will be investigators and will be selecting an item to analyze, either from outside or from a selection you provide. They will spend time looking carefully and drawing what they see.

Procedure

- If possible, take students on a walk outside and have them select an item that catches their eye and that they want to investigate further. If it's not possible to go outside, bring in a collection of small items from nature and ask students to select one item to study.

- Demonstrate how to use the magnifying glass to examine an object closely.

- Allow students adequate time to examine their items closely.

- Demonstrate the process of documenting by drawing a detailed illustration of an object as seen through a magnifying glass. Reinforce the idea of looking closely and drawing the details that make each object unique. If possible, project the drawing on the class whiteboard and make references to the visual alphabet as the depiction takes shape.

- Once the drawing is complete, lead a discussion about what else this object looks like. Give examples: "A rock can look like mountains or a building or a piece of fruit."

- Students will then draw a detailed illustration/depiction of their objects, using the magnifying glass to closely examine the object. They can refer back to the visual alphabet while drawing.

- After drawings are complete, students can take turns in small groups sharing what each item looks like. Ask everyone to offer suggestions and feedback on their group members' renderings.

- To wrap up, have students take a walk around the classroom to view other specimens and fellow students' drawings and written responses.

In the example, the student chose to study and draw a strawberry. Fresh fruit and vegetables always make good options for a first botanical drawing. And, if there are leftovers, the class gets to have a tasty, healthy snack too.

Assessment/Evaluation
Formative Assessment: Ask students why they chose their items. As they make observations, notice how they describe their objects. Do they use descriptive language? Are they using vocabulary appropriate both to a study of botany and visual curriculum?

Summative Assessment: Can students point out specific features in their illustrations that represent parts of the specimens they chose? Did students make successful and pertinent observations of their specimens? Can students relate their specimens to other things? After students have produced their drawings, assemble them into a collection of student work. A binder containing all the drawings can serve as a class reference on carefully depicting items in nature.

LESSON 2 TAKING OUR NATURE JOURNALS TO THE GARDEN

Subject: Science, Botany/Gardening Grades K–3

Duration: 1 hour and ongoing throughout the year

Materials Required
blank paper or nature journals, pencils, colored pencils, outdoor garden or place to set up an indoor garden

Key Vocabulary
observation, specimen, scientist

Description
To develop and foster an appreciation for nature, students need time to observe, document, collect, and reflect on what they see in the field. Students need to engage in questioning, reflection, and analysis to synthesize their appreciation and understanding of nature. Slowing down and closely examining living objects fosters the disposition to look deeply into the details of nature. In this lesson, we apply the skills of studying an inanimate object to observing and documenting the growth of plants.

Learning Objectives
- Over time, students will study one plant in the class garden—an indoor or outdoor garden—and create a nature journal entry to document their observations.

Visual Objectives

- Students will analyze the features of plants in the garden.
- Students will illustrate the plants—with multiple drawings in sequence and over time to demonstrate growth—in their nature journals and illustrate parts of the plants labeled with botanical nomenclature.

> You can find science kits—like the Root Viewer Garden that comes with peat pellets, seeds, and multiple planting tubes—online. These kits are an exciting option for an indoor class garden since the plants can be observed growing above the soil line, and their root systems can be seen through the clear tube they are planted in.

Lesson Introduction

Ask students the following questions: "What does a scientist do?" "How do scientists learn?" Present the idea that we are all scientists and that we will be learning about nature and the world outside our classroom.

Procedure

As a class, or in small groups, invite students to visit the class garden (indoor or outdoor garden) to choose a plant to study and depict. (You may choose to assign a plant to each student or allow the students to choose a plant to study.) Multiple students may study the same plant.

- Explain to students that they will be making several entries in their nature journals—with illustrations—while their chosen plant continues to grow.
- Guide students in recording their initial observations in their nature journals. Students will be directed to format their journal entries using the appropriate fields from the following list. Feel free to include other directions for the nature journals according to your class needs:
  - Date
  - Place
  - Weather
  - Time
  - First impressions
  - Close-up observations
  - Bird's-eye observations
  - Drawing and labeling of individual items
- Give students time to draw, label, notice, think, and record their initial entries in their nature journals. Students can elaborate on their drawings and label essential features at a later time if need be.
- If time permits, encourage students to share their work with their classmates.

Repeat this process several times throughout the "growing season," so students can document their observations as their plants grow. At the culmination of the lesson, students can share their findings within small groups or with the entire class.

In this example, the student was viewing a young plant in a Root Viewer Garden. The student used a magnifying glass to get a closer look at what was happening under the soil. This student not only made observations about the plant, but also documented his or her curiosity and intent to check back in.

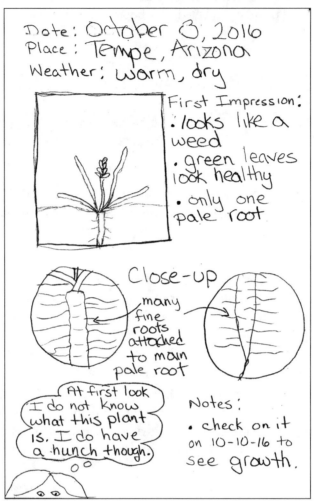

Assessment/Evaluation

Formative Assessment: Observe students as they record their observations of their chosen botanical specimens in their nature journals, looking for detail in depictions and noting students' impressions and observations.

Summative Assessment: Have students write in their nature journals using the following prompts:

- What plant specimen did you observe and what did you notice about it?
- What did you learn about this plant specimen over time? What changes occurred?
- What other questions came up for you?

Evaluate students on how they describe their plant specimens, the changes they observed in their specimens, and what questions this lesson sparked for them.

"Using handheld magnifying glasses while looking closely at and sketching items from nature has literally changed our classroom and my students' learning. Students look at things from a different vantage point. They observe more closely and they sketch more thoroughly while analyzing and hypothesizing about the specimen they are studying."

Jenna

Who Am I? Heritage, Culture, Traditions of Me: Grades 2–3 Social Studies

The primary grades are an opportune time to help students identify how they are similar and different from their peers while at the same time embracing their unique selves. The ability to see oneself in others and the ability to appreciate the differences we all bring to our community are addressed in the next unit.

Unit Narrative

Building a classroom community is at the top of every teacher's checklist. The more connected, integrated, and knowledgeable we are about one another in the culture of our classroom, the richer the learning and learning environment will be throughout the year. As children learn about the world, it's important for them to learn about themselves as well. By focusing on the self, students can use this new understanding of "identity" to build self-confidence, further their awareness of the world, and appreciate their classmates' diversity.

Some students may not know their own heritage, culture, or traditions at this age. Others may have been steeped in their family's culture from birth. Either way, this unit is about exploring these personal areas with the support of their families. They will need to take time to look back, acknowledge what milestones they have already experienced, and find out how their family's past might have shaped who they are today. A larger awareness of their family and what makes them unique will enhance students' abilities to understand who they are.

Curriculum Map

Subject: Social Studies Grades 2–3

Unit/Theme: Who Am I? Heritage, Culture, Traditions of Me

Essential Questions
1. What are the elements of a culture?
2. What is *heritage*?
3. What about our past is important to know?
4. How are people alike and different?

Common Core State Standards and/or State or Provincial Content Standards	Content Topics
CCSS.ELA-Literacy.RL.2.2 CCSS.ELA-Literacy.RL.2.3 CCSS.ELA-Literacy.RL.2.5 CCSS.ELA-Literacy.RL.2.7 CCSS.ELA-Literacy.RL.3.1 CCSS.ELA-Literacy.RL.3.2 CCSS.ELA-Literacy.RL.3.3 CCSS.ELA-Literacy.RL.3.7 CCSS.ELA-Literacy.SL.2.5 CCSS.ELA-Literacy.W.3.2.A CCSS.ELA-Literacy.W.3.2.B CCSS.ELA-Literacy.SL.3.4	Trace family history Artifacts Photographs Conduct interviews Compare and contrast your past Timeline of your life Autobiography

Unit Questions

1. Who am I and where do I come from?
2. Who are my ancestors?
3. Does my past make me who I am today?
4. How can I compare my past to others?

Skills	Visual Skills	Projects/Products
Identifying attributes	Illustrating	Illustrated timelines
Interviewing	Doodling	Picture books
Classifying	Painting	Family trees
Comparing/contrasting	Drawing	Family posters
Identifying relationships	Collage	Heritage museums with photos and family artifacts
Designing	Storyboards	
Inventing	Outlining	
Drawing conclusions	Framing	
Note-taking		
Researching		

LESSON 1 LOOKING BACK AND VISUAL TIMELINES

Subject: Social Studies Grades 2–3

Duration: 45–60 minutes for lesson, with extended time for students to work on their visual timelines as needed (estimate one hour).

Materials Required

- A picture book that focuses on an important event in a child's life. I recommend any of the following:
  - *Amber on the Mountain* by Tony Johnston and Robert Duncan
  - *Ira Says Goodbye* by Bernard Waber
  - *Sarah Morton's Day: A Day in the Life of a Pilgrim Girl* by Kate Waters
  - *Rachel's Journal: The Story of a Pioneer Girl* by Marissa Moss

- "Plot Outline," "Visual Alphabet and Six Essential Design Elements," and "Autobiography Visual Timeline Homework" handouts for each student (see pages 227, 220, and 248–250), visual learning notebook or blank paper, paper cut into half sheets for each student to make their timelines, pencils, pens, colored pencils, crayons to add color to visual timelines

Prep Work

Create a visual timeline of important events in your life to share with the class to provide a model of a timeline. Your sample visual timeline should span five to six years and should include the period of time when you were the age of your current students.

Key Vocabulary

timeline, milestone, memories, past

Description

Students will read about a character's life and the important events that character has experienced. From that reading, they will fill in the three panels of the "Plot Outline" with events that took place in the character's life, identifying three key milestones. Share your visual timeline of important events from your past. Students will create their personal visual timelines with milestones they can remember. Point out that important events will be different for each of them.

Learning Objectives

- Students will document important events that have taken place in a character's life from a book.
- Students will interview family members about the students' births and early lives.
- Students will understand their own pasts, milestones, and events that have shaped who they have become.
- Students will sequence events from their own lives.

Visual Objectives

- Students will place significant events from their lives on personal visual timelines.
- Each year of their lives will be illustrated and have a caption next to it.

Lesson Introduction

Discuss that each of us has a unique past that has helped shape who we are today. Remind students that there are different cultures, heritages, languages, and human experiences and that there is a lot of diversity in their class too. Students will learn more about themselves, who they are, and what past events have shaped them.

Procedure

- After the introduction, make a list of some of the big events people might experience in their lives, such as losing a tooth, breaking a bone, the birth of a sibling, and so on. As students share their ideas, record them on the whiteboard.

- Choose a picture book to read from the suggested list or choose one about a character that goes through small or big life changes during the story.

- After reading the book, add examples from the book to your list of events.

- In small groups, ask students to complete the three panels on the "Plot Outline" by choosing events that shaped the character in the book. Give them less than ten minutes to illustrate and write short captions under each of the three events.

- Display all of the plot frames and ask students to walk around the room and look at each others' frames. Students should focus on observing, not commenting or talking. Everyone should simply look at the different events people chose to depict.

- When finished, show students the visual timeline of a five-year span of your life when you were little (for example, when you were five, when you were six, when you were seven, when you were eight, when you were nine). On your visual timeline, you should have the year listed, a drawing/doodle of an event that happened that year, and a short caption of the drawing.

- Have students examine your timeline. Ask them to share what they see and explain how the timeline is sequenced by years and how each year has a strong visual to illustrate that milestone or memory.

- Have students make a quick doodle of some important events that have taken place in the last two years of their lives.

- Give students class time to start creating their current year's page. Assign the "Autobiography Visual Timeline Homework" so parents, relatives, and friends can help students brainstorm milestones from their pasts when they were four and under.

- Here are some sample questions students might ask their relatives and caregivers as they fill out the homework:

  ○ When and where was I born?

  ○ Where did we live? What was our home like?

  ○ What schools did I go to? Did I like school?

  ○ Who were my friends?

- What was my favorite thing to play? Did I like to play alone or with friends?
- Did we do anything special with our relatives?
- What holidays did we celebrate? Did we make or eat special foods? Did we have special traditions?

- When students (and their parents, relatives, and friends) have completed the "Autobiography Visual Timeline Homework," students can use this information to finish their visual timelines spanning from birth to the present day. The following example is from a completed Autobiography Visual Timeline Homework page.

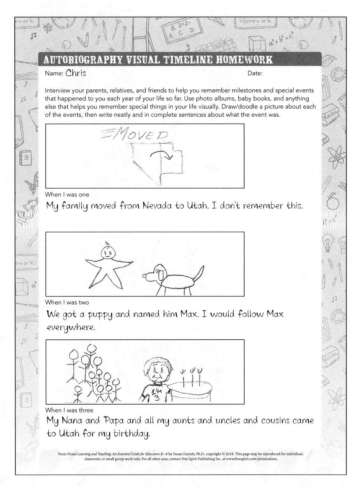

- Have students create a half-sheet entry for each year of their lives (as seen in the example on the next page). Each entry should have an image depicting an important milestone from that year along with a sentence or two describing the milestone. Remind students to label the pages with their age at that time (1 years old, 2 years old, and so forth).
- After the pages are complete, have students arrange them sequentially either horizontally or vertically to create a visual timeline.
- Ask students to tape the pages neatly to each other to create a horizontal or vertical timeline.
- Display finished timelines in the classroom as desired.

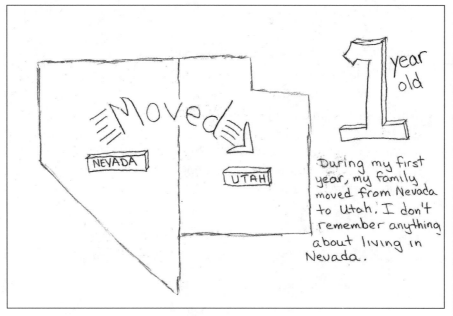

Assessment/Evaluation

Formative Assessment: As students complete their timelines, observe which events they identify. Prompt students to justify why they have chosen these events. Does their sequencing of events make sense?

Summative Assessment: An assessment or self-assessment checklist could include:

- Did students complete their autobiographical homework?
- How did this "research" help them complete their timelines?
- How do students understand time and important or defining events?
- Can students explain how these events influence who they are today?
- Can students explain the sequence of events?
- Can students calculate the year of events in relation to their ages?

LESSON 2 HERITAGE/CULTURE/TRADITIONS AND ME, CREATING A FAMILY PICTURE BOOK

Subject: Social Studies Grades 2–3

Duration: Several weeks as needed

Materials Required
- teacher-made picture book to share and model; "Autobiography Visual Timeline Homework" handouts completed by each student; "Visual Four-Square" graphic organizer (see page 231); a blank, six-page picture book for each student (two pieces of copy paper folded down the middle and stapled along the spines); and pens, crayons, colored pencils to illustrate the books
- Also, have one or more picture books about families, such as:
  - *The Family Book* by Todd Parr
  - *Families, Families, Families!* by Suzanne Lang
  - *The Great Big Book of Families* by Mary Hoffman
  - *And Tango Makes Three* by Justin Richardson and Peter Parnell

Key Vocabulary
traditions, research, heritage, and interview

Description
Students will develop a picture book about themselves that shows their family's traditions through food, games, clothing, hobbies, and traditions.

Learning Objectives
- Students will apply information gathered from their family research.
- Students will reflect on their daily lives and who they are now and contrast that with what their families were like in the past.

Visual Objectives
- Students will create a picture book that includes text, drawings, collages, photographs, or other visual resources.

Lesson Introduction
Discuss with your class: What makes each of us unique? Share ideas and make a list of students' answers. Create a graphic organizer where students can write down words and create doodles about what makes them who they are.

The "Visual Four-Square" graphic organizer works well for this activity. It includes spaces for sketching people, events, and "big ideas." There is a square for key vocabulary and space to write about the subject at the bottom of the page. Another option could be to have students create mind maps with connections related to their families: family members, homes, traditions, foods, hobbies or pastimes, pets, and anything else your students are interested in.

Students will complete several graphic organizers with information about themselves and their families. When they are finished, hang these around the room so students can observe the similarities and differences among their classmates. Over several class sessions, students will complete a rough draft and then a finalized picture book.

Procedure

- Read the picture book about families you have chosen. After reading, partner students to discuss: "What makes a family?" It's important to begin by discussing common aspects of families and then discuss different types of families. This helps students understand basic features of families and ways in which their families may differ, including: parents, stepparents, siblings, extended family members, homes, foods, traditions, and so on.

- Draw two columns on the whiteboard. First, ask the class, "How are all families similar?" and write their responses in the first column. You might hear answers like, "Families play games together" or "Families eat meals together."

- After you have a good-sized list, ask "How are each of our families unique?" Write down students' thoughts in the second column. Discuss differences among families based on the list in the first column. For example, you might say to your class, "We've listed that families play games. Let's talk about the different types of games families play and how that might be related to their heritage."

- Ask partners to discuss these topics as they relate to each of their families.

- Ask students to select five topics from the list generated by the class. Explain that they will devote one page of their picture books to each of the topics. So, if they choose "family games," they will make a page in their picture book about the games their family plays.

- Have the students fill in a visual four-square graphic organizer with doodles/sketches and ideas about each of the five topics as related to their own families. Students should keep these organizers to use as an outline for their family picture books.

In the following example, the student has brainstormed about family traditions and what they mean.

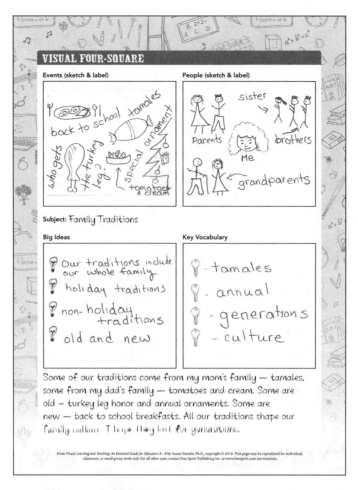

- Show students your completed sample picture book. Explain that students will create eight pages: the cover, the inside front cover (which has a table of contents listing each of the five topics in the book), pages one through five (each page covering one topic about their family), and the back cover.

- Instruct students to use their completed visual four-square organizers (five total) to make a rough draft of each page in their picture book. They should create illustrations with a small place for writing a caption or keywords about the pictures they drew.

- When their rough drafts are finished and you have reviewed them, students can begin their final drafts of their books. When everyone has finished their books, ask students to share what they wrote as an oral presentation in front of the class. This could be held after school when parents could attend or contribute to the presentations.

The following example shows a cover, table of contents, and first page of one student's picture book.

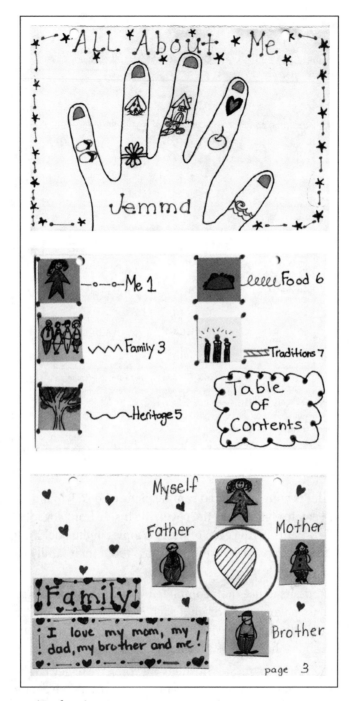

Assessment/Evaluation

Formative Assessment: Can students define *family*? Can they list things common to all families? Can they list things that make families unique?

Summative Assessment: Did students complete a book that discussed their families' backgrounds and heritages? Have students write reflections about their works, answering the following prompts: "What did I learn about how I grew up? What did my relatives remember about my childhood that was different from my memories? What did they remember that was the same? Was there anything that surprised me about my life up until now?"

"For nonwriters, the act of using letters/words to express themselves is extremely difficult. That doesn't mean they don't have anything to say. It just means that they are not proficient in using written language to express themselves. I had one student who couldn't write at all. He had challenges with speech and fine motor skills. But when I showed him how to draw cartoons, his world changed. In the picture book lesson, he was able to tell his family story through his simple pictures. The picture book gave him the courage and confidence to push through when it was difficult for him to express himself. What gratification he experienced producing a book about himself and his family!"

Moving On

Creating curriculum units and supporting lessons isn't always completed in a direct path. Each unit can and will take a shape of its own over time. You do not need to set out to create a unit that incorporates visual teaching and learning from scratch. Many teachers have found that they are able to weave in visual products and projects to some of their favorite existing unit studies. By doing so, teachers don't diminish what they are already teaching but are able to enhance the lessons as students participate in their learning through the essentials of the visual triad model: See it, imagine it, depict it.

Visually Integrated Curriculum Grades 4–8

It's important for students to have visual learning and teaching as a regular part of their school experience, optimally starting in preK or early elementary. But what about for students who haven't had that early grounding? For example, a student transfers from a school that didn't have an inherent visual component to the curriculum. It's not too late to introduce visual teaching and visual learning in the intermediate and middle school grades. Almost everyone has an implicit understanding of visual language. Remember, these are not new skills or new ways of learning. Intermediate grade and middle school students simply need their visual abilities *refreshed* and *reawakened*.

The following curricula work well with students in fourth through eighth grade, whether or not they have a firm foundation in visual learning.

"I was at the school before the start of the school year, and a student and her parent came to help. After some small talk, I asked the student if she had any questions for me, and she asked, 'Can I doodle in class?' 'Yes,' I replied and told her it's part of what we do in class—all students would be doodling. She smiled a happy, contented smile. During the school year, she was one of the students other students naturally went to for inspiration or ideas when they had 'doodle block.' Her willingness to 'give it a try' and her supportive nature were things her peers appreciated."

Novel Studies—Exploring Friendship Through Literature: Grades 4-8 Literature

Friendships typically become more important during preadolescence through adolescence when young people start to reach out beyond their families for close connections with at least one other peer. These relationships provide support socially, emotionally, and intellectually. Trading ideas, sharing stories, and designing projects with friends may also support creative thinking. Many friendships support physical development through participation in sports and games. Further, research has indicated that students who have a good friend are more likely to do well in school. In the following unit, we'll explore tight-knit relationships through novel studies, a natural fit for students in grades four through eight.

Unit Narrative

This novel study unit focuses on the theme of friendship. All of the recommended novels grapple with concepts and difficulties related to friendship. These include:

- similarities and differences
- disagreements and allegiances
- adventures, challenges, and dependability
- changes, growth, and loss
- abilities and disabilities

Students will explore these themes and concepts through character studies and a creative project.

Curriculum Map

Subject: ELA, Literature Grades 4–8

Unit/Theme: Friendships in Novels

Essential Questions

1. Why are friendships important to people?
2. What qualities describe friendships?
3. What events shape friendships?

Common Core State Standards and/or State or Provincial Content Standards	Content Topics
CCSS.ELA-Literacy.CCRA.R.2 CCSS.ELA-Literacy.CCRA.R.3 CCSS.ELA-Literacy.CCRA.R.7 CCSS.ELA-Literacy.RL.4.3 CCSS.ELA-Literacy.RL.4.10 CCSS.ELA-Literacy.RL.5.3 CCSS.ELA-Literacy.RL.5.10	Friendship Character qualities Conflict

Unit Questions

1. In what ways is friendship important to the characters in your book?
2. What positive personality traits do your characters have and how do the traits affect their friendship?
3. What events shaped the friendship of the characters in your book?

Skills	Visual Skills	Projects/Products
Literary analysis	Imagining	Character study
Interpretation	Depicting	Illustrated timeline
Character analysis	Translating text to image and image to text	Illustrations
	Visually representing significant events	
	Illustrating	

LESSON 1 A LOOK AT THE CHARACTERISTICS OF MAIN CHARACTERS WHO ARE FRIENDS

Subject: English Language Arts, Literature Grades 4–5

Duration: 1 hour for the lesson, not including the time needed to read the novel

Materials Required

- A fourth- or fifth-grade novel about friendship; you may assign the same novel to the whole class or allow each student to choose a different book. Use any novel with the theme of friendship. Here's a list if you need ideas.
  - *Bridge to Terabithia* by Katherine Paterson
  - *Dead End in Norvelt* by Jack Gantos
  - *A Dragon's Guide to the Care and Feeding of Humans* by Laurence Yep and Joanne Ryder
  - *11 Birthdays* by Wendy Mass
  - *Holes* by Louis Sachar
  - *Liar & Spy* by Rebecca Stead
  - *My Last Best Friend* by Julie Bowe
  - *The One and Only Ivan* by Katherine Applegate
  - *Serafina and the Black Cloak* by Robert Beatty
  - *Summer of the Gypsy Moths* by Sara Penny Packer
  - *The Year of the Dog* by Grace Lin

- "Character Portrait" and "Visual Alphabet and Six Essential Design Elements" handouts (see pages 239 and 220), and pencils, erasers, black pens, color pencils

Key Vocabulary

character, personality, characteristics, compare, contrast

Description

In this lesson, we are looking at characters who are friends. Students will complete a "Character Portrait" handout that includes a visual depiction and a list of personality traits for each character. This will provide a catalyst for discussion of students' interpretations and understandings of the two characters. As students explore novel characters and friendship on a deeper level, they are reinforcing their comprehension of the verbal text. This lesson expands on that learning and enables students to practice their visual literacy skills by translating the written word into an integrated visual and verbal product.

Learning Objectives

- Students will depict and describe the personalities of two friends in the novel.
- Students will list at least four personality traits for each character.

Visual Objectives

- Students will imagine what the characters look like based on the descriptions in the novel.
- Students will create a simple portrait of each character on the "Character Portrait" handout.
- Students will illustrate and describe in text the character traits that contribute to the characters' friendship.

Lesson Introduction

Tell students that this will be the first of two novel study lessons. Explain that the focus will be on identifying at least four traits of two characters who are friends. If everyone is reading a different book, remind students that although the theme of friendship unifies all the novels, the friends and friendships depicted will most likely have significant differences. Students will be learning about these differences as the lesson unfolds.

Procedure

- After students have read their novels, discuss the friendship theme as a class. Ask students what traits friends have. Record their responses on the whiteboard and save them for future reference.
- Distribute a copy of the "Character Portrait" handout to each student. Direct students to first use pencil to fill in the sheet. Once they are happy with their overall depiction and design, they can go over the pencil lines with pen. The final step is erasing stray pencil lines and filling the page with color.
- Tell the class to complete the "Character Portrait" handout by drawing a simple portrait depicting how they imagine each character would look using the boxes located at the top of each of the two columns. Encourage students to look past the images that may appear on the book covers and have them rely on how the characters came to life in their own imaginations.

- Remind students that the portrait should also visually represent the character's personality as well as their physical appearance. If students find this step difficult, they may choose to depict items around the portrait that help the viewer get a sense of the character's personality.
  - Adventurous: hiking boots/walking stick
  - Trustworthy: handshake
  - Dramatic: comedy/tragedy theater masks
  - Fair/balanced: balance scales
  - Popular: figure surrounded by many others
  - Athletic: sports equipment
  - Artistic: art supplies

- In the spaces provided below each column, students list personality traits that make the characters unique and contribute to their friendships.

The "Character Portrait" handout gives students a chance to use fonts to enhance the visual nature of the assignment. Ask students to find space within the portrait area to write the character's name in a font style that represents the character's personality. Similarly, they can write out the name of their novel along with its author in the space at the top of the "Character Portrait" handout using a font that represents the overall theme of the novel.

- When the assignment is complete, students will meet in small groups to share their worksheets with each other.

- Finally, discuss as a class what everyone learned from this activity. Are their thoughts and ideas on friendship and the personality traits that friends have any different than before? Refer back to the list of traits you made at the beginning of the lesson and add more traits as students offer them.

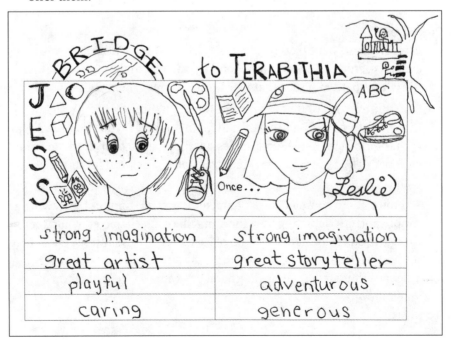

In the example student work, two characters from the novel *Bridge to Terabithia* are depicted—each with a small portrait and depictions of their individual personality traits—and described in terms of personality traits and abilities that contribute to the friendship of the two. They have some traits in common, for example, they both have strong imaginations. They have some traits that are unique, for example, Jesse draws all the time, and Leslie is a talented storyteller and writer. Jesse has large, deep eyes and is portrayed as playful and caring. Leslie seems to have a slightly mischievous smile and a twinkle in her eye that indicates she is adventurous.

Assessment/Evaluation

Formative Assessment: Walk through the room and ask students questions about their portraits and the personality characteristics they list. Listen and observe for details, evidence of interpretation from the text, and accuracy.

Summative Assessment: If desired, have students write a descriptive essay about the two characters with references to the text of the novel to support their interpretation of the two characters illustrated on their "Character Portrait" handout.

LESSON 2 ONE PAGER—A DAY IN THE LIFE OF YOUR CHOSEN CHARACTER

Subject: ELA, Literature Grades 4–5

Duration: 2 to 3 class periods

Materials Required
a novel about friendship, white paper for rough draft designs, 8.5" x 11" card stock for final pages, pencils, erasers, black pens, markers, colored pencils and/or crayons, index cards

Key Vocabulary
significant, event, point of view

Description
Students will design a one pager from the point of view of one of the characters with images and text illustrating, describing, and reflecting on the events of a significant or important day that the friends shared.

Learning Objectives
- Students will identify scenes that have significance for the developing friendship in the story.
- Students will analyze the events of the chosen day—from the perspective of their chosen character—and design a way to express these events in images and writing on their one pagers.

Visual Objectives
- Students will design a one pager that illustrates an important day or event for the two characters in the novel.

- Students will depict both friends on the page with mock photographs made on index cards.
- Students will use images and text to show and tell about the importance of the day or event.
- Students will use frames to set images apart on the page.

Lesson Introduction

Tell students that for this next activity, they will create a one pager to illustrate and describe an important event or day from the story as told from a single character's point of view. The page should also include text that might have been written by the character.

Procedure

- After the introduction, ask students to start thinking about what important event they want to document and from whose perspective.
- While students are thinking, project the "One Pager Worksheet" (see page 232) on the whiteboard and remind students that they need to plan a design that will combine both visual and verbal content.
- Distribute supplies: white paper for draft, card stock for final, and index cards for portraits.
- Have students write their chosen event and character on one side of the plain draft paper.
- Students will make a plan and create a sketch of their design on the other side of the plain draft paper. The following items should be included on their draft:
  - Title: This is not the title of the novel. This is a title that best represents the event, day, or experience that the character is documenting. For example, the title of a scene from *Bridge to Terabithia* might be "Leslie Finds Janice Crying."
  - One to two portraits: Incorporate some hand-drawn portraits that capture memories of the event. The portraits should be created on index cards rather than on the one pager. This gives students the opportunity to create drafts of their portraits before choosing the ones to add to the one pager.
  - Text blocks: The text shouldn't be a retelling of the event the way it was portrayed in the novel but rather a personal reflection of the event written from the character's point of view.
- When students have finished their one pager design, they should get feedback from you and your okay to proceed to the final page.
- With approval to proceed, students re-create their one pager on their final cardstock. They should address the following issues:
  - Re-create the portraits on blank index cards, first in pencil, then go over the lines in pen and add color as needed.
  - Create frames from color construction paper and attach portraits to frames with adhesive. The good thing about this method is that index cards can be redone, if needed, to make adjustments or corrections much more easily than working directly on the final one pager.

- Transfer pencil layout to the final one pager. Once happy with the layout, go over it in pen and use an eraser to remove any stray pencil lines.

- Continue with transferring the title and the text blocks onto the final one pager. Again, first with pencil and then in pen.

- Tell students to get creative and add color and embellishments to their final pages.

- When students are done, the one pagers can be displayed in the classroom, or students can give a quick three-minute presentation to the class sharing their character's memorable event.

In this example, the student chose to record Christmas in Terabithia from Leslie's perspective. The mock photos depict the images that Leslie would have wanted captured, and the text is written from a very personal point of view documenting what Leslie wanted to remember from that day.

Assessment/Evaluation

Formative Assessment: Look at rough sketches and discuss them with students to learn about their thinking—analysis, interpretation, and design—and provide them feedback.

Summative Assessment: Evaluate final one pagers for:
- representation of a significant event
- organized layout design
- images that accurately document the event, day, or experience
- text that is in the voice and perspective of students' chosen character
- text that describes the experience of the significant event

Martin

"My students were skeptical when I mentioned we were doing a novel study about friendship. They accused me of trying to sneak in another book report. But after I shared the lesson introduction with them, they were excited about getting started. They enjoyed picking their own books about friendship, with several of them picking the same book so they could have their own 'book club.' They enjoyed talking with their classmates who chose different books and comparing the novels and their characters. The visual activities brought even more excitement to the lessons, and even my reluctant readers were more engaged with having a creative outlet to show what they know. All my students were able to depict the character's personality and the theme of friendship using anything from the most basic of doodles to more detailed sketches."

Redesign Our Schoolyard— Applying Perimeter and Area: Grades 4–8 Mathematics

This unit integrates several visual learning and communication strategies, mathematics, design thinking, problem-solving, collaboration, and public speaking.

Unit Narrative

Students will apply mathematical knowledge to a contextualized, higher-order practice: redesigning their schoolyard. Students will choose the creative aspects of the project, including the concept and visual representation of their chosen designs. At the same time, the collaborative aspect ensures that group members' opinions are validated. After reviewing the concepts and mathematical properties of perimeter and area, students will apply this knowledge to optimize the redesign of their schoolyard space. They collaborate to brainstorm new designs for the available space, create a blueprint of their planned schoolyard revisions, and share their design and rationale for their chosen layout in a brief class presentation.

Design Thinking

The "Redesign Our Schoolyard" unit is an excellent example of design thinking. Design thinking involves working with a real-world problem or question that requires a creative and useful solution. That solution most often involves collaborating with others to design a product or complete a project. John Spencer and A.J. Juliani, authors of *Launch: Using Design Thinking to Boost Creativity and Bring Out the Maker in Every Student*, speak at length about the higher-order thinking skills incorporated in the design thinking process and say that "creative thinking is as vital as math or reading or writing."[19] Design thinking involves problem-solving and experimenting; it incorporates both creative and critical thinking. It also requires the visual thinking skill of imagining—or envisioning—possibilities in the design process, analysis of those possibilities, selection of the best option, and the creation of a finished product that could be applied in the real world.

In the case of the "Redesign Our Schoolyard" unit, the culminating project includes a blueprint for a newly designed schoolyard and a presentation to an audience of peers. Design thinking is a powerful learning process as students apply creative and critical thinking skills and also come to consider themselves makers, inventors, and creators.

Curriculum Map

Subject: Mathematics

Unit/Theme: Redesign of Our Schoolyard. Applying Perimeter & Area

Essential Questions

1. How can math skills and visual data be used in the real world?
2. How can math and visual data be used for design, problem-solving, and creating change?

Common Core State Standards and/or State or Provincial Content Standards	Content Topics
Mathematics (4.MD.A.3) CCSS.ELA-Literacy.CCRA.R.7 CCSS.ELA-Literacy.CCRA.SL.2 CCSS.ELA-Literacy.CCRA.SL.4 CCSS.ELA-Literacy.CCRA.SL.5 CCSS.ELA-Literacy.RI.4.7	Measurement Perimeter Area Scale drawing/ blueprint rendering

Unit Questions

1. What are perimeter and area, and how are they related?
2. How are perimeter and area measured/determined?
3. How do formulas for perimeter and area help us?

Skills	Visual Skills	Possible Projects/Products
Apply knowledge of perimeter and area to produce original, to-scale plans for a remodeled schoolyard. Find the total perimeter and area of the space, breaking an irregular shape into smaller, regular regions if necessary. Place new playground equipment based on available square footage and create a design that allows for ease of use. Present plans to the class, who will informally appraise use of the space and the mathematical soundness of calculations of perimeter and area.	Sketching Evaluate mathematical ratios and represent them in illustrations Represent elements of proposal in blueprint using simplified, standardized symbols	Visual vocabulary chart Area calculations Blueprint Presentation

LESSON 1 THE MATH OF DESIGN

Class: Mathematics

Duration: Approximately two class periods

Materials Required
satellite image of school, "Redesign Our Schoolyard" handout (see page 251), straightedges, pencils/crayons, grid paper, blank paper

Key Vocabulary
side, shape, rectangle, perimeter, area, measurement, diagram, proposal, blueprint

Description
In this project-based mini-unit, students propose a redesign for their schoolyard, applying mathematical knowledge. Developed as an extension to a unit on measurement, perimeter, and area, this project replicates the process of research and design. Students identify and communicate an authentic need in their environment or in their community.

After students have assessed the total square footage of their schoolyard, they will wipe the slate clean and start over by adding all new equipment. They can place the equipment wherever they choose, provided it fits in the available space. Students will present their proposed changes to their classmates for discussion and then reflect on the unit as a whole.

Learning Objectives
- Apply knowledge of perimeter and area to produce original, to-scale plans for a remodeled recess space.
- Judiciously place new playground equipment into the redesigned schoolyard, knowing how much space each piece of equipment takes up within the total space available.

- Render scale blueprints of real-life space.
- In groups, present plans to the class who will informally appraise use of the space and the mathematical soundness of calculations of perimeter and area, and other visual and geometrical reasoning.

Visual Objectives
- Represent mathematical concepts using visual note-taking.
- Render scale blueprints of real-life space.
- Evaluate mathematical ratios and represent them in illustrations.
- Represent elements of proposal in a blueprint using simplified, standardized symbols.

Lesson Introduction
Review the concepts of perimeter and area of rectangles and irregular shapes.
- Visual vocabulary: Give students blank "Visual Vocabulary Chart" handouts (see page 224) and ask them to illustrate or write what they know about perimeter and area and how to find these measurements.
- Ask: How does this help us in real life? Could perimeter and area help us build something?

Procedure
- Explain to students that they will design their "dream schoolyard." They can add whatever playground equipment they want as long as: (1) it fits within the space available, and (2) it takes into account the needs of *all* students, not just what the designer wants. To start, students must first figure out the total square footage of the current schoolyard.
  - Show the class a satellite image of the school and schoolyard using a document camera if possible. Ask: What do you think this is?
  - Explore the image. Point out streets, the office, their classroom, and so on.
  - Mark off the schoolyard. Ask students what shape it is. If the schoolyard is an irregular shape, break it down into smaller, regular shapes to make calculations easier.
  - Ask: How do we determine how much space we have to work with?
  - Ask: Could perimeter and area help us do that? How?
  - Using Google Maps or your own measurements, give students the perimeter measurements and have them assess the total square footage.
- Once students have determined the square footage, tell them to imagine the current schoolyard completely empty. It will now be their jobs to fill it.
- Introduce an example. "I redesigned a city park to show you what you'll be doing with the schoolyard." Say to students:
  - This is my finished project. (Show diagram and read proposal.)
  - What do you notice in the diagram?

- How is the space used? What are the main areas?
- What would be most important about this space for local residents? Why?
- Do you have other ideas? How would you re-create this space?

- Assign students to collaborative groups.
  - Using one sheet of graph paper per group, ask students to use pencils and straightedges to draw the outline of the existing schoolyard. Be sure to give them some sort of scale to work with. (For example, one square of graph paper equals 5 square feet or 10 square feet. Depending on the available space, you may have to be creative with the scale you use.)
  - Pass out "Redesign Our Schoolyard" handouts.
  - Explain that the handout lists different types of schoolyard equipment, including some from the existing playground.
  - Explain that every piece of equipment takes up a certain amount of space. Students' job is to design a playground with any types of equipment they want, provided it all fits within the existing space.
  - Go over the "Redesign Our Schoolyard" handout and note that each piece of equipment is represented by a geometric shape. This is the shape they must draw on their graph paper within the confines of the schoolyard. Again, be sure to tell students the scale they are working with (which may vary given the size of graph paper) so they know how many squares a particular piece of equipment will take up.
  - Ask students to create a sketch of the proposed space made to scale.

- Introduce the following rules.
  - Students must leave 5 to 10 square feet between each piece of equipment. (Use your discretion here. This will depend on the scale you end up using.)
  - They must account for walkways in the playground. (How can you get to the merry-go-round on the other side if a wall of swing sets is blocking the way?)
  - They need to take into account the needs of *all* students. For example, if the student is a soccer player and the schoolyard is 1,500 square feet, not all 1,500 square feet can be made into a soccer field! Students should address many types of activities and interests for all classmates.

- Before students start, tell everyone that they will be presenting their proposed new schoolyard to the rest of the class to explain why they chose the equipment and placed it the way they did.

- For an extension, encourage students to think about anyone with special needs. Even if no one in the class uses a wheelchair, how can students design the schoolyard so it is accessible to those who do? Or think about younger or older students. What might interest them?

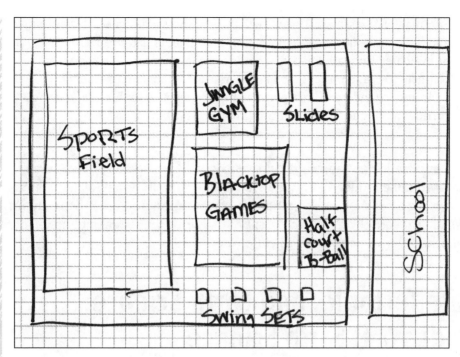

- It may be a good idea to end here and let students brainstorm overnight. Devote another class period to let them confer with group mates and begin experimenting with designs.

- Once students finish designing their new schoolyards, they can present what they came up with. Explain to students that while their classmates will be listening to their presentations, their classmates will have two jobs:

  1. They will take notes on what they liked about and learned from the presentation.

  2. They will ask questions about the choices made in the designs.

- Closure/reflection. Ask: How do perimeter and area help us in real life?

- Visual learning strategy: Ask students to illustrate one thing that went well during this process and one thing they would change.

You can use the "Redesign Our Schoolyard" handout or create your own. Be prepared for students who want to use equipment that isn't listed on the handout. (Let's say you have a track and field enthusiast who wants a pole vaulting area.) You can either ask them to stick to the equipment listed (saying it's all the school has access to) or you can create (on the fly) an approximate square footage for the requested equipment. If you choose the latter, be sure to list it on the board so all students have access to the new information. Warning: While this may encourage creative thinking in students, you might also be inundated with requests for special equipment. Proceed with caution.

Assessment/Evaluation
Formative Assessment: During group work, teacher will look for proper usage of measurement/geometrical principles.

Summative Assessment: Groups will present their redesigned playgrounds and their work showing calculations of perimeter and area. Group work will be evaluated for mathematical soundness, completeness of ideas, visual competences, and presentation skills. Assess students individually for their understanding of area/perimeter concepts prior to this lesson using curriculum-aligned or curriculum-provided content assessments.

"In application to teaching contexts, visual learning strategies have offered me avenues to engage students in a multimodal fashion, and, in turn, assess their understandings in ways that are authentic to them. Reluctant verbal communicators, be it in writing or speaking, are afforded another way to contribute to classroom discussion."

— Kipp

Plate Tectonics and Earth Science: Grades 6–8 Earth Science

As we focus on incorporating visual teaching and learning into the upper elementary and middle school grades, we start to see greater emphasis on layers of understanding, depth of complexity, and attention to detail. To see how visual learning can convey more multifaceted subject matter, let's look at a sample earth science unit.

"Visual learning strategies work well with content that is new to students. For example: visuals can help teach social studies and history by depicting information about places, times, and so forth. In science and math, diagrams help students understand parts of the whole or placement of one thing in relation to another."

— Toni

Unit Narrative

Earth science and the study of plate tectonics lend themselves well to projects and products that include visual elements. From making models, posters, or diagrams to graphic texts, slide shows, or movies, students can create and be creative in the projects and products they design and construct. It's important to clarify content expectations and the amount of accuracy required before projects begin. This contributes to straightforward assessment even within the variety of products created.

Most units on plate tectonics include diagrams of Earth's layers, plate boundaries, types of volcanoes, as well as maps of Pangea, continental drift, and more. When students create their own visual content, even if it's just copying provided images, it helps internalize the information and solidify their understanding of geological concepts.

Creating a timeline is a good introductory lesson to connect visual learning with earth science. In doing so, students gain perspective of the human place in the context of geologic time and geologic processes and events over time.

Curriculum Map

Subject: Earth Science Grades 6–8

Unit/Theme: Plate Tectonics

Essential Questions

1. What is the relationship between time and Earth systems?
2. What are the processes that shape the earth?
3. How does our understanding of change and making meaning of changes develop over time?

Common Core State Standards and/or State or Provincial Content Standards	Content Topics
CCSS.ELA-Literacy.RST.6–8.4 CCSS.ELA-Literacy.RST.6–8.7 Next Generation Science Standards MS-ESS1-4 Earth's Place in the Universe MS-ESS2-2 Earth's Systems MS-ESS2-3 Analyze and interpret data on the distribution of fossils and rocks, continental shapes, and seafloor structures to provide evidence of the past plate motions. MS-ESS3-1 Earth and Human Activity	Geologic time Fossil evidence Layers of earth Plate tectonics Earth systems Continental drift Sea floor spreading Mountain formation Earthquakes Volcanoes

Unit Questions

1. What is geologic time?
2. What is continental drift?
3. What evidence made continental drift go from a hypothesis to a theory?
4. What part of the earth actually moves?
5. What causes the earth to move?

Skills	Visual Skills	Projects/Products
Comprehending nonfiction texts Note-taking Building vocabulary Reading and understanding maps Reading and understanding diagrams	Visualizing time Diagramming structures Modeling interactions Illustrating conceptual understanding Reading and understanding maps Reading and understanding diagrams	Geologic timeline of the earth Visual vocabulary chart Depicting diagrams Research and presentation of project

LESSON 1 GEOLOGIC TIMELINE

Subject: Science, Earth Science Grades 6–8

Duration: One to two class periods

Materials Required
adding machine tape, pencils, pens, markers, tapes, a meter stick for each group, a copy of the "Directions for Geologic Timeline" (see page 252) for each group, a premade timeline of a much shorter time period as a sample

Key Vocabulary
geologic time, geologic periods, scale, ratio, billion, Pangea

Description
Students will develop a deeper understanding of geologic, or deep, time by creating their own timeline of the history of Earth complete with visuals. By using a length of adding machine tape, students will mark and illustrate key geologic events and time periods. Through this experience, students will analyze and compare passage of time in geologic terms showing the timeline of humans and the timeline of the universe.

Learning Objectives
- Students will develop a deeper understanding of the enormity of geologic time and the relationship of human participation during that time.

Visual Objectives
- Students will model and visualize geologic time through scale, developed with a premeasured strip of tape.
- Students will illustrate key geologic timeline markers.

Lesson Introduction
Earth is commonly believed to be 4.5 billion years old. But this length of time is extremely difficult to grasp and human participation is such a small blip in that span of time. This lesson helps students understand the enormity of time and how little a role humans have played in the bigger view of Earth's history.

Procedure
- Discuss timelines with students. Remind them how their personal timeline would begin on the date they were born and would continue up until today's date. You may wish to illustrate this on the whiteboard, adding dividers at equal distance for each year. Allow students to see the visual of how much space it takes to display ten to thirteen years.
- Tell students that Earth is 4.5 billion years old. Ask them how large Earth's timeline would be. Get them thinking about the scale of 4.5 billion versus the ten to thirteen years they see before them.
- Divide students into work groups and give each group a premeasured strip of adding machine tape that is 5 meters long, along with the "Directions for Geologic Timeline" handout to guide them in their creation of the timeline.
- Tell the class that this strip of paper represents all of time from the creation of Earth to the present day. So, each meter represents almost 1 billion years.

- Have students break into their groups and find a location where they can spread out with their timelines and begin the directions on the handout.

- Once groups have marked their timelines, lay them all down on the floor, one above another, to compare and discuss.

  ○ Are there variations in the timelines? Discuss. Why might that be?

  ○ Was this a challenging assignment? What was challenging? What was difficult?

  ○ What did you notice while making your timeline?

  ○ Did any questions come up for you?

Even with specific instructions and dates for the construction of the timeline, the groups always have some variety in how they place events. When students discuss the variation in their timelines, it highlights the need for precision. Discussions should include the need for scale, ratios, and accuracy in measurement and marking. Students should also talk about what strategies were used to ensure accuracy and how they checked the accuracy of their timeline placements.

The events to be marked on the tape can be modified to fit your class discussion and level of background knowledge. Students will need to discuss, analyze, and plan how and where to mark the tape. Even when students know that dinosaurs went extinct 65 million years ago, they will still have to calculate where this lands on the timeline of Earth.

Assessment/Evaluation

Formative Assessment: Observe students' discussions during and after the creation of timelines. How do students explain and justify their placements in marking events on their timelines? Do they connect their discussions to concepts being introduced? What vocabulary is being used? How has their understanding of time shifted?

Summative Assessment: Students reflect on the following questions in writing and/or with a doodle:

- What do you understand about geologic time from creating your own Earth timeline?

- How did your thoughts about the role of humans in the history of Earth change after discussing and evaluating geologic time?

- What is the difference between time as a measure of just yesterday or last week as compared to time measured in billions of years?

- What thoughts do you have about how short the human role has been in Earth's history?

LESSON 2 PLATE TECTONICS

Subject: Science, Earth Science Grades 6–8

Duration: One class period

Materials Required
blank paper, pencils, pens, markers, crayons or colored pencils, and "Visual Alphabet and Six Essential Design Elements" and "Visual Note-Taking Form" handouts (see pages 220 and 225)

Key Vocabulary
Generate a list that pertains to the curriculum. Some suggested vocabulary terms that relate to plate tectonics may include, but are not limited to: asthenosphere, continental drift, convection (currents), convergent (plate boundaries), divergent (plate boundaries), lithosphere, and mantle.

Description
Students will work in pairs to create a classroom visual glossary of plate tectonic vocabulary. Terms will then be shared around the class. Vivid and clear depictions are essential to learning these terms and concepts.

Learning Objectives
- Students will express the meaning of terms, incorporating visuals with text, and build a common understanding of key vocabulary and concepts.

Visual Objectives
- Students will depict key concepts of the unit vocabulary and essential concepts with a graphically designed one pager.

Lesson Introduction
Explain to students that they will be creating a visual glossary for the terms they encounter in their study of Earth's crust. The integration of visual and verbal will help students with recall and retention. Working in pairs will help promote collaboration and cooperation.

Procedure
- Working with a partner, students will pick a word from the word list to illustrate and define. (Words will come from the current unit of study.)
- Give students time to research their word (search online, reference a dictionary or their science textbook, or other sources) and have them use a "Visual Note-Taking Form" to take notes and sketch images.
- Encourage group members to collaborate on the best way to represent their words. Brainstorming and viewing each other's note-taking forms is helpful.
- Give students plain white paper and read the following directions aloud. Students will have the same directions, but how the groups design their pages will vary as they interpret the directions and make design decisions.

- Once groups are finished with their one pagers, they can share them with the class. Students may also choose to give a brief presentation on their key vocabulary term using the one pager as a visual aide.

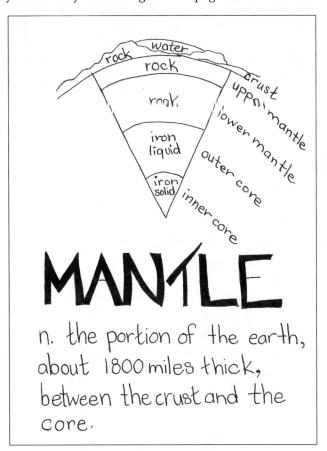

Assessment/Evaluation

Formative Assessment: Observe how students use vocabulary. Accurate use of terms in projects and presentations illustrates the student's understanding of content vocabulary.

Summative Assessment:

- Is the primary vocabulary term written/represented clearly on the page in a way that catches the viewer's eye?
- Are the parts of speech and definition included? Is the definition effectively restated in student's own words?
- Are the illustration(s) and caption(s) used to depict the word relevant to the definition of the word?

Additional evaluation can include informal assessment of verbal understanding of terms and/or concepts through class discussion or a more formal follow-up quiz.

Jenna

"My team loops our grades, meaning I get my classes for two years. So, I just got my class back for their second year together. Over the first couple of weeks of this school year, students created one pagers. The topic was the recent solar eclipse and this was their first one pager of the school year. As I looked at these first projects, it was obvious to me that there was clear and measurable progress in the quality of their one pager work. I could see improvement from last year in the content and organization of their information in both the written components and the visual images. It was an 'aha' moment for me that I could visually see the growth in this skill set of dual language."

Moving On

The teachers throughout this book collaborated to create these units that have been implemented with excellent student outcomes. Students in kindergarten through eighth grade have shown the ability to depict their knowledge, comprehension, understanding, interpretations, and the content of their imaginations with everything from simple doodles to highly detailed and elaborate sketches. With these approaches, visual learning takes place alongside verbal learning.

You may find that you want to use one of these curriculum maps and the lessons provided as a foundation for a unit in your own class. Or, you may want to refer back to these units as models for designing your own visually integrated units. Either way, these sample units can help you on your way to developing more visually integrated curriculum.

CONCLUSION

Looking Forward

While I've been writing this book, I have had the good fortune of working with many teachers who have piloted the visual learning and teaching strategies and activities presented here. I have spent time with teachers and students in kindergarten through eighth grade who have readily integrated visual and verbal learning. Yet, I also know that verbal modes continue to predominate and there is much work yet to do.

My hope is that you too will find these strategies and activities applicable to your setting and that you can use them flexibly and adaptably in ways that work for you and your classroom. This transition will not happen overnight. Perhaps you will start by doodling with your class and then introduce visual note-taking. The possibilities are abundant for how you might continue to enhance visual learning and teaching in your classroom.

Keep in mind that it's important to be both flexible and persistent when working with visual learning and teaching. For example, if you teach a brief lesson on doodling and it doesn't go as well as you had hoped, please don't give up and think, "Well, that didn't work." I hope you will persist with these approaches and try again. Make them your own. Find the best approaches that work for you and your students and build on them.

Please share this book and its supplemental resources with your colleagues. Consider creating a book group and working together with your teaching team to discuss and develop ways to integrate visual learning and teaching into your existing curriculum. By talking about visual learning and teaching at staff meetings, PLCs, and other team meetings, you will be helping visual learning and teaching have a place in discussions and curriculum planning alongside verbal learning and teaching.

I hope that you will find new applications for visual literacy skills and new ways to meet the visual learning needs of all your students. When I run into some of you at conferences or while visiting different school districts, I'll look forward to seeing how you are incorporating visual learning and teaching in your classrooms.

I hope you will consider sharing some of your work with me. I'd love to see samples of how you are applying these methods.

So, please open your notebook to a blank page and make a frame large enough to contain the following text:

Susan Daniels
c/o Free Spirit Publishing Inc.
6325 Sandburg Road, Suite 100
Minneapolis, MN 55427
help4kids@freespirit.com

And that can be the beginning of a mind map. Over time, as you are incorporating the visual tools and texts into your classrooms, and as your students are strengthening their visual literacy skills, you'll undoubtedly have moments or memories that you will want to share. Questions, ideas, feedback, and even new strategies—record and depict them here. Once the page is full, photocopy it, scan it, or take a picture of it and send it my way. I welcome the opportunity to hear about your experiences exploring visual learning and teaching.

Wishing you all the best; go forth and doodle!

Susan Daniels

ACKNOWLEDGMENTS

First, I want to acknowledge Free Spirit president, Judy Galbraith, who shared my vision for this book, and the following Free Spirit authors and editors: Richard Cash, whose encouragement was invaluable, and Brian Farrey-Latz and Meg Bratsch, the best editorial team I could hope for. Both Brian and Meg have extensive experience and insight to bring to the editing process and were dedicated to making this book the best it could be.

Julie Cortez devoted two years of her life researching, curating images, editing first drafts, and discussing visual learning and teaching with me for literally hundreds of hours. This book would not have happened without her. Elizabeth Ringlee gave important feedback during the last few months of writing and helped bring the manuscript together for final submission. Dr. Patrick MacAfee was a cherished mentor whose insights, encouragement, and care were essential to the process of writing the book.

Dozens of teachers have participated in and informed this work for more than twenty years since I wrote my dissertation on image use and creativity. Most recently, the teachers and administrators from Discovery School in San Jose piloted instructional strategies and helped create curriculum with a visual emphasis that appears in the final chapters of this book. Several of these teachers appear in the book as well. Carol Baker, Jenna Bryon, Jenny Hare, Martin Lewis (from Piedmont), Toni Sindelar, and Kipp Trieu pop up throughout the chapters sharing insights and words of wisdom with numerous doodles and quotes. Other teachers who contributed to the development of the manuscript include: Carol Bauerle, Colleen Lewis, and Paula Simka. Discovery School administrators, Debby Perry and Dale Jones, opened the doors of the school to me and provided time to work with the dedicated and creative staff at Discovery. The K–8 students at Discovery loved their visual learning time and readily shared their work and their ideas with me. Elizabeth Bell, a sixth-grade teacher in southern California and one of my former graduate students, contributed several illustrations and mind maps.

Dr. Linda Silverman, a brilliant scholar of visual-spatial learners and their needs, shared her work with me, as did Sunni Brown and Dave Gray, two great visual thinkers from the worlds of business and design. Heartfelt appreciation goes to all. Thank you.

ENDNOTES

Introduction

1. Sunni Brown, *The Doodle Revolution: Unlock the Power to Think Differently* (New York: Penguin Group, 2014).

2. Linda Silverman, *Upside-Down Brilliance: The Visual-Spatial Learner* (Denver, CO: DeLeon Publishing, 2002).

3. Richard E. Meyer, *Multimedia Learning* (New York: Cambridge University Press, 2009).

4. Jerre Levy, "Possible Basis for the Evolution of Lateral Specialization of the Human Brain." *Nature* 224 (1969): 614–615.

5. Howard Gardner, *Frames of Mind: The Theory of Multiple Intelligences* (New York: Basic Books, 2004).

6. Allan Paivio, *Mind and Its Evolution: A Dual Coding Theoretical Approach* (New York: Lawrence Erlbaum Associates, Inc., 2007).

Chapter 1

7. Timothy Gangwer, *Visual Impact, Visual Teaching: Using Images to Strengthen Learning* (Thousand Oaks, CA: Corwin Press, 2009).

8. Robert H. McKim, *Thinking Visually: A Strategy Manual for Problem Solving* (Palo Alto, CA: Dale Seymour Publications, 1980).

Chapter 2

9. Jackie Andrade, "What Does Doodling Do?" *Applied Cognitive Psychology* 24, no. 1 (2009): 100–106.

10. Sunni Brown, *The Doodle Revolution: Unlock the Power to Think Differently* (New York: Penguin Group, 2014).

11. Andrew J. O. Whitehouse, Murray T. Maybery, and Kevin Durkin, "The Development of the Picture-Superiority Effect," *British Journal of Developmental Psychology* 24, no. 4 (2006): 767–773.

12. Jackie Andrade, "What Does Doodling Do?" *Applied Cognitive Psychology* 24, no. 1 (2009): 100–106.

13. Carrie Barron and Alton Barron, *The Creativity Cure: How to Build Happiness with Your Own Two Hands* (New York: Scribner, 2013).

14. Steve Moline, *I See What You Mean: Visual Literacy K–8* (Portland, ME: Stenhouse Publishers, 2011).

Chapter 4

15. Michael J. Gelb, *How to Think Like Leonardo da Vinci: Seven Steps to Genius Every Day*, (New York: Random House, 2009).

16. Jeffrey Wammes, Melissa Meade, and Myra Fernandes, "The Drawing Effect: Evidence for Reliable and Robust Memory Benefits in Free Recall." *Quarterly Journal of Experimental Psychology* 69, no.9 (2016): 1752–1776.

Chapter 5

17. William Playfair, *The Statistical Breviary* (London: T. Bensley, 1801).

Chapter 9

18. Diane Heacox, *Differentiating Instruction in the Regular Classroom: How to Reach and Teach All Learners* (Minneapolis: Free Spirit Publishing, 2012).

Chapter 11

19. John Spencer and A.J. Juliani, *Launch: Using Design Thinking to Boost Creativity and Bring Out the Maker in Every Student* (San Diego, CA: Dave Burgess Consulting, 2016).

REFERENCES & RESOURCES

Allsburg, C. V. (1985). *The Polar Express*. Boston: Houghton Mifflin Co.

Andrade, J. (2009). "What Does Doodling Do?" *Applied Cognitive Psychology* 24 (1): 100–106.

Applegate, K. (2015). *The One and Only Ivan*. New York: HarperCollins.

Armstrong, T. (2017). *Multiple Intelligences in the Classroom*. Alexandria, VA: ASCD.

Avgerinou, M., and Ericson, J. (1997). "A Review of the Concept of Visual Literacy." *British Journal of Educational Technology* 28 (4): 280–291.

Banyai, I. (1995). *Zoom*. New York: Penguin Books.

Barrie, J. M. (1954). *Peter Pan & Wendy*. Leicester: Brockhampton Press.

Barron, C., and Barron, A. (2013). *The Creativity Cure: How to Build Happiness with Your Own Two Hands*. New York: Scribner.

Becker, A. (2013). *Journey*. Somerville, MA: Candlewick Press.

Becker, A. (2014). *Quest*. Somerville, MA: Candlewick Press.

Becker, A. (2016). *Return*. Somerville, MA: Candlewick Press.

Bowe, J. (2007). *My Last Best Friend*. Orlando: Harcourt.

Brett, J. (1989). *The Mitten*. New York: G.P. Putnam & Sons.

Brown, S. (2014). *The Doodle Revolution: Unlock the Power to Think Differently*. New York: Penguin Group.

Christie, A. (1934). *Murder on the Orient Express*. Glasgow: Collins Crime Club.

Columba, L., Kim, C. Y., and Moe, A. J. (2009). *The Power of Picture Books in Teaching Math, Science, and Social Studies Grades PreK–8*. Scottsdale, AZ: Holcomb Hathaway, Publishers.

Common Core State Standards Initiative. www.corestandards.org.

D'Acquisto, L. (2006). *Learning on Display: Student-Created Museums That Build Understanding*. Alexandria, VA: ASCD.

Defoe, D. (1719). *Robinson Crusoe*. London: W. Taylor.

dePaola, T. (1989). *The Art Lesson*. New York: Putnam.

Deviney, J., Duncan, S., Harris, S., Rody, M. A., and Rosenberry, L. (2010). *Inspiring Spaces for Young Children*. Silver Spring, MD: Gryphon House.

Easel.ly. www.easel.ly.

Eastman, P. (1960). *Are You My Mother?* New York: Random House Publishing Group.

Eckhoff, A., and Urbach, J. (2008). "Understanding Imaginative Thinking During Childhood: Sociocultural Conceptions of Creativity and Imaginative Thought." *Early Childhood Education Journal* 36 (2): 179–185.

Eilam, B. (2012). *Teaching, Learning, and Visual Literacy: The Dual Role of Visual Representation.* New York: Cambridge University Press.

Emberley, E. (1972). *Make a World: Learn to Draw the Ed Emberley Way!* New York: Little, Brown and Company.

Essley, R. (2008). *Visual Tools for Differentiating Reading & Writing Instruction: Strategies to Help Students Make Abstract Ideas Concrete & Accessible.* New York: Scholastic Inc.

Essley, R. (2010). *Visual Tools for Differentiating Content Area Instruction: Strategies That Make Concepts in Math, Science & Social Studies Accessible—& Support All Learners Across the Curriculum.* New York: Scholastic Inc.

Fetter, B. (2012). *Being Visual: Raising a Generation of Innovative Thinkers.* Elgin, IL: Grape Lot Press.

Finley, T., and Wiggs. B. (2016). *Rethinking Classroom Design: Create Student-Centered Learning Spaces for 6–12th Graders.* Lanham, MD: Rowman & Littlefield.

Fisher, A.V., Godwin, K. E., Seltman, H. (2014). "Visual Environment, Attention Allocation, and Learning in Young Children: When Too Much of a Good Thing May Be Bad." *Psychological Science* 25 (7): 1362–1370.

Fitzhugh, L. (1964). *Harriet The Spy.* New York: Harper & Row.

Frey, N., and Fisher, D. (2008). *Teaching Visual Literacy: Using Comic Books, Graphic Novels, Anime, Cartoons, and More to Develop Comprehension and Thinking Skills.* Thousand Oaks, CA: Corwin Press.

Fulton, L., and Campbell, B. (2014). *Science Notebooks: Writing About Inquiry.* Portsmouth, NH: Heinemann.

Gandini, L., Hill, L., Cadwell, L., and Schwall, C. (Eds). (2015). *In the Spirit of the Studio: Learning from the* Atelier *of Reggio Emilia.* New York: Teachers College Press.

Gangwer, T. (2009). *Visual Impact, Visual Teaching: Using Images to Strengthen Learning.* Thousand Oaks, CA: Corwin Press.

Gardner, H. (2004). *Frames of Mind: The Theory of Multiple Intelligences.* New York: Basic Books.

Gelb, M. (2009). *How to Think Like Leonardo da Vinci: Seven Steps to Genius Every Day.* New York: Random House.

Glogster. www.glogster.com.

Golding, W. (1954). *Lord of the Flies.* London: Faber & Faber.

Guardino, C., and Fullerton, E. (2010). "Changing Behaviors by Changing the Classroom Environment." *Teaching Exceptional Children* 42 (6): 8–13.

Gurian, M., and Stevens, K. (2004). "With Boys and Girls in Mind." *Educational Leadership* 62 (3): 21–26.

Haddon, M. (2003). *The Curious Incident of the Dog in the Night-Time*. New York: Doubleday.

Harvard College Writing Program. writingprogram.fas.harvard.edu.

Heacox, D. (2012). *Differentiating Instruction in the Regular Classroom: How to Reach and Teach All Learners*. Minneapolis: Free Spirit Publishing.

Hemmingway, E. (1952). *The Old Man and the Sea*. New York: Scribner's.

Hoffman, M. (2011). *The Great Big Book of Families*. New York: Dial Books for Young Readers.

Huxley, A. (1932). *Brave New World*. London: Chatto & Windus.

Jacobs, J., and Cauley, L. B. (1980). *Joseph Jacobs' The Story of the Three Little Pigs*. New York: Putnam.

Jensen, E. (2003). *Environments for Learning*. San Diego, CA: The Brain Store.

Johnston, T., and Duncan, R. (1994). *Amber on the Mountain*. New York: Puffin Books.

Koester, M. (2015). *Science Teachers Who Draw: The Red Is Always There*. Blue Mound, WI: Deep University Press.

Lainez, R., and Lainez, M. (2015). *Familia, Familia, Familia*. New York: Random House.

Laws, J. M., Lygren, E., Breunig, E., and Lopez, C. (2010). *Opening the World Through Nature Journaling: Integrating Art, Science, and Language Arts*. Sacramento, CA: California Native Plant Society Press.

Leedy, L. (2000). *Mapping Penny's World*. New York: Henry Holt and Company.

Leslie, C. W. (2015). *The Curious Nature Guide: Explore the Natural Wonders All Around You*. North Adams, MA: Storey Publishing.

Levy, J. (1969). "Possible Basis for the Evolution of Lateral Specialization of the Human Brain." *Nature* 224: 614–615.

Lewis, C. S. (1950). *The Lion, the Witch and the Wardrobe*. London: Geoffrey Bles.

Lin, G. (2006). *The Year of the Dog*. New York: Little, Brown and Company.

Margulies, N., and Valenza, C. (2005). *Visual Thinking: Tools for Mapping Your Ideas*. Norwalk, CT: Crown House Publishing.

Mass, W. (2009). *11 Birthdays*. New York: Scholastic.

Mayer, R. E. (2009). *Multimedia Learning*. New York: Cambridge University Press.

McCloud, S. (2006). *Making Comics: Storytelling Secrets of Comics, Manga, and Graphic Novels*. New York: William Morrow.

McKim, R. H. (1980). *Thinking Visually: A Strategy Manual for Problem Solving.* Palo Alto, CA: Dale Seymour Publications.

Media Matters for America. www.mediamatters.org.

Melville, H. (1851). *Moby Dick.* New York: Harper & Brothers.

Milne, A. A., and Shepard, E. H. (1926). *Winnie-the-Pooh.* London: Methuen Publishing.

Moline, S. (2011). *I See What You Mean: Visual Literacy K–8.* Portland, ME: Stenhouse Publishers.

Moore, D. M., and Dwyer, F. M. (Eds.). (1994). *Visual Literacy: A Spectrum of Visual Learning.* Englewood Cliffs, NJ: Educational Technology Publications, Inc.

Moss, M. (1997). *My Notebook (with help from Amelia).* Middleton, WI: Pleasant Company Publications.

Moss, M. (1998). *Rachel's Journal: The Story of a Pioneer Girl.* Orlando, FL: Harcourt.

Moss, M. (1995). *Amelia's Notebook.* New York: Simon and Schuster Books for Young Readers.

Mueller, J. Authentic Assessment Toolbox. jfmueller.faculty.noctrl.edu/toolbox.

"NCTE/IRA Standards for the English Language Arts." National Council of Teachers of English. www.ncte.org/standards/ncte-ira.

Next Generation Science Standards. www.nextgenscience.org.

Paolini, C. (2003). *Eragon.* New York: Knopf.

Parr, T. (2010). *The Family Book.* New York: Little, Brown and Company.

Paterson, K. (1977). *Bridge to Terabithia.* New York: Crowell.

Paivio, A. (2007). *Mind and Its Evolution: A Dual Coding Theoretical Approach.* New York: Lawrence Erlbaum Associates, Inc.

Pennypacker, S. (2012). *Summer of the Gypsy Moths.* New York: HarperCollins Children's Books.

Piktochart. piktochart.com.

Pillars, W. (2016). *Visual Note-Taking for Educators: A Teacher's Guide to Student Creativity.* New York: W. W. Norton and Company.

Playfair, W. (1801). *The Statistical Breviary.* London: T. Bensley.

Potter, B. (1902). *The Tale of Peter Rabbit.* London: Frederick Warne & Co.

Pullman, P. His Dark Materials series. (*Northern Lights,* 1995; *The Subtle Knife,* 1997; *The Amber Spyglass,* 2000). New York: Scholastic.

Purdue Online Writing Lab (OWL). owl.english.purdue.edu.

ReadWriteThink. www.readwritethink.org.

Roam, D. (2008). *The Back of the Napkin*. New York: Portfolio.

Roam, D. (2014). *Show & Tell*. New York: Portfolio.

Rohde, M. (2013). *The Sketchnote Handbook: The Illustrated Guide to Visual Notetaking*. Berkeley, CA: Peachpit Press.

Ruef, K. (2003). *The Private Eye (5X) Looking/Thinking by Analogy: A Guide to Developing the Interdisciplinary Mind*. Seattle, WA: Private Eye Project.

Scholastic. www.scholastic.com/home.

Schulten, K. (2010, Aug. 23). "Teaching with Infographics | Places to Start." *New York Times*. tinyurl.com/26kxu93.

Scieszka, J., and Smith, L. (1989). *The True Story of the 3 Little Pigs!* New York: Penguin.

Sendak, M. (1963). *Where the Wild Things Are*. New York: Harper & Row.

Seuss, D. (1972). *The Lorax*. New York: Random House.

Seuss, D. (1957). *The Cat in the Hat*. New York: Random House.

Seuss, D. (1960). *Green Eggs and Ham*. New York: Random House.

Seuss, D. (1990). *Oh, the Places You'll Go!* New York: Random House.

Silverman, L. K. (2002). *Upside-Down Brilliance: The Visual-Spatial Learner*. Denver, CO: DeLeon Publishing.

Slobodkina, E. (1940). *Caps for Sale*. New York: W. R. Scott.

Spencer, J., and Juliani, A. J. (2016). *Launch: Using Design Thinking to Boost Creativity and Bring Out the Maker in Every Student*. San Diego, CA: Dave Burgess Consulting.

Stead, R. (2013). *Liar & Spy*. New York: Yearling Books.

Stevenson, R. L. (1882). *Treasure Island*. London: Cassell.

Sweeney, J., and Cable, A. (1996). *Me on the Map*. New York: Crown Publishers.

Swift, J. (1726). *Gulliver's Travels*. London: Benjamin Motte.

Tolan, S. S. (2002). *Surviving the Applewhites*. New York: HarperCollins.

Tolkien, J. R. (1937). *The Hobbit*. London: Allen & Unwin.

Tolkien, J. R. (1954). *The Lord of the Rings*. London: Allen & Unwin.

Vasquez, J. A., Comer, M. W., and Troutman, F. (2010). *Developing Visual Literacy in Science K–8*. Arlington, VA: NSTA Press.

Venngage. Venngage.com.

Verne, J. (1873). *Around the World in Eighty Days*. France: Pierre-Jules Hetzel.

Verne, J. (1873). *Twenty Thousand Leagues Under the Sea*. Leicester: Thorpe.

Viorst, J., and Cruz, R. (1987). *Alexander and the Terrible, Horrible, No Good, Very Bad Day*. New York: Simon & Schuster.

Waber, B. (1988). *Ira Says Goodbye*. New York: Houghton Mifflin.

Wammes, J. D., Meade, M. E., and Fernandes, M. A. (2016). "The Drawing Effect: Evidence for Reliable and Robust Memory Benefits in Free Recall." *Quarterly Journal of Experimental Psychology* 69 (9): 1752–1776.

Waters, K. (1989). *Sarah Morton's Day: A Day in the Life of a Pilgrim Girl*. New York: Scholastic Inc.

Wells, H. G. (1896). *The Island of Dr. Moreau*. London: Heinemann, Stone & Kimball.

White, E. B. (1952). *Charlotte's Web*. New York: Harper.

Whitehouse, A. J. O., Maybery, M. T., and Durkin, K. (2006). "The Development of the Picture-Superiority Effect." *British Journal of Developmental Psychology* 24 (4): 767–773.

Wiesner, D. (1991). *Tuesday*. New York: Clarion Books.

Wiesner, D. (2006). *Flotsam*. New York: Clarion Books.

Wurm, J. P. (2005). *Working in the Reggio Way: A Beginner's Guide for American Teachers*. St. Paul, MN: Redleaf Press.

Young, E. (1989). *Lon Po Po: A Red-Riding Hood Story from China*. New York: Penguin Putnam Books for Young Readers.

APPENDIX

Reproducible Forms

VISUAL TRIAD MODEL BREAKDOWN

	See	Imagine	Depict
Actions	*Decode*	*Manipulate mental models*	*Encode*
	Look View Perceive Observe Inspect Examine Identify Analyze Contemplate Investigate Evaluate	Picture Visualize View in mind's eye Envision Conceptualize Interpret Design Foresee Inspire Invent Dream	Doodle/draw/diagram Represent Reproduce Chronicle Communicate Illustrate Display Model/map Compose/recompose Express Create
Questions	What did you see? What is and isn't there? Are you able to think about parts and wholes about what you see? What insights have you had about your observations? What did you discover in your observation?	Have you used mental images in your thinking? What did you discover? Are you able to manipulate your mental images to develop a new idea? Do you have thoughts about how to express what you have imagined?	Did you visually depict an idea, concept, or feeling? Are you able to use simple methods of depiction—especially doodling—to depict your thoughts and convey meaning? Are you able to elaborate your depictions to convey a more detailed meaning? Would a viewer understand your intended meaning?

VISUAL TEACHER CHECKLIST

☐ I provide regular opportunities for students to view and decode visual images, documents, and texts.

☐ I provide regular opportunities for students to doodle, draw, and otherwise visually depict their learning.

☐ I model visual expression by purposefully doodling and writing while delivering class lessons (without apologizing for my lack of skills or talent).

☐ I provide regular opportunities for students to apply and further develop their abilities to organize images for effective display.

☐ I provide regular opportunities for students to substitute words with images.

☐ I provide regular opportunities for students to expand their understanding and use of visual language.

☐ I provide regular opportunities for students to combine images with text—picture writing—to share ideas more expressively.

☐ I provide regular opportunities for students to integrate images into live presentations to communicate more purposefully and effectively.

☐ I provide regular opportunities for students to manipulate and transform existing images to imagine and create something new.

☐ I incorporate the judicious use of technology while incorporating images and visual media in the classroom.

VISUAL ALPHABET AND SIX ESSENTIAL DESIGN ELEMENTS

VISUAL ALPHABET

•			∧	⌒	⊙	ℓ
Point	Line	Angle	Arc	Spiral	Loop

⬭	⬮	△	▭	⌂	☁
Oval	Eye	Triangle	Rectangle	House	Cloud

SIX ESSENTIAL DESIGN ELEMENTS

1. Letters and Numbers

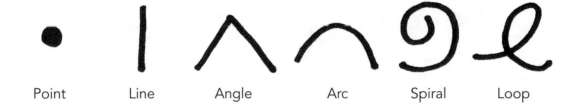

abc 123

2.

fonts

3. Bullets

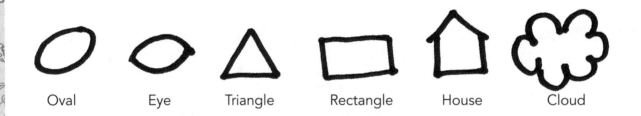

4. Connectors and Separators

5. Arrows

6. Frames

SQUIGGLE DOODLE

Continue these squiggles, and create a doodle using your imagination.

_____

_____

_____

_____

VISUAL ALPHABET DOODLE EXERCISE

apple	book	cat	dog
Earth	house	igloo	light bulb
car	bug	toy	mother
pencil	toothbrush	roses	umbrella
cupcake	airplane	firefighter	mittens
bus	phone	watch	school

DOODLE FIGURES ACTIVITY

standing	walking	sitting
reaching	sleeping	eating
reading	walking a dog	mother and child
teacher	tennis player	chef

VISUAL VOCABULARY CHART

Word/Definition	Sketch	Word/Definition	Sketch	Word/Definition	Sketch

VISUAL NOTE-TAKING FORM

Topic:

Key Words & Phrases

Doodles & Sketches

SEE-HEAR GRAPHIC ORGANIZER

Instructions: List a topic you want to brainstorm in the oval. Next, write one thing that topic makes you think of on each of the eight lines around the oval. In the boxes at the bottom of the page, doodle/sketch something memorable about the topic (based on your brainstorming) and list what sounds you might associate with the topic.

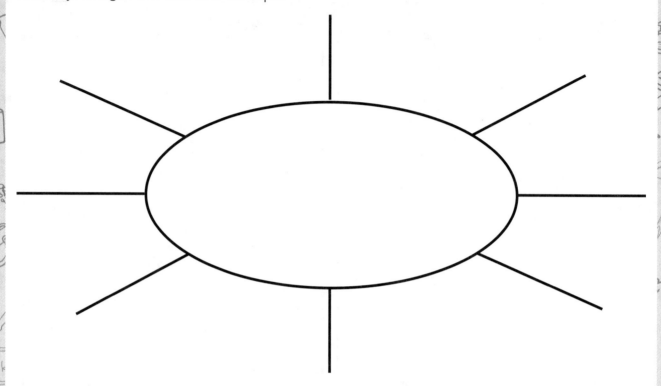

SEE 👁	HEAR 👂

PLOT OUTLINE

Title:

Beginning	Middle	End

STORYBOARD—COMICS

STORYBOARD—NARRATIVE

STORYBOARD—NINE PANEL

VISUAL FOUR-SQUARE

Events (sketch & label)

People (sketch & label)

Subject:

Big Ideas

Key Vocabulary

ONE PAGER WORKSHEET

Thumbnail Sketch

Step 1: Develop a list of keywords, phrases, and ideas related to your one pager.

Step 2: List key visuals that will be depicted in your one pager.

Step 3: Select or create quotes as required for the assigned one pager.

Step 4: Create a thumbnail sketch of your design idea for your one pager in the space provided above.

ANALYTIC DIAGRAMS

Diagram Type	Definition	Example
Enlargement/ Exploded view	Enlargement diagrams depict at a larger scale what is too small to see clearly. Exploded-view diagrams depict the order of assembly of the various components or parts of an object.	isotonic blood cell enlargement Exploded Diagram
Floor plan/ Blueprint	Floor plans are drawings of a physical structure or space that shows the view from above. These are typically drawn to scale and show the relationship between the various areas and spaces of a structure. Blueprints are a design plan (technical drawing) of a structure and are typically used in the building or creation of an object or structure.	DESK
Cutaway/ Cross-section	Cutaways are three dimensional representations that have selected exteriors removed so that the inner workings of an object can be seen. Cross-sections are diagrams showing what would be exposed by making a straight cut through something. A cross-section of Earth would reveal all the layers of the planet.	Peach cross-section Human brain cross-section

PROCESS DIAGRAMS

Diagram Type	Definition	Example
Basic flowchart	A flow chart shows the step-by-step actions that are taken in any specific procedure or process by means of using basic geometric shapes and connecting lines.	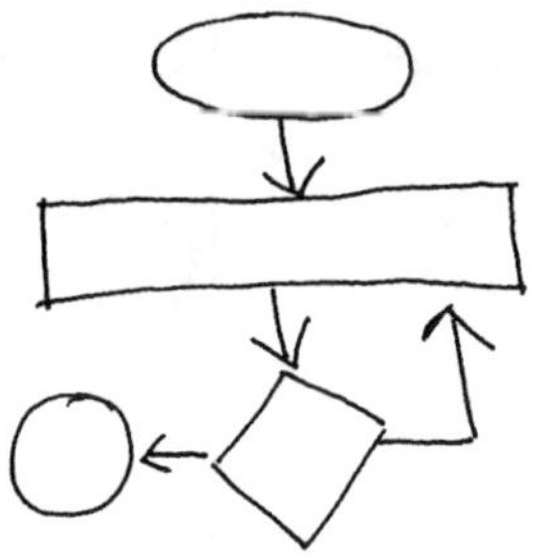
Storyboard	A storyboard uses images or illustrations in sequence to visualize the stages of a procedure, process, or story.	
Cycle	A cycle diagram depicts how items are related to one another in a repeating cycle with no beginning and no end.	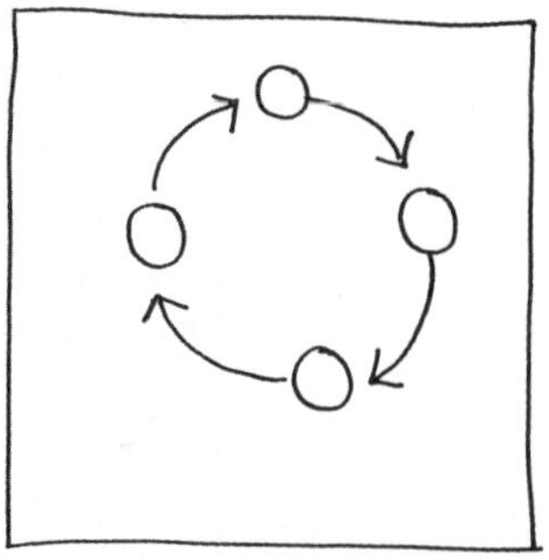
Play diagram	A play diagram is used mainly in sports. Players are represented on a playing court or field with a series of symbols (X and O). Arrows and lines depict motion or movement so players can visualize their relation to other players and their relation to a specific location on the field.	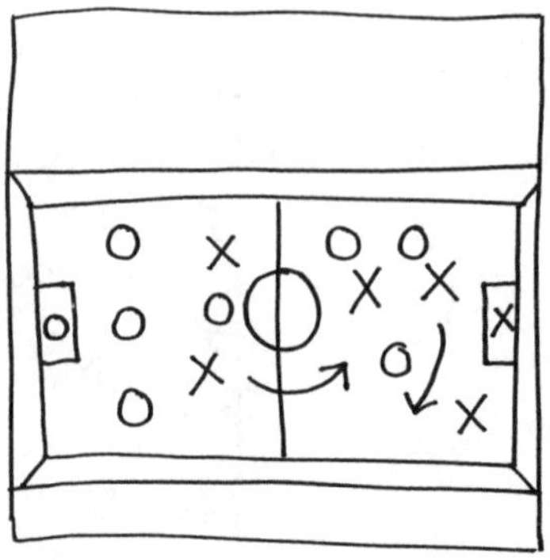

STRUCTURAL DIAGRAMS

Diagram Type	Definition	Example
Venn	A Venn diagram uses circles to designate and represent data sets and their relationship to each other. Venn diagrams are used to compare and contrast data.	
Pyramid	Pyramid diagrams are mostly used to depict and relate data that is hierarchical. A common elementary pyramid diagram is the food web energy pyramid.	
Web	Web diagrams visually represent relationships between concepts, actions, or things through the interplay of words, shapes, connectors, and other visual elements.	
Tree	A tree diagram has branching connecting lines that represent different relationships and processes.	
Tables	Table diagrams organize and display facts or figures in columns and rows.	

ILLUSTRATED TIMELINE

INFOGRAPHIC POSTER COMPONENTS GUIDE

Parts of an Infographic Poster	Definition	Example
Headings	Title and subtitles that name the subject of the data being presented.	
Sidebars	A short vertical area located to the side of the page that highlights related data.	
Illustrations	Images, depictions, doodles, clip art, and other pictures that connect the data on a visual level.	
Graphs	A diagram showing the measurable relation between variables.	
Timelines	A graphic representation of the passage of time as it relates to the data.	

CONTINUED ▷

INFOGRAPHIC POSTER COMPONENTS GUIDE, CONTINUED

Parts of an Infographic Poster	Definition	Example
Icons	A simple picture, image, or depiction that represents a noun, a verb, or a concept/idea.	
Forms	Visual shapes that create structure within an infographic.	
Facts	Data, evidence, or pieces of information that have been researched and cited.	

CHARACTER PORTRAIT

Character Name:

Describe the character.

How does the character act?

How does the character relate to other characters in the story?

SETTING

Illustrate or sketch the setting in the box below. If the story has several settings, choose your favorite.

Describe the setting and include details.

ILLUSTRATED PLOT PYRAMID

Name:

Story:

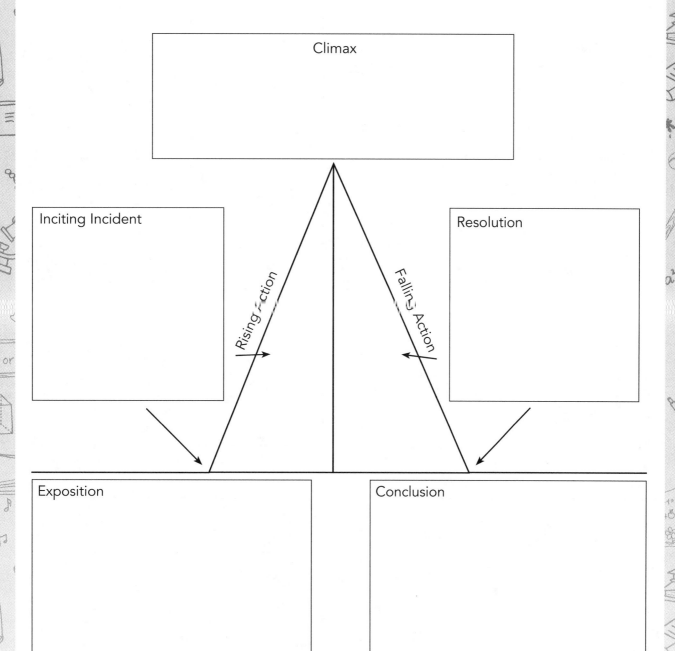

TWO-PAGE SPREAD LAYOUT

Page _____

Page _____

fold here

Page _____

Page _____

Page _____

Page _____

HOW TO CREATE YOUR PICTURE BOOK

1. Decide what kind of story you want to tell. It may be based on something from your life, or not. It may come straight from your imagination. Imagine what your story might sound and look like.

2. Write out your idea for the story in two long paragraphs. The story should match the points on the plot pyramid.

3. Complete the "Illustrated Plot Pyramid" handout with simple illustrations of the exposition, inciting incident, rising action, climax, falling action, resolution, and the conclusion.

4. Use the narrative storyboard handout with text in one column and an image in the other. Break up the story so that a sentence or two goes with each picture.

5. Sketch an image that goes with the text.

6. Once you know how many pages your story will be—based on the template—fold a few sheets of paper in half and place them inside one another. For example, if you have a six-page story, you'll need two pieces of paper. This will create three two-page spreads. If you have a ten-page story, you'll need three pieces of paper.

7. You might have an odd number of pages. If so, you may want to include pages for a dedication to someone, a page for "About the Author," or perhaps a page for acknowledgments.

8. Sketch the first draft into your blank book. This draft of your text and illustrations should be in pencil.

9. Once you've received feedback on your sketches and text, trace them with a black pen for the final version and color them, if you choose to do so.

10. Make a front and a back cover.

11. Staple the pages and the covers together.

12. And, hooray! You are done.

VISUAL LEARNING PORTFOLIO SELF-ASSESSMENT

Name: Date:

Self-Created Goals Growth/Progress	Attempting/ Beginning	Strong Effort	Meeting Self-Expectations	Exceeding Self-Expectations
Depictions match the image in my mind				
I want to become comfortable using the visual alphabet				
My work balances visual depictions and verbal phrases				
My visuals convey meaning and help me remember				
My images show thoughtful design				
I want to learn how to give and take clear feedback				

Self-Reflection: (May be chosen from list provided or self-created.)

1. Do I feel comfortable using doodling and other types of drawings?

2. What are my goals for the design and writing in my_____?

3. What are my future goals for my visual portfolio?

VISUAL LEARNING PORTFOLIO ASSESSMENT RUBRIC

Name: Date:

Class:

Assignment:

Directions: Teachers should complete a rubric for each student on a regular basis. For example, complete a portfolio rubric at the end of a unit, month, or grading period. Points are awarded for completeness, accuracy, neatness, and growth. The assignments may include notebook or journal samples, class assignments, lab reports, and homework. Each item is scored on a scale of 1–5. Total the points and provide comments on each criterion. The space at the bottom is for ongoing feedback.

Criteria	Excellent 5	Good 4	Average 3	Needs Help 2	Little Effort 1	Comments
Completeness						
Accuracy						
Neatness						
Growth						

Total Points   /20

Areas of growth:

Suggestions for improvement:

CURRICULUM MAP

Subject:

Unit/Theme:

Essential Questions:

1.

2.

3.

4.

5.

Common Core State Standards and/or State or Provincial Content Standards	Content

CONTINUED ▷

CURRICULUM MAP, CONTINUED

Unit Questions:

1.

2.

3.

4.

5.

Skills	Visual Skills	Projects/Products

AUTOBIOGRAPHY VISUAL TIMELINE HOMEWORK

Name: Date:

Interview your parents, relatives, and friends to help you remember milestones and special events that happened to you each year of your life so far. Use photo albums, baby books, and anything else that helps you remember special things in your life visually. Draw/doodle a picture about each of the events, then write neatly and in complete sentences about what the event was.

When I was one:

When I was two:

When I was three:

CONTINUED ▷

249

AUTOBIOGRAPHY VISUAL TIMELINE HOMEWORK, CONTINUED

When I was four:

When I was five:

When I was six:

CONTINUED ▷

When I was seven:

When I was eight:

When I was nine:

REDESIGN OUR SCHOOLYARD

This is your chance to design the playground you've always wanted!

On a piece of graph paper, draw an outline of the schoolyard to scale. Show the location of the school in relation to the schoolyard.

Using the shapes below as a key, add whatever playground equipment you choose in any design.

The only rules are:
- You must leave _____ to _____ square feet between each piece of equipment.
- You must make sure the playground has places to walk.
- You must think about *all* the students and what you think other students would like.
- You must stay within the confines of the schoolyard.

When finished, you will present and explain your design to the rest of the class.

Happy building!

Scale: 1 square foot of graph paper = _____ square feet

KEY:

Swingsets

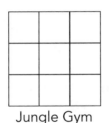
Jungle Gym
(monkeybars, rings)

Tetherball

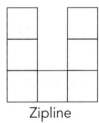
Zipline

Slide

Wheelchair
Accessible
Equipment

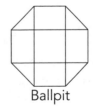
Ballpit

Teetertotter

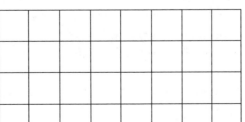
Half Basketball
Court

Sports Field (soccer, football, baseball)

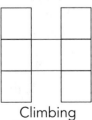
Climbing
Equipment

DIRECTIONS FOR GEOLOGIC TIMELINE

1. Record all group members' names on the front of the tape.

2. Also on the front of the tape, add a measurement scale with several measurements. Start your scale with the following information: 1 meter = 1 billion years

3. Measure out 4.5 meters on your strip of adding machine tape. This stretch of tape represents the time from Earth's formation to the present. (Alternatively, you can connect multiple pieces of paper—each representing 500 million years—together.)

4. Mark each measure of 500 million years along the entire timeline. Calculate this measurement and add it to your scale.

5. Mark on the tape and depict with a simple drawing when humans appeared on Earth. Calculate this timeline location using the following data:
   • Australopithecus afarensis first appeared approximately 3.85 to 2.95 million years ago.
   • Homo neanderthalensis lived approximately 400,000 to 40,000 years ago.

6. Mark on the tape and depict with a simple drawing when the dinosaurs lived. Place the span on the timeline using the following data:
   • Dinosaurs first appeared approximately 248 million years ago.
   • Dinosaurs lived until approximately 63 million years ago.

7. Mark on the tape and depict with a simple drawing when the Pangea era occurred. Place the span on the timeline using the following data:
   • Pangea formed approximately 270 million years ago.
   • Pangea began to break up approximately 225 to 200 million years ago.

8. Mark on the tape and depict with a simple drawing when the Jurassic period occurred. Place the span on the timeline using the following data:
   • The Jurassic period began approximately 199.6 million years ago.
   • The Jurassic period ended approximately 145.5 million years ago.

9. Mark on the tape and depict with a simple drawing when the Cambrian period occurred. Place the span on the timeline using the following data:
   • The Cambrian period began approximately 541 million years ago.
   • The Cambrian period ended approximately 485.4 million years ago.

10. Mark on the tape and depict with a simple drawing when the Ancient Egypt era occurred. Place the span on the timeline using the following data:
    • Ancient Egypt started approximately 4000 BCE.
    • Ancient Egypt ended approximately 1000 BCE.

11. Check with your teacher to see if any other major events need to be marked.

INDEX

Italics denotes figures; **bold** denotes reproducible handouts

To download the reproducible forms and other digital content for this book, visit **freespirit.com/visual-forms**. Use the password **toolbox**.

ABOUT THE AUTHOR

Dr. Susan Daniels is a professor, an author, an international consultant, and an educational director of a psychoeducational center that specializes in the needs of gifted, creative, and twice-exceptional children. She has been a professional development specialist for over twenty years, regularly providing workshops and training on creativity and visual learning and teaching. Susan is an avid doodler who enjoys working visually in her journals, and she is dedicated to supporting teachers' development of visual literacy and enhanced understanding of visual learning and teaching strategies. She lives in Berkeley, California.

Other Great Resources from Free Spirit

Teaching Gifted Kids in Today's Classroom
Strategies and Techniques Every Teacher Can Use
(Updated Fourth Edition)
by Susan Winebrenner, M.S., with Dina Brulles, Ph.D.

For teachers and administrators, grades K–12.

256 pp.; paperback; 8½" x 11"; includes digital content

Making Curriculum Pop
Developing Literacies in All Content Areas
by Pam Goble, Ed.D., and Ryan R. Goble, M.A. Developed in partnership with NCTE

For grades 6–12 teachers, administrators, curriculum directors.

224 pp.; paperback; 8½" x 11" includes digital content

Advancing Differentiation
Thinking and Learning for the 21st Century
(Revised & Updated Edition)
by Richard M. Cash, Ed.D.

For teachers and administrators, grades K–12.

240 pp.; paperback; 8½" x 11"; includes digital content

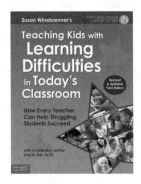

Teaching Kids with Learning Difficulties in Today's Classroom
How Every Teacher Can Help Struggling Students Succeed
(Revised & Updated Third Edition)
by Susan Winebrenner, M.S., with Lisa M. Kiss, M.Ed.

For K–12 teachers, administrators, higher education faculty.

288 pp.; paperback; 8½" x 11"; includes digital content

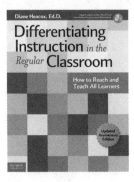

Differentiating Instruction in the Regular Classroom
How to Reach and Teach All Learners
(Updated Anniversary Edition)
by Diane Heacox, Ed.D.

For grades K–12.

176 pp.; paperback; 8½" x 11"; includes digital content

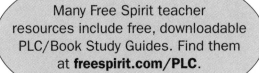

Many Free Spirit teacher resources include free, downloadable PLC/Book Study Guides. Find them at **freespirit.com/PLC**.

Making Differentiation a Habit
How to Ensure Success in Academically Diverse Classrooms
(Updated Edition)
by Diane Heacox, Ed.D.

For teachers and administrators, grades K–12.

192 pp.; paperback; 8½" x 11"; includes digital content

Interested in purchasing multiple quantities and receiving volume discounts?
Contact edsales@freespirit.com or call 1.800.735.7323 and ask for Education Sales.

Many Free Spirit authors are available for speaking engagements, workshops, and keynotes. Contact speakers@freespirit.com or call 1.800.735.7323.

For pricing information, to place an order, or to request a free catalog, contact:

Free Spirit Publishing Inc. • 6325 Sandburg Road, Suite 100 • Minneapolis, MN 55427-3674
toll-free 800.735.7323 • local 612.338.2068 • fax 612.337.5050
help4kids@freespirit.com • www.freespirit.com